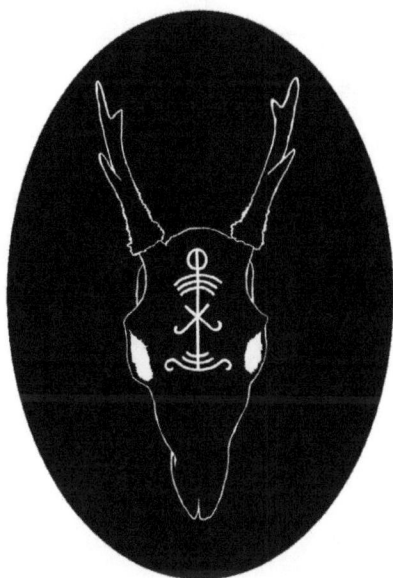

# THE CLOVENSTONE WORKINGS

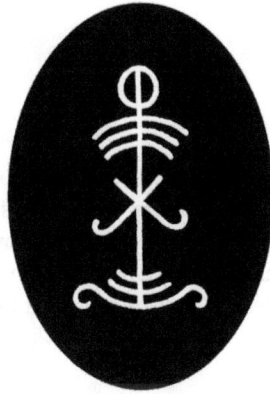

# THE CLOVENSTONE WORKINGS
## A Manual of Early Modern Witchcraft

A Handbook of Practical Sorcerous Transformations
And Feats of Art, based on reports of 17th Century
Witching Deeds and Aesthetics, Empowered by Channeled
Guidance and Experiential Knowledge

*By*
## Robin Artisson

*With Fine Interior Illustrations by*
## Molly McHenry

∞
Written and Assembled
In the year 2020 of the Common Era
*At* Ledgewood House
And the Surrounding Countryside

**ISBN:** 978-0-578-33048-8

**BLACK MALKIN PRESS**
*Hancock County, Maine*


www.robinartisson.com


Molly McHenry's works online:
www.instagram.com/artharpy

*This book is dedicated
To the Strange Souls of the World
That I have known and loved;
Those departed,
Those still here,
And those I am yet to know.*

If you doubt the reality of occult arts
Put this book aside;
It is not here to convince you.
If you fear damnation,
Or dismiss what you cannot see,
Abandon this book. Walk away swiftly.
If you seek only power and a cruel will over others,
Do not read further.
Destroy this book or give it away;
It will *harm* you if you continue.


The Devil is **'Aye gude to his ain'**,
And his *ain* know themselves without fear or shame.
They may not know *how* they know,
But they know.

# CONTAINED HEREIN

# INTRODUCTION

"They are undenyably reproveable, who, instead of covenanting with God, do covenant with Satan, we mean here, witches, those renegade witches, of which it is storied, that they enter into an express compact with the devil, formally renouncing their baptismal covenant, and all their claim to Christ, and from the crown of the head to the sole of the foot, devote themselves to him."

*—James Clark, 1702*

## Witchcraft

Witchcraft is a mysterious kind of engagement, born in a compact between a human being and non-human persons who inhabit the Unseen dimension of this world. This compact or relationship can assume many forms and come about in many ways. Despite endless amounts of shallow or inaccurate modern depictions of Witchcraft—the many ways it has been re-imagined and sold to a modern audience—history leaves no room to doubt that Witchcraft in pre-modern times was not a matter of a man or woman being born special, nor 'gifted', nor psychic, nor anything of that nature.

Witchcraft, though it certainly appealed to stranger souls who lived within human communities, was always a form of extraordinary relationship or engagement that was largely *sought out* by the people who would become Witches. A meeting (or meetings) with spirit-persons of some power or influence within the local landscape, the spirits of the dead, or an encounter with even more mysterious spirits of greater power—and the initiatory transformations bestowed upon a man or woman by those spirits in those meetings—was the gateway into historical Witchcraft.

These transformative or initiatory meetings with spirits might come seemingly unbidden or unprovoked; many men and women confessed to going about their daily affairs as they would on any other day, when they met with a spirit that introduced them to the destiny of Witchcraft and spirit-aided sorcery that awaited them. Others, lured to the idea of being able to transform their lives in ways they deeply desired, were taught by other human beings certain methods or means of inaugurating spirit-contact or even methods of creating states of mind (possibly in ritually incubated dreams) in which initiatory meetings with spirits could take place.

Persons born with the 'special gifts'—persons born with extraordinary capacities which allow them to (at times) gain knowledge or insights about our world and persons within it *without recourse to the ordinary sensory means of doing so* (psychics and those of that nature) may have historically been placed on the roster of persons often suspected of harboring unsavory connections with the Unseen world, but there is no formal connection between the psychic and the Witch who, through the agency of spirit-helpers, familiar spirits, and empowering compacts with certain other spirits, gains the ability to affect this world or its people in extraordinary ways.

*Mediums*, or those who have some ability to sense the presence of deceased human beings (or other such beings) likewise do *not* automatically occupy the ranks of Witches. A psychic or a medium who becomes a Witch does so in the same manner that anyone else does: in a spectral or powerful meeting with spirits from the Unseen world in which they undergo a real initiatory experience of some sort at the hands of those spirits.

"Witchcraft" always historically refers to a person-to-person engagement with spirits or preternatural entities. This engagement is usually ongoing; but even if historical witches only confess to meeting spirits a *single time*—such as a single reported meeting with the "Queen of the Elves", in which she hands the Witch a bottle of healing ointment—that person's later career as a healer (using that ointment) satisfies the criteria that makes them **Witched:** touched by Otherworldly forces and given special benefits, powers, knowledge, insights, abilities, or extraordinary help of some kind, to accomplish something in the human world that they would not otherwise have been able to accomplish.

The nature of the compact between the Witch and their empowering spirits is very subtle and layered. We will discuss it more in the following section and in portions of this work to come, but at this point it must be stated that the Early Modern Christian cultures of Europe greatly over-simplified the dimensions of the Spectral Compact, seeing *all* of these agreements or relationships established between humans and spirits as a *Devil's Pact*, or reducing all such relationships to the equivalent of a formal deal with the Theological Devil—a covenant or agreement by which the Witch surrendered their soul to the Devil in exchange for dark powers. It doesn't matter if the empowering spirits were reported to be the ghosts of dead humans, or fairies, or even beings described as "saints" or "angels", depending on the time and place; all were seen to be disguises taken by the Enemy of Mankind and his demonic helpers, to lead the Witch astray.

As we shall see, this over-simplification is based in part on a significant spiritual reality, but also on many social and cultural forces that coalesced to create a false view of Witchcraft as a singular and unified demonic threat to society in Early Modern Times. The social and cultural forces in question arose in a background of political and religious strife and deep uncertainty, and in times of rapid social transformation within Early Modern societies. This birthed a paranoia within many communities which led to a need for forms of socio-psychological decompression, of *expiation of evil* and cleansing, followed by a kind of rebirth for those communities. Targeting those accused of the ultimate moral corruption, torturing them and killing them (thus banishing the evil from the wounded human group) was a collective coping mechanism of a very grim sort—but not a mechanism that is unknown, or even that unusual throughout recorded history.

Witchcraft has always existed on the margins of societies—and this is true for Early Modern Christian societies as well as the medieval societies that preceded them, and even the Pagan societies that were in place long before Christian cultural hegemony came to transform Europe so fundamentally.

Witchcraft before Christianity assumed many cultural forms in the many Pagan societies that then existed. But sorcery—the act of human men and women gaining access to the spirit world or the Unseen, and gaining special powers or insights from that world—while a truly universal practice, was *not* a warmly-embraced vocation within the Indo-European Pagan world. There was always a degree of suspicion and perceived danger inherent in such unusual activities as sorcery, always a social *wariness* between sorcerous practitioners with their obscure spirit-helpers and larger societies ordered around the cults and traditions of tribal and national Gods.

The act of people introducing "religious innovations" to Pagan societies could be met with severe punishment. The celebrated philosopher Socrates was sentenced to death on the charge that, by honoring and taking advice from his *daimon* (the personal guiding spirit he claimed to have access to) he was somehow breaking his belief in the Gods of the Athenian state and showing impiety, which could be a criminal matter in all pre-Christian Greek city states.

Among the stories attributed to Aesop, we find mention of "mages" and other users of magic and sorcery being condemned to death. In one story, a "woman mage" is brought to trial because she claimed to be able to placate the anger of the Gods with her incantations. She did well for herself for a while, until people accused her of foisting unknown or newfangled religious ideas onto people, and she was executed.

The storied men and women who managed to accomplish strange and powerful partnerships with unknown or little-known spirits were *not* commonplace. The sorcerer or the Witch has *never* been "commonplace" within polite society or dominant social circles, not even in Pagan times. Further, the *Witch* and the Iron-Age Pagan *priest* or *priestess* of the various historical Godly cults were **not** part of the same spiritual or vocational realm; they were not interchangeable people with similar social roles.

The Pagan priest or priestess was a trusted public ritual functionary whose sacred task it was to maintain temples, shrines, and various important sanctuaries to the Gods of a community or culture, and to facilitate sacrifice rituals to those Gods on behalf of the community. Such a person was a trusted and respected pillar of Pagan society. Sorcerers and Witches would have been seen as belonging to a much less reputable segment of society; the Pagan sorcerer or Witch was the man or woman to whom you might go with requests that you could not make of the Gods publicly, or before the eyes of your community. Clandestine matters were their specialty.

The *seeresses* that we hear tales of in Pagan societies—such as the *Pythia* at Delphi, the *Veleda* among the Celtic peoples, and the *Volva* among the

Germanic peoples—were socially revered for their helpful abilities to gain prophecies and were *also* very distinctive figures from the sorcerer or Witch. I will own that the spirit-singing *Volva* probably had more in common with a sorceress or Witch than most ancient cultural seership-authorities, but in general, seeresses occupied a particular place of honor in Pagan societies, above and distinctive from the sorceress or Witch.

It may come as a surprise to most modern people, but Pagan cultures were just as willing to execute Witches or sorcerers as Christian cultures were. Before Christian culture was established throughout Europe, laws in ancient Greece and Rome (to make two examples) were in place listing penalties, up to and including the death penalty, for people who used sorcery to manipulate others or harm them.

Witchcraft in its original historical sense remains now what it always was: a universal human *cultural activity,* an activity of extraordinary engagement with the Unseen world, that has taken many forms over time. Perhaps in times before the Pagan Iron Age, and before the Christian era, sorcery or Witchcraft might have been more accepted or acceptable in the now-lost societies of prehistory. Or perhaps, owing to its natural strangeness and the fact that only strange-souled people tend to be drawn to its extraordinary (and sometimes maddening) voyages of mind and soul, Witchcraft has always been somewhat mistrusted and kept at a cultural arm's length.

By the time Christianity's long shadow fell over the world, Witchcraft had been for ages in the darkness of social margins, and from that darkness Witch-men and women performed healings, exorcisms, curses, hexes, and other such works for clients who paid them appropriately. This same activity for Witches is on clear display well into Christian times, even if the darkness the Witches lived in by then had become deeper and more scandalous. And the activity of Witches continues today.

It is not the popular or celebrated Witches of modern Neopagan religions of which I am speaking; I am talking about those who have undergone a certain transformation of the soul which empowers them to be in league with entities who dwell on the Nightside of our world. This occult realm of experience is both *rare* and *risky* to the (often) fragile modern psychologies of the men and women who might chance it—and that's before one considers the many social dangers it can still invoke in the lives of those who succeed (to whatever degree) in becoming *Witched*. Why any modern persons would chance the crooked pathway towards the hidden reality of *Witching* shall be discussed soon.

## The Dark Ecology of the Devil

The Devil, as the primary "empowering agent" of Early Modern Witchcraft in the minds of Christian elites and authorities (and the minds of most common folk, too), is a deep and traditional presence in any record of European Witchcraft and in the relevant folklore of the same. While it has become quite a popular opinion that the Devil is a later insertion, a false theological boogeyman inserted by Christian cultural authorities into a (far more natural or harmless) background of Pagan culture, this is only true to a certain extent. Modern scholarship now draws a distinction between the Theological Devil and what is called the *Folkloric Devil*—the Devil as the arch-enemy of God and man, who seeks to corrupt souls just in time for judgment day, versus the Devil who appears to be a continuation (in folklore, folktales, and other aspects of folk-culture) of various earlier, pre-Christian figures.

Christian culture, as it transformed Europe, would not tolerate the presence of competing spiritual or cultural worldviews. Any and all Pagan Gods and Goddesses, followed by any "Pagan" spirits—whether they were the local spirits of springs, wells, mountains, or rivers, or just the Ancestral spirits of Pagan peoples, were lumped together as Satanic forces, as masks of the Theological Devil and his demons. To belong to Christian culture was to reject *all* of these spirit-beings and replace them in devotion and belief with God, Jesus, the angels and the saints.

This was how deep cultural transformation was carried out; the destruction of the *Ancestral element* of Pagan culture was particularly necessary in this regard. But as we know, deep cultural transformation of this nature is not so easy to accomplish. Far from a "clean" transformation, European cultures all transformed into metaphysical messes, enormously complex matrices of blended beliefs and conflicting, even contradictory worldviews in which many tapestries of preternaturalism and supernaturalism combined alongside a new Christian universal moralism.

We have been led to believe that after the transformation into Christian culture, Europeans had fairly cohesive, consistent, and more-or-less shared understandings about the nature of this world and the next, the nature of spirits, and the nature of good and evil. Scholarship now has shown that nothing could be further from the truth.

Perhaps at the level of theological elites, at the level of priests, popes, and intelligentsia, there was a consistent understanding of theology and the Christian worldview as approved by church authorities. But the further one moves down the ladder, towards the common and less educated people who inhabited the folk-landscape, there is a massive breakdown, a great adulteration of the Christian beliefs preached from the pulpit with many strains of leftover Pagan and other folk beliefs. This blending—captured so well in the recorded trials of Witches—is the chaotic background in which the figures of the Theological Devil and the Folkloric Devil emerge and blend together.

The Theological Devil is enormously real in the minds and imaginations of Christians and Muslims. The Folkloric Devil is very real in the pages of folklore, folk tale, and in the stories and trials of Early Modern Witches. If we strain to examine the pre-Christian figures who make good candidates for later being called "The Devil", we find many: mischievous spirits, Underworld Gods, fertility Gods, and other beings occupying the reaches of what we call "myth" now make perfectly viable candidates on account of their darker nature, their associations with death, with deception, sorcery, sexuality, and other such things.

Christians declared certain beings to be "The Devil" for more reasons than just a pursuit of cultural religious dominance. Surely that pursuit of dominance led them early on to call *all* Pagan entities demonic, but *certain* Pagan entities stood out in character and nature, making them natural matches for what Christians imagined the Theological Devil to be like. "Satan" or "Devil", or "Diabolical" was a descriptor applied very generally at some points, but very specifically at others.

Then one day, the distinctions all vanished. Perhaps during transitional times, in times when cultures were not yet thoroughly Christianized, it was easier for people to see that a powerful Christian faction was calling the Old Gods devils, or the Chief God of the former Pagan culture "The Devil." But those transitional times came to an end, long ago. The language of polytheism was banished just as thoroughly as Pagan cultures were, and what remained was the absolutist language of the One God. Remnant Gods of the Pagan world were no longer *consciously recognized* as former Gods; they were spirits, or devils, or demons in the minds of our Ancestors. In some places they became seen as *fairies*— but as the records of witch trials show, *fairy* and demon or devil were entirely interchangeable in the minds of judges and clergymen, as well as in the minds of ordinary people.

"Theological Devil" and "Folkloric Devil" are academic distinctions that we make in the very modern day; they are not distinctions that people made a hundred years ago, or three hundred years ago, or at any point in the past. To a priest in 17th century Scotland, The Devil was just the Devil, and it didn't matter what shape he appeared to people in—and he could appear in many shapes.

To a peasant in the same era, it was much the same, though their understanding of what place the Devil cosmologically inhabited might not have been as detailed as the priest's.

Where the priest might cringe in terror at the idea of meeting the Devil, the peasant might also; but the peasant may just as easily decide to make a bargain with the Devil for more food or security; after all, the cohesive, super-clear religious cosmology and conviction held by the priest was likely *not* held by the peasant. Where the priest had studied theology in seminary or a university, the peasant had only heard folk-stories of the Devil around hearth-fires.

In those stories, the Devil could be oafish, comical, easily fooled, or even (at times) a protagonist acting against the greedy, wealthy, or powerful. The Devil was the great enemy of God, and surely the peasantry understood that God was the highest power—but God and the Devil's great aeonic struggle was between *them*, and these cosmological titans probably didn't concern themselves with lowly peasants overly much.

The preachers regularly insisted that all souls were precious to God, even those of the lowly peasant—and they further insisted that the foul Devil *absolutely* desired to corrupt even the lowly peasantry—but this breathless certainty, this awe and terror of the Cosmic Contest of Souls and Eternity, was not easy to transmit from the pulpit down to the hungry peasant who had watched half his family perish in the winter before. Such spiritual certainty was a *privilege* of the educated and well-fed ministers; it was just another story, hard to believe or even understand, to the dirt-scraping peasant of Early Modern Europe.

The Devil could be presented as cunning, as a great gentleman, and as someone you might turn to when you needed a favor or help that the Church and its ministers weren't willing to give. Just as before, in Pagan times, people needed a *less reputable* source of help and aid at times, and there were always shadowy places one might sneak off to, to find it.

Whether or not dealing with the Devil might mean the forfeiture of one's soul was likely not a major concern of ordinary or uneducated people in Early Modern times, either—beliefs on the afterlife were also not uniform and neat across Folk Europe. The idea of taking up residence in the Fairy World after death (to make an example) was a genuinely held belief among many people in the British Isles in the Early Modern period. This was a complete alternative vision of the afterlife which stood alongside the official narrative that one either went to "heaven or hell" when they died.

In the rich blend of folk-Christianity, one might evade contracts or bargains made with the Devil or demons by simply confessing to a priest before death, repenting, and trusting the power of Jesus to save one from the contract—after all, in common belief, Jesus or God were surely more powerful than the Devil. It was worth the risk to have one's family delivered from sickness, poverty, or hunger—a thing that God and the saints were clearly unable or unwilling to do much of the time. Their cosmological enemy might be willing to do that favor in exchange for some allegiance.

And if not the Devil, there were other powerful spirits that one might deal with. The King of the Fairies—and the Queen of the Fairies—both feature as encountered beings in many narratives of fairy belief and Witchcraft. Of course, the blending of belief being what it was, in many minds the Fairy King was none other than the Devil, albeit an example of a *Folkloric Devil* as we have discussed here.

Most people reading this book will be direct inheritors of Western Christian culture. Even though much has changed, and the power of churches has faded, a vibrant blending of our Ancestral myths and stories, alongside various (often confusing) iterations of the Christian cosmological worldview lives inside of all of us. Even in this post-Christian era, even among those who claim no beliefs in the supernatural or preternatural at all, the name of *Satan* or the Devil means something. More than intellectual meaning, it carries an emotional meaning.

To us modern Westerners, the Devil is *real*. He has always been real to us, and will remain so until some uncertain point in the distant future when the history of Christian culture is itself almost like a legend, half-remembered, and forgotten. For us, in our culture-soul, in our culture-minds, the Devil is a real person. We may come up with countless ways to interpret The Devil; we may secularize him into a psychological shadow of repressed, dark material, or we may say he's simply a figure invented by Christians to scare Pagans into conversion. We may say that he's a fallen angel, indeed, but that his rebellion against God was righteous, and that he's not such a villain after all, in a very Miltonian way.

We can say that The Devil is many things, just as people in Early Modern times did. But he's always *something* to us.

We can be as academic and intellectual as we wish to be when it comes to the Devil, or as skeptical as we wish, or we can embrace a belief in him with full force, hating him as the arch-enemy of God and hoping to never end up in hell with him, but we always have to make an *answer* to the cultural reality of The Devil. And his very name still has the power to provoke some kind of emotional response deep inside us, whether it is a secret shudder, or a sudden alarm bell of danger, or a mocking laugh at what we *hope* is the unreality of such a monster.

We become considerably more powerful and considerably more free the day we recognize that the Devil is *real*. He may not be real exactly as the local minister or priest says, and he may not be real precisely as the Early Modern priests and preachers said, but he is a real feature of our cultural psychology, a real feature of our history, and a real feature in our general realm of Western occult understandings.

Studying history, and the transformation of European cultures from Pagan to Christian, *does* supply much material to make an airtight case that The Devil, if he could be met on the road behind your house tomorrow, would probably be a pre-Christian spirit of some great power, perhaps even once worshiped by Pagan cultures as some kind of God. The being you'd meet would very likely *not* be leading a band of evil demons about, intent on corrupting your soul and leading you into eternal damnation; and yet, you'd have very little choice but to feel that you've encountered a dangerous, potentially even *evil* entity.

Our cultural Christian conditioning cannot allow us to feel much otherwise when The Devil is on the stage. There's a lot of people who don't believe in the Devil anymore, and yet, paradoxically, *everyone* truly believes in the Devil in a deeper cultural-psychological sense.

We are deeply hindered by our cultural conditioning when it comes to grasping or understanding who this powerful spirit-person is—this powerful person that Christians specifically (and perhaps rightly) called "The Devil." Whoever or whatever he was before Christians came around, he was powerful; he was tricky; he was wise beyond comprehension, and he could lead men and women to great wisdom or great peril. He could do things that were frightening, or even malicious-seeming. He was inscrutable, he was mercurial, and he was beyond anyone's attempt at a human moral code. He could be helpful, he could be distant, or he could be destructive.

This complex figure must be approached by each person to the best of their ability. Ultimately, it doesn't matter what you believe about Him. If you sincerely believe he's the force of cosmic super-evil, you probably won't be walking down to the local crossroads to attempt to meet him or one of his representatives and make any deals. Or perhaps you might; like so many people in ages before you might think you know a loophole that will get you out of the consequences of your actions.

If you believe that the Devil is a mysterious character, a figure in our cultural metaphysical narrative created from many different older cultural strands and stories (some of them theological, some of them folkloric) all blended together, you're just smarter than the average person. But even you can't evade the "stench of evil" that our culture bestowed upon the Devil, and if you met him, you'd be on your guard. And perhaps that's wise.

Those who will be following the instructions in this book, instructions which might lead them to the Unseen side of our world and into face-to-face meetings with spirits of different sorts, will have to come to terms with The Devil in their own understanding.

The attempt to say *"I'm not afraid of The Devil, because I don't accept the Christian worldview, I don't believe in hell or sin, and I think the Devil is probably just Pan or Dionysos or some Pagan God like that, given a bad rap by Christians"* seldom works as well as people think it will. Neopagans—who are still Western Cultural Christians, even if they reject their cultural Christianity—have been declaring some version of this story for decades; what it gives back to them intellectually, it certainly robs from them emotionally. It also places them in a subconscious place of emotional denial.

Ironically, while it is *rationally* important (in some circles) to contest the propagandistic claims of historical Christians who once called the Gods of the Pagan world "devils', doing so *doesn't make for very good modern Witches*. A person will gain more power—and more depth of experience—feeling *afraid* of the Devil they meet, than trying to put an essay about how Christians "made the devil up" between themselves and the dark encounter with the great and mysterious Other. A defensive reaction laced with rationality and a history textbook really *will* kill the moment. But fear, awe, and the sublime regions of mind and experience one might reach if they are brave and if they surrender their desire to explain everything away—that's a treasure beyond value.

Any understanding of The Devil will allow one to proceed with the work of this book, with the exception of one: the idea that he is completely fake, that he does not exist as a person (nor a collective of persons) who might be met in the same way that you might meet a stranger during a walk in a park. That belief will *not* act as an empowering corridor of understanding and emotion which can potentially open deeper Unseen metaphysical doors.

After decades of pondering the Puzzle of the Devil, I can say what my conclusions are regarding him—and my conclusions don't have to be adopted by anyone reading this. I no longer think of The Devil in terms of "the person" whose nature or ultimate origins we are trying to unravel. I think of the Devil as a person of unthinkable, unimaginable spiritual power, but *also* as a name given to an **Ecology of Power**, an ecology of powers and forces which is far more ancient than any human culture or civilization.

When I say "ecology of power", I do not mean that Devil is only a name given to a collection of powers, though from the perspective of history, we know that many powers and spirit-persons were, in fact, *all* called "The Devil" by Christian cultural authorities.

The stories of The Devil, found in folk-tale, in folk culture, in fairy tales, and in other places (the stories that form the core of the layered Folkloric Devil motif) present him in precisely the manner you'd imagine a natural ecology being presented: ambiguous, unpredictable, sometimes foolish, sometimes very clever; extremely powerful; sometimes hostile, sometimes helpful. That describes our experience of Nature very well. And indeed, from within the body of Nature, we can envision a spiritual figure of great mystery and power emerging, worshiped or revered as far back as humans have existed—and we can further see that quasi-natural force/person assuming a rulership role in the later pantheons of Pagan peoples.

And we can see how such a force, such a person—a shape-shifter, with many names, with many entities subordinate to him and serving him, deeply associated with the carnal nature of humans and animals, with the fertility of the land, with the vitality of nature itself, with the destructive powers and the generative ones, could finally end up excoriated as *The Devil* by a Christian culture that was trying to lead humans *away* from Nature—which was declared sinful and fallen—and away from "The Lord of this World", and towards a transcendent heaven; a clean, pure place beyond the grasp of dirty bodies, or of sex, sin, violence, vice, and injustice.

It was a transcendent God of justice and peace that people wanted. Perhaps they were tired of the timeless cycles of blood and death, of sex and betrayal, of vain empires and the forever *ebb and flow* of toil and misery. Abrahamic religions reject the world; they reject that death should be natural, and see our world as only a temporary misery to be endured before entering into an eternal reward. This is a very predictable and even understandable psychological reaction to a world of pain. But that *doesn't* make it real, nor does it mean that the transcendent God they propose is real.

What *is* more likely real is what has always been here: the timeless cycles of blood and death, of sex and searching for food, of wellness and sickness, of loves and hurts, risks and adventures, failures and successes, rewards and disappointments. And within the mighty organic matrix of sensual life which makes *all* of this possible are powerful spirits, some of whom have obtained much influence over the organic systems and cycles of life.

The "Lord of this World" might refer to the ecology of vital life in this world, and the devious, clever indwelling intelligences that permeate it. We can call them *spirits*, if we want, and we can see that among them, there is an eldest, or perhaps a group of eldest powers running back to the ancient roots of all life. Perhaps they have the most influence, and it is to *Them* we must look if we wish to understand the mystery of the "Gods" of the Pagan world, and the Spirits of the Foretime in general.

And one of them, so stridently clever and cunning, so full of life-force and himself the dreamer of the first stories that so many Ancestral life-forms were influenced by, may well stand at the center of this ecology. He may be flanked by other powers similar to him, and by countless others lesser somewhat in strength or power, but convicted to his resonance, to his presence, and acting as his *mediators* to greater reaches of this ecology—his serving spirits.

He may be our Devil, after all. And he may put on cultural masks and names, and take them off again, as rapidly as we change our own clothes from day to day. He may laugh at the stories told about him by so many peoples, or he may not—he may barely notice them at all, and instead sit in timeless contemplations in trance-states or states of perception that we can't begin to imagine.

Whatever he *is*, whatever he *does*, whatever he is called, he is *feared* by our culture and our civilization—he and the ecology of powers that surround him, the very ecology of which we are all a part. We deny our belonging to this ecology, but we are still parts of it. We hope to escape it, but I do not believe that is possible; **this ecology is reality** and there is nothing outside of it to escape to. We can only become powerful within it, become more capable, insightful, or wise within it, or remained scared, isolated, and unaware within it. This is a fundamental crossroads that we all face eventually.

Because this ecology is feared, and because the dark Master and other great powers sitting at its center are so dreaded or denied, we are privileged to know one more thing about it: **this is the ecology and these are the powers that make men and women into *Witches***. These are the powers that Witches approached, in defiance of social norms and conventions, in defiance of the fears they had learned from their own cultures, and with bravery and trust in the darkness beyond ordinary comprehension, they joined the *Witched*—they gained extraordinary sight in the darkness, and extraordinary helpers.

They approached reality as it is: raw, hungry, relational, risky, desirous, ambiguous, and full of the intensity of life-force, and they gained power and wisdom. If it wasn't the Devil who met them and bestowed initiation upon them, it was one of the powers in his ecological kinship—or one of the other greater powers, such as (in European folklore and certain witch-trials) the *Good Lady of Elfhame*, whom we are about to discuss.

Not all men and women have minds that can handle this. Most minds are too fragile these days, and most souls too weak. Though this timeless and dark ecology is a great combination of *Nature* and *Preternature*, though it is natural and preternatural joined together in blissful eternity, and though it is our *true home* and the origin of these bodies and souls, we now live in an age of isolation from it and its eternal truths. Our cultural truths are lies compared to its pre-human and other-than-human truths. And few among us are ready for the Truth.

Having said that, it is important to point out that the natural, eternal truths of our world are not straining to "become known" by human beings. We humans are not engaged in some cosmological contest to "figure out the truth"; the entire notion of the "purpose" of human life being to discover deeper and greater truths about things—about ourselves, about the world—is civilized mythology, and arrogant mythology at that.

The World is not waiting for us humans to know it. Living beings naturally know the world, through an ancient matrix of sense and sensual inherence in the world. Instincts allow us to feel and sense the eternal truths about our world, which are announced in every moment of instinctive and sensory perception. That *we* have lost touch with this, that *we* have lost touch with our dreams, with our bodies, with our souls—this is not the fault of the Great Ecology to which we belong.

If all these things we have lost due to our unwisdom provoke a desire in us to seek them out again and find them, that's quite okay. But to decide that "the cosmos" or Fate or destiny or God intended for us to be embarking on this search, and that completing this search successfully somehow exalts us above all other beings is childish—entirely laughable. Finding what we lost in the first place is just that; it's not cosmological or profound to anyone *except* us. And yet, we have created endless myths about it, and even whole religions and philosophies devoted to the idea. The frogs lazily sitting in the dark water and under the cool sky outside my window have never lost any connection to the Great Living World that my fellow humans feel so disconnected from, or terrified by.

To return to the Eternal Truths of Nature, or of the Ecology of which I have spoken, to meet and mingle with its living powers, ever more ancient than our own kind, is not to win some cosmological game. It is a quiet sanity that is restored, if we can overcome our fear and ignorance. It is not fireworks that explode in our heads, nor a great light of enlightenment that bathes us; it is the same lazy lap of the water and brush of the wind that the frog outside is enjoying, wordlessly and fully.

Sad to say, when a man or woman is carried beyond the lies and errors of their culture or society, and when they see the vast, dark spaces of the ecology that we descend from, and when they see the reality of the Gods, of the spirits, of the human flesh itself, and all the flesh of life, they *may* feel a certain peace, a certain rest, a certain freedom—but those who have not overcome the same fears and seen the same dark and ancient spaces will fear them or hate them.

There's only one thing really worse than the lies and terrors that imprison us, and that's the men and women who don't suffer them alongside us. They might as well be alien beings from another world, and indeed, the attained Witch becomes (partly) *precisely that*. They are, after all, the

*Devil's Own*. They don't become all-wise sages; they just become more free than others, in the deepest sense of that word. And that might make all the difference in the world.

## The Good Lady of Elfhame

Most of the Early Modern accounts of Witchcraft and trials related to Witchcraft focus on the Devil, and for quite understandable cultural reasons. Whether he was called *The Devil, Christsonday, Robin, Mahoun, Auld Hornie, Old Nick, Old Hobb, Old Splitfoot*, or simply the *Gudeman* (the Good Man) or the *Hynd King* (the Kindly King), his ubiquitous appearance can't conceal the other beings who worked their way up into the official records of history from the dark bedrock of Folk culture.

The Witches Alison Pierson, Andro Man, Isobel Gowdie, and Jean Weir (alongside many others) all gave accounts of meeting the Queen of the Elves, or the Fairy Queen. Two of these testimonies are from the 16th century (Pierson and Man) and the other two are from the 17th century, indicating a persistent folk tradition. But that a folk tradition concerning the Queen of Elves or the Queen of Fairies existed in Britain is not in question at all; the *Romance of Thomas Rhymer*, dated to the 14th century, gives the most detailed and popular account of a mortal man meeting the Fairy Queen and being taken into her realm and there, undergoing mysterious transformations which endow him with the power of *prophecy* after he returns to this world.

The *Survey of Scottish Witchcraft*, one of the most important modern sources whose insights are critical to any real understanding of the subject of Early Modern Witchcraft, has produced a superb body of information which reveals some of the lost treasures of Early Modern Witchlore. Before the Survey's results were published, the legendary Queen of Elves or fairies—the *Queen of Elfhame* (or *Elphame, Elphane, Elphyne*, or *Elfhome*, depending) was never given much in the way of a formal name in Folk Tradition. *Nicneven* certainly emerges as one of the best candidates, at least from Scotland; but the Survey showed that twenty-one accused witches named the Elf-Queen **Antiochia**, and described her as *"the gentle wife of the Devil."*

The strange name "Antiochia" is probably based on some unknown older root. Joyce Miller, who mentions the name in her seminal essay *Men in Black: Appearances of the Devil in Early Modern Scottish Witchcraft Discourse*, does not believe that Antiochia connects in any way to Saint Margaret of Antioch, an obscure Turkish saint. *Antiochia* is one of the only names arising from deep British Isles Folk tradition that we have for the powerful female counterpart to the *fierce and fell* Devil, She who fills our soul-imaginations with so many wonders through the vehicle of her romances, folk-tales, fairy tales, ballads, visionary encounters, and other stories.

Such is the nature of an ecology, and of the localist nature of our Folklore and folk-culture, that powerful female-appearing spirits, even those described as "Fairy Queens", do not all necessarily refer to the *same* entity; and yet, such is the nature of inter-connectedness and relationship (particularly as we see in geographic cultural kinship) that certain figures spread across the fund of different stories or accounts *might* well be.

Andro Man, who was executed for Witchcraft in 1598 when he was in his 70's at least, confessed that he had met the "Queen of Elphen" when he was a boy. Before long, he had become her lover, and over the decades of his trysting with her, he claimed he had several children with her. The Queen of Elphen was certainly the primary source of Man's power; though she killed one of his cows on a hill called *Elphillock* (Elf-hill), she promised him "only good" after this. She told Man he would have the power to know all things, to heal, and that while he would be "well looked after", he would wander all his life, and have to "seek his meat" or food before he died, as Thomas Rhymer—the most famous legendary consort of the Fairy Queen—was said to do. Thomas Rhymer was one of the ghosts or departed humans that Man claimed to meet in the presence of the Fairy Queen, his patroness and provider of his power.

Man's testimony was unusually detailed, much like that of two other arch-famous Witches: Isobel Gowdie and Bessie Dunlop. The generous layers of detail given by all three confessors to "trafficking with spirits" allow for incredible cosmological depths and insights to be unlocked in the unique worldviews each of them had during life. Their worldviews overlapped in many significant ways, pointing to a more-or-less cohesive form of folk animism they had inherited from their own cultural times and places.

Andro Man is one historical Witch (but not the only one) who identified the male partner of the Fairy Queen as a powerful spirit-being named *Christsonday*. Man called Christsonday the *Gudeman*, or the husband of the Fairy Queen, and considered him to be his "Master"—but he was also very clear that Christsonday was The Devil, forever engaged in a "thraw" or quarrel with God. This would be another instance of the folkloric overlap of the Fairy King and Devil figures, and again certainly not the only one. Man said that while Christsonday had "all power under God", it was the Queen of Elphen who had a "grip", or total command, over all of the arts of Witchcraft.

Man further reported that the Queen of Elphen could be "young or old as she pleased"—a trait clearly displayed in the *Romance of Thomas Rhymer*, and in other strains of old lore—and could "make any that she pleased into a king"—a hint of an ancient sovereignty-granting power that suits the Great Queen dwelling inside the Land, in a fairy-Underworld or otherwise. She was also able to "make love to whomever she wished"; the supreme Venusian power being granted to her rounds out a folk understanding of whom and what this primal Queenly figure might be.

The power of the Good Lady of Elfhame stood behind the careers of many Early Modern Witches. Bessie Dunlop, executed in 1576, gained her power to heal, find stolen objects, and the like through the aid of her familiar, Thom Reid—the ghost of a man slain some decades before she met him, at the Battle of Pinkie. Dunlop met Thom at a time of great distress in her life, with a newborn baby on the edge of death and her husband taken ill. She was bringing their cattle in when she met Thom—and the relationship that began between them would define the next four years (which were the last four years) of Dunlop's life. When she asked Thom why he chose to come to her and endow her with the powers he had, he responded that the *Fairy Queen had sent him* to act as her familiar.

Thom was clearly an agent of the Queen of Elfhame—a Queen to whom his soul was bound (along with many other fairy beings) since the time of his death. He was a kind, if strange familiar to Bessie, at times asking her to renounce her Christian baptism and yield her soul to the Queen. Some consider Thom Reid to be a ghost, but it's clear from the records that he was a fairy man—a thing that only confuses people who do not understand that fairies in the Early Modern British Isles were very often seen to be the post-mortem entities of dead human beings. The Queen of Elfhame is, indeed, the Queen of Spirits or Souls, those who have died and descended into the interior dimension of our sensual world, which is the origin-dimension of life itself.

It was an act of kindness to the Queen of Elfhame that apparently won Bessie Dunlop the reward of a familiar spirit, who empowered her to four very legendary years of preternatural adventures and fame: when Bessie was in labor with one of her children, a "stout carline" came to her door begging for a drink, and Bessie obliged her. This seemingly ordinary traveler was the Fairy Queen in human form. The Queen could assume any shape or form, including attractive, middling, or even hideous human shapes.

Isobel Gowdie met with the Elf-Queen in one of her many journeys below the Downie Hillock (or below the Downie Hills), in the *"Elfe's Howsses"*—and Gowdie said that the Queen was "handsomely clad in white linens and white and brown clothing", and her generosity was second to none; Gowdie said she *"got meat there from the Queein of Fearrie... mor than I could eat."* This report of the Elf-Queen or Queen of Elfhame being dressed in white coincides with her deeper role as the *White Phantom Queen* which can be detected in the annals of British Isles pre-Christian culture. And *whiteness*, as a ghostly or otherworldly motif, re-occurs with the Queen in historical records. Marion Grant, a Witch who was either part of Andro Man's coven, or spiritually aware of him through some kind of spectral dream-cult that joined together witches in Old Aberdeenshire, described the Queen of Elfhame as *"A fine woman, clad in a white walicot."*

The Good Lady of Elfhame bestowing special treasures or enchanted items (or medicinal charms) onto people who meet with her in her underground realm is a common motif. Even King James VI records, in his work *Daemonologie*, an interlocutor asking how Witches claim that *"they have been transported with the Phairie to such a hill, which opening, they went in, and there saw a Faire Queene, who gave them* a *stone which had sundrie virtues...*" The "stone" in question here is of course a stone used in healing workings—stones that were at times captured as evidence in trials against Witches. But other stories recount the Queen giving other talismans, such as a talismanic white powder which gave a Witch the power to heal humans and beasts.

The connection between ghosts and fairies has already been mentioned, and the connection of both ghosts and fairies with the Fairy Queen and (of course) the Fairy King is plain. It's quite telling how often ghosts, or deceased humans now in the "fairy" condition act as emissaries or messengers for the greater, deeper powers and rulers of *Elfhame*, which in this case can be thought of as a name not only for the fairy-world specifically, but for the whole of the Unseen world into which living, breathing beings must one day perish.

The term *Elf* itself is a direct equivalent in the Germanic cultures from which it was born to the concept of *Fairy* in Celtic lands. Elf, extending as it does from *Alf*, rooted in *Alb*, refers to a *white one*, or a *pale one*, one of the dead. It may be a poetic reference to the bones of the dead, bones calcinated white by funerary pyres, or simply to the ages-old connection between otherworldly beings and the color white or pale. The notion of an "Elf-hill" or an *Elphillock* is clearly a circumlocution for a burial mound. The dead are below the ground, merged with the land through the burial of their remains, whether their remains be interred whole or deposited as ashes and bone fragments.

Alison Pearson, who was tried in 1588 for "*haunting and communing with the gude neighbours and the queen of Elfland*", reported not only going below the hills and into the Fairy Underworld (Elfland, Elfhame), but receiving a familiar who was a ghost—the deceased entity of William Simpson, who assisted her in her Witchcraft, a craft which was largely concerned with healing and exorcism.

Isobel Haldane reported, in 1623 that she had been carried to a "hill which opened"—and she remained underneath it for three days until a gray-bearded man brought her out again. She invoked this man thereafter when she performed her Witchery, and he came to assist her. In 1628, Steven Maltman told his judges at Stirling that his healing gift (for which he was presumably on trial) came from *the Fayre Folk*. In 1572, Janet Boyman explained that her healing powers came from the ghost of a woman who had taught her to heal, and who "came to her like a blast of wind" when she called upon her.

These accounts are legion. I could fill this book up in mentions of them—but the point is made. Both the Devil and the Good Lady of Elfhame cast their timeless shadows into the accounts of Early Modern Witchcraft, and if we lift our eyes to other lands and other shores, we find easily recognizable cognate and parallel figures and similar activities of spirit-aided sorcery in other places during the same period.

This is all part of a universal experience of sorcery, of Witchcraft, of *humans relating to spirits for extraordinary outcomes* which was ancient long before the Early Modern period. And most critically for those reading my words here, **these great powers are still active today**, and they or their serving-beings *might* (if certain fortunes hold) be met in extraordinary ways. Relationships with them can be formed.

It is clear that familiar spirits are often in the service (in some manner) of greater spiritual authorities or powers, granting skills or favors on their behalf. There are no hard-and fast "rules" for the Spirit world or the Unseen; but if historical accounts can teach us anything, there are powers and beings with different degrees of influence who can be appealed to and *asked to send forth spirits in their service* to our aid. It may be that very powerful beings always extend their blessings, curses, or influences through the vehicle of entities bound to them, and always have in any age of the world. This will be useful to ponder, and to know.

## The Devil's Own

We stand to gain a good deal of insight into the *Strange Souls* of our modern day—those men and women who might find themselves walking the hidden road into the spectral experience of the eldritch forces who forge Witches from the flesh of humankind—by investigating who the Witches of the past were themselves. Human life and society is an intimately connected story that extends branches of its great narrative into all manner of places: the past, the present, and the timeless *hidden past* that the true present is based upon.

Our story of time and wandering life is rhizomic; it has many branches and roots that overlap at odd angles and coincide at unexpected points. Who we are right now is entwined deeply with who we were, and all that we might have been, or will be.

Who were the Witches of Early Modern Times? Who are they now? These two questions are quite distant in some regards, and merged together in other surprising ways.

One of the most important insights that emerges from *The Survey of Scottish Witchcraft* is that Witches were not a persecuted minority. In previous decades, there was a popular narrative created that "witches" were subjected to a mass slaughter or a holocaust of types, resulting in *millions* of deaths in Early Modern times—claims were made that anywhere from seven to nine million people were executed for Witchcraft. Thankfully, we now know that this was not the case.

The Survey of Scottish Witchcraft took into account every recorded Witch trial in Scotland between 1563 and 1736—the nearly 200 years that saw the heyday of the "witch hunts" in European history. Due to the turbulent politics and social and religious strife that consumed Scotland in these times, witch hunting and witch trials/executions were *more common* there than in other European nations. The Survey shows that 3,837 men and women were accused of witchcraft in Scotland in this time frame. The Survey further (tentatively) concludes that possibly 67% of those accused were executed—2,570 people. That comes to roughly 19 people being executed for Witchcraft a year, for nearly two centuries in Scotland.

If we attempt to extrapolate from this data how many people might have been executed across Europe in the same period (bearing in mind that Scotland was a bit more heavy-handed in executions than most other places) and when scholars take into account what is known about witch trials in other regions, the best estimate of how many men and women lost their lives in Early Modern times to Witchcraft accusations comes to about 60,000. That's about 300 people a year, Europe-wide.

This hardly represents a historical holocaust; and while (most) modern people will never find it acceptable for even *one* person to be executed for what amounts to spiritual differences, or folk-charms or spells or what have you, the belief in the spiritual menace behind these things was extreme and everywhere common in Early Modern times. Whatever the case, it remains undeniably true that people were *infinitely* more likely to be executed for theft than they ever were for Witchcraft in the Early Modern era. And despite the outbreaks of witch-hysterias or mass arrests and executions that *did* occur from time to time, Early Modern life was not characterized by endless frequent accusations of Devilry or Witchcraft between neighbors, as so many modern people assume.

Alongside the discredited myth of "millions" being killed for Witchcraft, we find two other assumptions worth looking into: the idea that Witch accusations largely targeted women, and were continuations of patriarchal aggression against women specifically, and the idea that certain professions often associated with women—such as herbalism, hedge-healing, or midwifery—were especially targeted for Witch accusations.

The idea that women were more likely to be accused of Witchcraft is borne out by evidence; the Survey of Scottish Witchcraft shows that 85% of the accused in Scotland were women. If the 67% execution rate holds, that means 2,185 women were executed over the two centuries in question, or about twelve women a year. This number has a way of changing fairly strongly by cultural region; Caroline Lea's research into Witch accusations and executions in Iceland between the years 1604 and 1720 revealed that of the 22 people executed for Witchcraft in that time, only one was a woman. Cultural variation plays an enormous role in this.

In the *Survey of Scottish Witchcraft*, it was found that of all the people accused of Witchcraft, only 9 were listed as midwives by profession, and for 10 others, midwifery was mentioned as part of their charges. About 4% of the cases—141 people—had any mention of "Folk healing" in their accusations. Healing was a fairly common practice and industry in those times, so it's surprising that so few accused Witches in Scotland were associated with it.

The Survey does mention that the gender division of accused and executed in Scotland appears to match what is known of the gender division in other parts of Europe, both in England and the mainland. It also points out that in places like Estonia, Russia, and Finland, the accused were just as likely, in some places, to be male as female.

As far as the cultural motif of the "old crone" goes, the idea that Witches were often older women, this notion probably belongs more properly to the realm of fairy tales or folklore than to actual legal realities or records of witch trials. Based on what the Survey of Scottish Witchcraft could record, 22% of the accused were between 30 and 40 years of age; 22% were between 40 and 50, and 31% were between 50 and 60. All other ages (younger or older) were outliers. That's not very many "crones" in the sense that is ordinarily meant by that term.

One thing that is held up by records is how *class-related* Witch accusations and executions were. Practically every person accused of Witchcraft in Scotland, or executed for it, was *not* from a wealthy background. The nature of wealth being what it is, we can be certain this was the case across Europe, generally speaking.

What *sorts* of people do writers from the Early Modern period claim that Witches were? As you might imagine, the people who had the education to write down statements that would survive to us today were likely to be members of the elite or upper classes, or members of the clergy, and thus, their descriptions of the personalities of Witches aren't likely to be very flattering. But this brings us to a critical point all on its own: Witches were overwhelmingly *not* members of the elite classes. They were not formally educated people. They were the common folk, the people of the Land, as it were—the everyday people who lived at the hearthside and in small villages and rural areas around Europe.

There is a metaphysical class division between the Witch and the figure of the *Mage*. Mages, the sorts of men (for they were almost always men) who kept libraries in their homes, who owned books of magic which include the famous Grimoires of Hermetic or Ceremonial magic that are so popular in occult circles today, were *not* Witches. These were men who had the money to own libraries of books, and the education to both read them and write them. They *could* be accused of Witchcraft just as readily as any Witch, for in the eyes of the Church their magic was diabolical too—even though it was done in the name of God, in the name of Christ and the angels and saints, it still inclined largely towards the conjuration of demons, and the obtaining of wealth, power, and knowledge thereby. In this *goetic* sense of diabolical conjury, so-called "High magic" could be quite sorcerous in nature.

But the educated and often upper-class men who owned these Grimoires typically had the money to protect themselves from prosecution for their strange occult pastimes. An enormous difference remains, aesthetically and metaphysically, between the Witch who obtains familiar spirits through meetings with The Devil or the Queen of Elfhame, and the Mage who, through appeal to Christ and the saints, *forces* a demon to serve them. A demon so bound by the faith of the Mage and his endless ecclesiastical incantations may help to bring about or accomplish extraordinary things for him, but the relationship of familiar to Witch is of a strikingly different sort.

The worldview of the historical Mage, arising from formal education, theology, and the arts and sciences of high culture, was of a *vastly* different tone and aesthetic from the worldview of the farmer or peasant. The folkloric cosmologies informed by lifelong encounters with local landforms, the tales and stories of resident or wandering storytellers, and the rich fund of folklore itself would have been scoffed at by the educated members of social upper-echelons. In this, we see the ultimate origin of the idea that Witchcraft and sorcery represent "low magic"—the magic of uneducated, backwards people intent on making their crops grow higher or robbing their rival neighbors of milk, versus the "sacred" magic of Grimoires being labeled "high magic", or the elite magic of civilized and educated men intent on reaching the heights of divine realization.

This distinction, which is still very much alive today, is a rancid artifact of classism that somehow managed to replicate itself into the modern day—and ironic too, as most of the people engaged in *Grimoiric* workings in 2020 are not often in any economic, educational, or social class higher than the vast majority of those engaging in what they believe is Witchcraft.

History, they say, is written by the winners; "winners" here is just a circumlocution for "the wealthy." The wealthy Medieval and Renaissance hobby of occultism via Grimoires and complicated and expensive ceremonies was privileged to survive (due to the literacy of its proponents) to the present day, where it deeply informs what we think of Early Modern magic. The nature, activities, and deeds of Early Modern Witches were lost almost entirely. The 100% conflation of "magic" (in the sense of Grimoire-based operations or metaphysics) with Witchcraft is *total* in most modern occult communities, and in the minds of most occult practitioners. The most popular and common groups of persons calling themselves "witches" today are practicing a form of ceremonial magic which ultimately arose from Ceremonial magic orders and practitioners in England in the middle of the 20<sup>th</sup> century.

So what did Early Modern sources actually say about the character of the individuals who became Witches? What forces were working on their persons and personalities, to lead to such strange (and in the eyes of the pillars of society, woeful) outcomes? The General Assembly of the Scottish Church declared in 1643 that the causes of Witchcraft "*are found to be these, especially: extremity of grief, malice, passion and the desire for revenge, pinching poverty, solicitation of other Witches and charmers, for in such cases the devil assails them, offers aid, and much prevails.*"

This straightforward declaration might be unpacked for days—it comes out and says that people who are stricken by poverty are naturally more open to offers of relief from their torment by preternatural forces. One might be sympathetic to people hammered down by class-related injustice seeking redress for that ages-old wrong, that ages-old aggression against ordinary people at the hands of wealthy elites, via alliance with the more ancient Unseen world. And this point lies at the heart of the fear and hostility we see on the part of the wealthy elites for Witchcraft: Elder forces and strange allies helped to 'even the social score' a bit, giving some ordinary people an eldritch sword with which to strike back at their oppressors. Certainly *part* of the horror was based on theology, on the prevailing religious norms of the day, but those were (as we have seen) religious norms that meant far more to upper-class elites than they ever did to the peasants they regularly exploited.

The mention of "extremity of grief" is telling, as well. The idea that in grief, after the loss of a child or family members particularly, a man or woman might be more receptive to spiritual influences connects to other reports of Early Modern Witchcraft. One story tells of a woman who lost three children, and was visited by their ghosts—or entities that might have been their ghosts—and she accepted them as familiar spirits after a rather harrowing interview with them. This woman's judges decided that these entities who appeared to her were not her children, but demons disguised as her children who were seeking a target of opportunity in a grieving mother.

The idea of *melancholy* often gets associated with Witches. Today we would call this depression, but what depression actually is, or how its many causes work together is far from known. It's safe to say that the 'pinch of poverty', alongside natural grief at the frequent loss of loved ones would be enough to do to people now what it has always done, and fill them with a deep melancholy about their prospects of happiness in this world.

The notion that people who are unable to cheerfully fall into their expected social place, into their class-related roles in life and to conform to their own social systems (for whatever reasons) are **in danger of being manipulated by forces from outside of their social system** is not a new idea. We see modern examples of this when we see people who refuse to accept the countless injustices of their capitalist societies entertaining socialist or communist notions; and goodness knows it wasn't long ago that another sort of savage witch hunt took place in the United States, with "communists" being the hidden Witches scattered about society.

The declaration of the Scottish Church essentially explains Witchcraft by (not surprisingly) associating it with every antisocial or sinful tendency in their own social and moral theology. But it goes further; it says that *other Witches* are sometimes the cause of a man or woman falling into Witchcraft—and that the Devil, when he does offer his aid to any of the many persons who might be in a situation to receive it, *often prevails*. This would suggest that the Devil was selling very effective cures for these men and women's social and emotional ills.

Malice, passion, and the desire for revenge—the strongest "negative" forces operating on the human person are connected to Witchcraft. Again, taking into account the hardships that people in Early Modern Europe lived through on the regular, taking into account the enormous quantities of injustice that were normalized in their lives, we have to see, in these words of the Elites, the typical elite condescension towards the emotional and tangible life-conditions of most ordinary people. Not all malice is without grounds. Not all desires for revenge are based on mere moral failing; sometimes outrages cry out for a revenge that extends itself from a deeper place of justice that transcends the justice systems of humankind, which have for ages been stacked in the favor of the wealthy elites. *Human nature*, and an even *deeper* nature, is being accused of being dangerously prone to Witchcraft by the aristocratic men who wrote this Declaration on the part of the Scottish Church.

And so it was, and so it remains—the emotional stresses, paradoxes, catch-22's, and the massive systems of social injustice inherent to both Early Modern and Modern societies create a **furnace of spiritual and emotional hell** which might produce misfits and rebels of many sorts— and despite their defamation at the hands of those who own most of the wealth and can insulate themselves from the heat of the furnace, we *must* be ready to understand how and why the misfit and rebel can belong to a different world of justification for who and what they are.

To understand the Unseen World, the Great and Ominous Other that *some* outsiders and *some* wounded or strange souls find their way to, we have to understand how much the narrative of elites and aristocrats shapes our understanding of what is proper, what is expected, and what is allowed: their voices (always hostile to people who found some way, however small or strange, of evading their corrupt reach) shape nearly every source we have from our common past that gives us insight into their social and philosophical opponents. *Their* notions of a well-ordered, Godly and "just" society are notions that favor their well-being over that of the vast majority of humankind. The *true* moral picture of human life and society is more complex. The real picture of the worlds Seen and Unseen is far more troubling to civilized human minds; its nuances are endless and its shades of gray run like long shadows into the indeterminate spaces of the Otherworld.

Beyond the neat and tidy official narratives is the *world as it is*—and that is the world of the strange souls who fall through the cracks and into the timeless and strange spaces of the Unseen. They've *always* been falling through those cracks; they are still falling. As the world suffers, the cracks only spread and grow deeper.

In the midst of all of this—now, as before—the figure of the Witch walks through the drama, not as a wise sage, activist, or leader who has seen through all of the political webs of social struggle, not as the great Wise One who knows the nature of all truth or the reality of all spiritual beings who might exist, but as a human being with strange connections that make them somehow stronger or more capable in certain ways. What they do with their capabilities is determined by the dense network of social, emotional, and spiritual factors pressing down upon them every day of their lives.

Witchcraft in the traditional sense of the word is not about "wisdom"; it was never about wisdom; vague or rarified philosophical appeals to wisdom are largely artifacts of educated elite culture or Biblical culture. It is about *flesh* and *blood*, about sustenance, about pleasure, local justice, and survival. It's about the ecstasy of knowing the extraordinary depths of the world. Any wisdom that is produced as a side-effect of this is certainly *not* anything that would be recognizable as such by the mainstream governing forces of this human social world.

The cauldron that produces Witches is about relationships forming between the Seen and Unseen reaches of the organic system of co-creative life that we call our world. These relationships have always been; they always will be, no matter how unfashionable, unbelievable, or scorned they become. The furnace of the world might provide the emotional wounding necessary to make some men and women more open to the experience, but men and women can come to it for reasons beyond some ordinary stress or strain produced by the human world.

Some—and I would say most—come to it for reasons that have no discernable logic at all. The world of *Witching* is beyond ordinary logic, and yet has been a regular resident of this world of arching sky and generous earth since the time when the first humans set foot within it.

**Sources Ordinary and Not So**

This work was born from many converging streams of ordinary and other-than-ordinary sources of insight and information.

The ordinary sources are drawn from the wide body of recently published (and very excellent) books and other works on Early Modern Witchcraft, beginning with the *Survey of Scottish Witchcraft*, which is available for researchers and other interested folk online. The (in my mind legendary) scholars responsible for that survey have published many related papers, edited collections, and reports; the first I obtained, and which still informs my thinking, is *Witchcraft and Belief in Early Modern Scotland*, edited by Julian Goodare, Lauren Martin, and Joyce Miller. Goodare edited and introduced a superb collection of papers called *Scottish Witches and Witch Hunters*, which I have relied upon immensely. Both of these works greatly informed the Introduction of this work.

Michael Ostling edited a collection called *Fairies, Demons, and Nature Spirits: 'Small Gods' at the Margins of Christendom*, which introduces a hidden world of perspectives regarding human and spirit-relations in the Early Modern period, and other critical insights. Edward Bever's book *The Realities of Witchcraft and Popular Magic in Early Modern Europe* is a groundbreaking and detailed analysis which helped to make my essay "Unawake and Unsleeping: Hypnagogic Prayer and Invocation in Witchcraft" (given in the Appendix of this work) possible. It is a wealth of powerful insights critical to these sorts of studies.

Emma Wilby's two seminal works *Cunning Folk and Familiar Spirits* and *The Visions of Isobel Gowdie* are together the two most important works, the true required reading for anyone who wants to cut to the heart of the phenomenon of Early Modern Witchcraft. My debt to Wilby and those two books is profound, both in regards to this present work and so many of my other works.

Daniel Ogden's *Magic, Witchcraft, and Ghosts in the Greek and Roman Worlds*, and *Scottish Fairy Belief* by Lizanne Henderson and Edward J. Cowan are two of the other supporting texts for my work at present that contain entire *worlds* of occult and historical insight into the emerging (and more accurate) picture of Witchcraft and other folk supernaturalism as a powerful pre-modern historical reality.

The work *Saducismus Triumphatus*, by Joseph Glanvill, is one of the main historical source-texts that informs this work. It is quite a lordly book, thick with many historical accounts of supernaturalism and Witchcraft, published posthumously in 1681. Its writing was an attempt on Glanvill's part to stem the rising tide of skepticism which came along with the "new sciences"—a skepticism about the supernatural that he felt would eventually lead to widespread atheism.

His goal in writing the book was to prove that Witchcraft—and the supernatural evil that empowered it—was *real*, and that a belief in these things didn't have to contradict newer worldviews. He made his case with reports of Witches and Witchcraft which preserved much extant Witchlore from his own time, though I'm sure he never meant for someone like me to use his book as a *guide* towards a revival of Witchcraft ceremony or ritual in line with Early Modern Aesthetics. But this is precisely what I have done.

Throughout these pages, readers will see how Glanvill's accounts, gained from informants in his own time, create starting points or even complete frameworks for the very potent and effective workings of Witchery found herein.

When it comes to the not-so-ordinary sources of this work, we find ourselves going back in time several years, as my own metaphysical and spiritual efforts and extraordinary explorations with Witchcraft intensified. At a certain point before the creation of this work, I set about to gain the attention and aid of *Wise and Helpful Spirits*, utilizing the power of certain ancient invocations, to reveal to me words of power that could breathe life into these Workings—***the Clovenstone Workings***, as I called them. A terrible dark barrier, like a boulder or stone of immense size which blocks all light and sound, stands between us and the treasury of hidden wonders that still echo to us from our esoteric past, for many reasons.

To cleave this spiritual and perceptual stone in two, I needed the help of spirits; and through extensive occult ritual work, and extensive divinatory work to guide and test the results of those works, I obtained my goal. Words of Power that could restore to life some of the legendary feats of Witches spoken of in Early Modern sources entered this world, and now will pass from me to the readers of this work. Their effectiveness is tested and verified.

The responsibility for their use lies with the people who scrutinize this book, find that it speaks to their own depths well enough, and are willing to do what is required to respond to its strange call.

In this, I wish the very luck of the Devil and his Good Lady to all who are brave enough.

Robin Artisson
August 13, 2020
Ledgewood House

# SOUL TRANSFORMATION

"I am that very witch. When I sleep, my spirit slips away from my body and dances naked with The Devil. That's how I signed his book."

—Thomasin, from *The VVitch*

## The Dark Glass: Seeing the Death

In order to assay the workings in this book to their fullest possible potential, a man or woman should be *Witched*—just as described in the Introduction. It is the *favor of the Unseen*, of entities within the Unseen World, which makes the wonders of sorcery or Witchcraft possible. If those reading these words have obtained some form of that hallowed state of *familiarity* with the Unseen, have gained familiars or established relationships with helping spirits, they should proceed to the *Workings* section of this book, and it is my hope that they will be able to gain much benefit and attainment from the operations of Witchcraft found there.

For those who have not, or for those who wish to re-focus or deepen their connections, this section of the book outlines a comprehensive method which might well bring about or increase that special condition within a person's mind and soul. What *sorts* of transformations this method can accomplish is an impossible question to answer; it will be different for all who succeed. These strange transformations are seldom one-time things; an initiatory transformation of any real strength will ineluctably lead to further experiences, and to a deepening of relationship with the subtle world over time.

Those who succeed at this task may discover that the beings that they have established relationships with can be of many natures. From the "double" or *Fetch*, the guiding and protecting Spirit who is said in ancient lore to accompany each person through life, to any number of serving-beings attached to the Greater Powers in the Unseen, and even the spirits of the dead or of local places in the landscape—the possibilities are many.

The 'rules' of relationships with Spirits are seldom simple or rational. In some instances, relationships may require various activities or offerings to maintain. Failing to engage them properly can cost a man or woman the relationship, and with it, the power or insights and special capabilities that it conferred. Some relationships can be based on a variety of other principles. Some relationships may be set to end after a certain period; some may be for the length of a person's breathing life. And some may be not only for the length of this life, but somehow continual into the state of existence that follows this life.

You must proceed—if it is your choice to proceed—as though the relationships you are seeking will not only be forever, but will alter your destiny to some degree within the boundaries of this life *and* beyond it. Even if this doesn't turn out to be the case, you should proceed as though it *will* be the case. My feeling is that the Unseen (generally speaking) has little time for those who do not approach it with an abiding sense of seriousness, and those who are prepared to give more, and thereby *receive* more, seem to be better candidates for extraordinary relationships and endowments.

Going into this with an "all in" attitude will make a person seem a more attractive potential partner to Spirits, many of whom wish to co-create with humans situations of mutual benefit, among other (perhaps stranger) goals.

You must banish from your mind most of the modern ideas people have about Witchcraft, and embrace the insight—the critical and everywhere fundamental insight—that Witchcraft, in its very essence, is a thing connected to *dreams*. The power to dream, to recall dreams, and to have a fertile, clear dream-life is *required* for this spiritual vocation. Dreams are the stage upon which most spirit-contact will occur, and the stage upon which many extraordinary feats of Witchery are performed. The pathway to becoming *Witched* lies in the activity of **incubating initiatory dreams**. And that is what this section of our manual is ultimately about.

If you succeed at this special task, you will find your interior life and awareness altered in some way. There's no way to describe the many shapes these alterations can take, but at some point in one or another, familiar spirits *will* arrive or assert themselves to your consciousness or awareness, and relationships with them will begin. This process will have a wide-ranging emotional impact upon you; it is inevitable. It will *not* always be a positive emotional impact, so those who suffer from emotional challenges of various kinds are in a paradoxical situation here: those challenges will either hinder them, or become exacerbated in negative ways by these activities, or (in strange irony) *help* them somehow.

In my experience, it's usually more on the harm side of things that the Fateful coin falls. Those who feel they are in such a condition of danger or emotional fragility should certainly reconsider reading any further.

To keep a firm grip on one's own ordinary condition of engagement with the human social world—a grip on one's sanity, to put it another way—is important. No degree of spectral attainment nor any spirit-relationships are worth much if one cannot *also* relate somewhat functionally in the human world. While we live, we are humans and we must have healthy human relationships to stabilize our lives in this world. Nothing else is possible without this.

The highly mysterious transformation(s) you are seeking, or putting yourself in special line to potentially obtain, *will* revise your dreaming life, the deep parts of your mind, and aspects of your personality. This revision can take countless forms, and will "play itself out" in your inner and outer lives in various ways. When it happens, it is unmistakable— but it is seldom a thing easy or even possible to explain to others. This is a topic we will talk about more soon.

When I stand outside at night, before the forest that surrounds my house, I can feel the immensity of the Otherness. The trees are giants—dark shapes looming high above me, and forever gazing downward at my small human body. The immensity of night itself should be enough to remind us all of what place we occupy in the greater scheme of things; but a nighted forest brings a new element, a new elaboration, to this ancient emotional encounter.

The forest is a complex, rhizomic, and super-layered world of countless lives all its own. It is a community of countless other communities, infinitely older than any human gathering that has ever existed. A Forest is much like the Unseen, and it resonates with that kind of depth and mystery. The night only accentuates this by *hiding from my eyes* what day reveals so easily. **To have one's senses taken from them, or restricted**, shocks the body into seeking new ways of sensing and becoming aware of the world. It is an ancient method of creating altered states of consciousness.

Anyone can feel the *Great Otherness* of a dark forest—this is an easy thing to feel, to sense, or to intuit; you only need to stand at the dark edge, hearing the owls in the distance and hearing the countless cracks and pops and hisses that a forest and its many creatures forever emanate. The great well of life that *is* the forest has a tangible, heavy and deep feeling; it takes no effort to sense it and encounter it. We spend most of our lives sensing and encountering countless things outside of ourselves; the pathway to the Initiatory Dream or dreams you are seeking now begins in introducing a *new* kind of encounter.

It's not the ordinary or even the extraordinary encounter of other things in the world (like the forest I just described) that we will seek, though these things *can* certainly serve to birth the Witching way in other circumstances; it's an extraordinary encounter of *yourself* that we shall utilize to shock deeper powers around you and inside you into a special awakening. I say "shock", but it's more like a firm boost or a small push. If it sets the right metaphysical rocks rolling, they *will* pick up speed.

**The confluence of forces that together you refer to as "yourself"** during the years of this breathing life has its own extraordinary aspects. We don't often see them because we are quite busy focusing (pretty instinctively) on the animate shapes all around us, keeping a sharp lookout for our help, our benefit, or things that might harm us. We can overlook subtle things that are closer to us.

We must exercise caution when we turn towards the confluence of "self" for special insights, because our human world is obsessed—entirely—by a foolish devotion to an invented notion, a false consciousness, of a hyper-individual *self-construct*. We live in a *self*-ish world, in which idealized notions of self are elevated to positions of psychological and social supremacy. Long gone are the days when the human self was shaped, known, and nurtured primarily in *relation to an intimate community*—a communal and relational situation in which selves could share with others, receive and co-create healthy support and healthy outcomes in ordinary circumstances.

When we seek to utilize our dynamic confluences of self for these special purposes, we are treading on a ground that easily gives way to dangerous obsessions with the idea of self, to false reifications of self, and to becoming lost within the ideas of self.

If that happens, **we lose the power to be open and flexible enough to the *Other*,** *and* to gain the kinds of extraordinary relationships we are seeking. Self-obsession already greatly hinders or renders impossible ordinary relationships in the human world; it can very easily do the same to relationships with any kinds of beings.

For the avoidance of doubt or confusion, it should be stated: "selves" are certainly real; we all know ourselves in many ways; they are simply far more relational and "soft", more mutable and connected to so many other beings and forces, than we often realize. Selves are not the "hard" things we are taught they are, or taught that they should be. They are *relational*, not isolated and cut away from everything else by impenetrable metaphysical walls. This needs to be embraced, remembered, and re-affirmed often if our work here is to be successful.

As another example of how *soft* and relational selves are, how vulnerable they are to being altered by influences from countless other places, *selves always change.* You have been changing all your life; you are changing now; and you will change. You are seeking a powerful change of a considerably rare and strange sort as you read these words.

Being what we are, with the sorts of storytelling minds we have, we don't often pay attention to our changing selves. Our stories tend to be stories of stability, of unchanging predictability, of achievement, or of the nostalgia of the past; we change and yet we don't notice our own changes. What we often notice happening in others is *certainly* happening in us, but since we are perceptually with ourselves every day, every hour, every moment, it's hard to see all that we have gradually become, and what we are becoming.

Aging (to make one example) happens at a crawl, at such a slow pace that we don't really notice it. And then one day we see an older picture of ourselves, or we meet someone who hasn't seen us in a long time, and that uncomfortable realization hits us of how profoundly we've changed.

It's time to use a special—and very accessible—technique to force yourself to face your changes. This is about more than just shoving a potentially uncomfortable realization into the forefront of your own consciousness; this is ultimately about *encountering the Other*. But it begins with the confluence of forces and life-vitality that you call yourself. You will, if successful, gain the power to tell the Other *who you are*, or at least, how you understand yourself to be at this point in time.

This will enable you to proceed with the methodology given in this section. But you *must* do this first, and you must do it as instructed here, as close to the letter as you can.

✳ ✳ ✳

You will now undertake to **See the Death**. This is an easy—though potentially disturbing—act of scrying. It is an act of *profane scrying*, meaning you will not be empowering this act of special seeing with sorcerous words, substances, nor any metaphysical empowering agents of any sort, by your own actions. You will simply *look* and see what you will see.

To perform this act of scrying, you will need an ordinary mirror. It should be a portable mirror, at least a foot across or tall, if not a few inches more. Too small of a mirror can hinder this, but in a pinch, with some finesse, you might be able to use a smaller mirror. This is an ordinary mirror, not one of the "black glass" scrying mirrors that are so often used for occult purposes. We will turn our attention to the black or dark glass scrying mirrors quite a bit later, but for now it's an ordinary mirror you need.

If you truly cannot obtain a mirror of the size I suggested here, it is possible to do this act of scrying in a bathroom mirror mounted on a wall, so long as you can stand or sit comfortably in front of it for a goodly while.

You will undertake this act of scrying on **three different nights**—and it *must* be at night—within the space of one week. You can do them on three consecutive nights, or skip a day between one or two occasions, so long as you do three scrying sessions within a week.

You will need the mirror, and a single candle which will be placed in a corner of the completely dark room that you do this work within. The key is to make it so that the light in the room is extremely dim. The flame of the candle **cannot** be visible in the glass of the mirror. When I sit at a table in my study to do this, I put the candle on the floor behind the table holding the mirror, and directly behind the mirror. If the room is very large, you will have to put the candle a touch closer, else the lighting will be too dim.

You want to set the mirror up such that you can sit comfortably before it, and there must be no unnatural light in the room—you can have one candle giving light only. Turn off all devices that are in the room. Close any windows to block out artificial outside lights as much as possible. Further, you must have silence—you cannot have commotion outside the door of the room you're doing this in. People cannot be outside talking or making noise; the sound of distant televisions or music or bumping about cannot be heard. For many people, this act will only be possible after family or roommates all go to sleep.

To be alone in a house, building, or dwelling place when you do this is ideal—a sense of isolation from other human beings will increase the power of this act tenfold. This could even be done in a tent in a forest at night, or some outdoors place that has a seat for you and place to put the mirror so that you can easily see into it—and a freedom from noise or intrusion. But for certain reasons, I find this is best done indoors in the conditions I stated above.

Get your mirror in place, your one candle of very indirect lighting in place, and then sit or stand before the mirror. Ideally, your face will be anywhere from 2 to 4 feet from the mirror.

Close your eyes, take a deep breath, then open your eyes and look directly at your reflection in the mirror. Your reflection should be blurry—with such low lighting, you might only see a vague, but softly colored outline of yourself, and you might make out your dominant facial features—the darkness of your eyes, your mouth, the curve and ridge of your nose.

Take another deep breath and fix your eyes—softly—on your eyes in the reflection. Just stare—but allow the tension in your eyes to do what it wishes to do. If your eyes involuntarily shift a bit to another spot on your reflection's face, that's fine; let them sit there for a bit, and when you feel ready, bring them back to the reflection of your eyes.

After a point, it won't really matter where your eyes flit off to. Just keep your fixed gaze on your face in the mirror. You need to relax a bit into this.

Then, probably sooner than you'd like, you'll begin to see things. Your face and figure in the mirror will become blurry; sometimes—and this is a good sign—your face and form in the mirror will go completely dark. It might even seem to disappear completely—but the darkness, or the "fade out", will not last forever. Your face and form will re-emerge from the darkness, or come back to visibility, but prepare yourself, for when it does, it may not look at all like you'd expect.

Your face may transform into something hideous, and it can be shocking to see. You may see your own "death face"—the face of yourself dead. You may see your face, though much older than you are now. You may see your own face in extreme decay, even the bones and tissues below your skin exposed. You may see a face that is not your own—and this can be the most troubling of all these visions.

As unsettling as these visions can be, this is *precisely* what you are attempting to see. This is *Seeing the Death*—seeing your own precious form subjected to the ravages of change, of age, of death itself. The experience (which you will almost certainly have) of seeing someone else's face—and sometimes not even a human face—suddenly rear itself out at you can be frightening, and send what feels like an electrical shock through your body, a shock of sharp fright or startle.

The moment you feel this feeling of shock from something you've seen (and it is an *unmistakable* feeling in your flesh, tissues, and nervous system) you have *succeeded* in a very important way with this technique. You have succeeded in obtaining the psychological depth-engagement, the other-than-rational wake-up jolt, but you are *not* yet finished.

You must, after the shock, continue to watch the parade of strange and sometimes horrific forms and faces that will emerge, again and again, out of your own face and form. As they appear, disappear, warp, and re-appear, you will have (likely without realizing it) **fallen into a form of light trance**. And then, after a short time, something special will happen: your own face and form will return to you in the mirror, but something will be different about it.

The eyes of your reflection will be gone, and replaced by voids of darkness. This image of you—the reflection with the eyes gone and replaced by darkness—will become stable; it will stay in the mirror for long periods of time. When this happens, you **have to address it as though it *is* the Other.** Think of this as some kind of preternatural force or reality that parallels your own ordinary body and selfhood. Think of it as some kind of "representative" of the entire Unseen world, here to listen to what you have to say.

It doesn't matter what it *actually* is; in this moment of psychological stress and trance that you will have created, your brain, body, and vitalizing soul will be in a kind of suspension state, a condition in which they have become temporarily unable to make full and accurate judgments about what is real and what isn't. They can still *mostly* make good judgments, but they're not operating at the top of their game anymore. Your situation will have stirred up emotional and deeper biological forces inside you that have gone into a state of high alertness, and infiltrated your ordinary rational awareness. What you say now matters in a new way, impacts you in a different way, psychologically.

When you are staring at the *Other* in this way, **say who you are**. It's a pretty telling thing, what people say when they're asked to say who they are. Of course everyone says their name, and you should too—say your name, and the name of the woman that gave birth to you; her first and maiden last name. Say it like this example given here, naturally replacing these names with your own:

*I am Anna Sutton, who was given life by Christine Smith.*

Then speak aloud a few other things about yourself. Most importantly, if you happen to be known by other names in different human groups or organizations, say that too. Say that "some humans know me as X.". Say where you live. Say some things about you that you feel really define you as the person you are at this moment. Don't *ever* lie.

Then tell the *Other* what you want. **You want to receive, from the Unseen World, the gift of friendship with spirits**. You want for the Great Powers in the Unseen to give you the boon of a familiar spirit, or spirits, so that you can become powerful through relationship to them. This is key; this is critical.

And you have to say why you want it. You want it because you will be better able to help and protect yourself and your loved ones, and your community, if you have this special empowerment. You want it because it is *right* that some humans should create allegiances with the other-than-human world. Make certain that you say so.

Once you've said what you need to say, gaze into the mirror a while longer, then close your eyes, take a deep breath, and turn away from the mirror. Don't look back into it. Get up, put out your candle, and put the ordinary lights back on.

You must do this three times, on three separate nights. You only need to obtain that feeling of "shock" in your system—that jolt of shock-fear—one time. Usually, it will happen in your first scrying session. It doesn't need to happen more than once, but if it does, that's fine. Your bravery for this activity will increase on your second and third performances. But remember—whatever you see, don't take it as some grand sign of your impending doom, or anyone else's. Profane scrying is not likely to result in potent visions of the future or anything of that nature; it's more about you, and your own emotional state. As disturbing as it can be, you must have the bravery to bare-knuckle your way through it.

If you found that you were *unable* to finish the first session, too frightened or too troubled by what you saw or felt, it is **important** that you put this book away for good. If you cannot mentally and emotionally bear what you see in a simple mirror in a dark room, you will *not* be able to handle more advanced works in which actual other-than-human persons bring their influences to bear on your mind and soul. It will drive you mad or harm you. With good grace and what amounts to real wisdom, you should end these activities now.

Otherwise, after your third completed session, you can continue on; because now, you and *Them* know who you are at this time, and what you want. You've made a clear and loud psychological statement of *both* things, under conditions that borderline on trance. Your more-than-rational mind has been poked awake. The stage is set for what comes next.

## The Lonely Soul

A person who proceeds from this point and manages to obtain extraordinary dreams of an initiatory nature will find themselves in a difficult situation with regard to the majority of their friends, family, and peers. If a person succeeds at becoming *Witched*, they will be in possession of something extraordinary: a strange metaphysical thing or sequence of things that will remain alive inside their memories, their minds, and tangibly resident inside their flesh and soul.

This strangeness has no ordinary way of being known, and it defies nearly all attempts at ordinary explanation. What may be one of the most valuable things within the collective human experience—a doorway of interaction and relationship between the ordinary world and the world's extraordinary dimensions—will seem fake, made-up, delusional, or otherwise nothing at all to most people.

A *Witched* soul is inevitably a lonely soul. However lonely or strange those people who become Witches may have been *before*, those qualities are only destined to increase within them as they proceed with creating alliances between themselves and Unseen powers.

Many modern occultists embrace a set of four qualities or principles—first written out by the ceremonial magician Eliphas Levi in the 19th century—which have (perhaps not surprisingly) become popularly known as the "Witches' Pyramid." These four qualities, which Levi claimed would lead to an attainment of the *Sanctum Regnum,* or the "knowledge and power of the magi", were "**to dare, to know, to will, and to be silent.**"

These four principles aim to create an occult personality that will manifest the discipline and discretion that Levi felt was instrumental to the ends of those who studied ceremonial magic. They have been expanded upon by generations of mage-occultists since Levi's time, and adopted by the modern Witches whose Witchcraft is a basic continuation of ceremonial magic. The rule of "keeping silence" is often sold as a cautionary rule about not talking about your 'magical workings', lest outsiders or outside forces somehow bring unwanted influences to bear upon your results.

I think that the strange souls of Witches in the older sense of the word are going to incline towards keeping silent simply because there's *no way* to really talk about what they have encountered, or about what they regularly experience. The ordinary tongue cannot shape ordinary words that can satisfyingly capture the richness or depth of the spectral compact, or of the strange life of surreal dream-visions and encounters that begin to proliferate around souls that have joined with great Otherworldly forces and persons in relational intimacy.

This comes with a great loneliness of the soul, because all beings wish to share with others of like mind and caliber the goodness or benefits that they have found or enjoyed, to some extent. But the *Witched* may discover none who will be able to understand the interior strangeness of Witching, not for hundreds of miles around. Only *Witched others* can truly satisfy this loneliness, and, such is the Fateful darkness of our day, *even* Witched others may not be able *or* willing to reveal themselves or become friends.

The concept of spiritual and tangible friendship between Witches brings us to the strange term Isobel Gowdie used—**Coven**—which indicates a gathering of Witches joined together for reasons of co-creating power, fulfilling relationships with certain Powers in the Unseen World, and celebrating the presence of other Strange Souls. More will be said on the topic of Covens later in this book.

To lack the ability to share with your ordinary friends and family the wonders that you have felt *and* seen might sometimes feel like a coal burning its way into your flesh—a thing you want to express, but cannot for multiple reasons. The *relief* of being able to reveal this to a rare person who understands is in a category all its own. But that relief may not be a thing many people ever really find. This burden is a **necessary part of the Witching vocation in modern times,** and must be accepted as such. In that gap of frustration and discomfort, in that increased space of alienation, one *might* offset these feelings of lostness via efforts to better oneself and work (secretly if needs be) to increase the safety and capability of friends, family, and community. It seems a waste indeed for anyone to willingly subject themselves to the preternatural challenges and dangers one must to obtain familiar spirits, and *then* to suffer the sense of alienation that will certainly follow or increase, if one isn't gaining something back for it—for themselves, or their loved ones.

One of the subtle traps created by the false consciousness that we call "self" in our society today is the idea of a spiritual or preternatural "practice" of some sort that benefits no one beyond a single occult-oriented person. The *occult hermit* notion, the idea of a secretly withdrawn occultist of great power whose knowledge and insight or attainment is great, but who never engages in any sort of practical work beyond the boundaries of their own private space or skin—assuming they engage in practical work at all—is a romantic ideal with nothing to recommend for it.

If one is fortunate enough to gain and use power of any Otherworldly sort, it is *dead* if not used to help others, or to increase one's own grasp on vitality and enjoyment in life. The Witch of Early Modern times was not a "sage" cloistered off in an occult monastery or hermitage. They brought strange influences to bear on themselves and others when the situation called for it—even if it was done in a clandestine way.

## The Witch Dreams

Now you will undertake to incubate and achieve dream-visions of an initiatory nature. They are called *initiatory* because a new life or a new flow of life-experiences begins, is formally *initiated* after you experience them. The metaphysical constituents and forces operating on your body and soul are altered in a (relatively) permanent manner by the experience of these dreams. They are *Witch Dreams* because they *Witch* the souls of people, making those people into Witches, people capable of extraordinary congress with the Unseen world.

You must understand the degree to which dreams are involved in the phenomenon of Witchcraft. Turn to the appendix of this book and read the essay **"Unawake and Unsleeping: Hypnagogic Prayer and Invocation in Witchcraft."** You do *not* need to utilize the Hypnagogic Prayer technique yet, but you must understand it fully. And you *must* understand how dreaming and hypnagogia are powerful tools of the art of Witchcraft—and how they always have been so.

After you have studied the essay and internalized its understandings, look to the *Workings* section of this book, and read the working called **The Gateway Ring.** Of all the workings in this book, it is the one that does not require relationships with familiar spirits to strongly empower it. Anyone who follows the instructions given for it will be able to achieve success with it on some level. Learn to create a Gateway Ring— internalize the whole easy method by heart, and obtain the things you'll need to make a Gateway Ring.

When you have read and understood the essay, and learned the Gateway Ring working perfectly, proceed.

## I. Creating the Breaching Talisman

Obtain a piece of paper, parchment, or a small piece of linen cloth of some light color. It should be about 3-4 inches across and tall, and can be square or circular as you desire, though circular would be better.

Get a calligraphy pen that writes in black ink, or a high-quality artist's pen, or a charcoal pencil, and upon the parchment, paper, or linen, draw this sign:

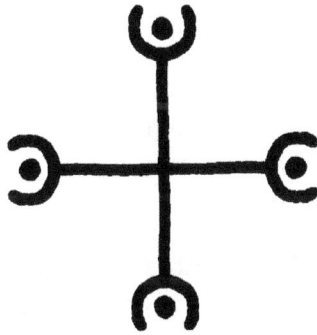

Let the ink dry or the image set—and when it is ready prick any finger on your left hand and make a streak of blood above the symbol, and a streak of blood below it. Let that blood dry. Then, roll up the parchment or cloth, fold it in half once, and use a small piece of string to tie the fold closed. Put this into a small leather bag or a cloth bag that will be attached to a cord, such that it can be worn around your neck. This is the **Breaching Talisman**.

At first opportunity, remove yourself to a place where you can privately and without interruption or disruption create a Gateway Ring. It would best be done outdoors and in the night, in some private place, but any place indoors or out will do, so long as it is quiet and private. Try to perform this at night or twilight.

Bring two bowls and a bottle of whole milk or a flask of whiskey or some strong spirit with you, alongside three straight branches a foot to a foot and a half long each, and the Breaching Talisman you made. Make your Gateway Ring. Then, pour some of your milk or liquor into one of the bowls, and say, while holding the bowl up:

To the Good Neighbors here, spirits of this place, take this offering and see me as a friend. Do not hinder my work here. Instead, lend your power and aid to me.

Then put the bowl off the side of your Ring somewhere.

Make a triangle with the branches that you brought somewhere inside your Gateway Ring. It would be best if it was in the northern region of your Ring, with the "upper" point of the triangle facing north, but it can be anywhere inside the Ring you need. Put the Breaching Talisman into center of the triangle.

Pour out the rest of your offering into the other bowl you brought along. Put it to the side of your triangle—either side is fine. Extend your hands palms-down in the air over the triangle (and thus directly over the Breaching Talisman) and say aloud:

SISOCHÔR, Ancient Son of the Abyss, Leader of the Spirit-Host, you I conjure by Bitter Necessity. Let my holy work here be received into the wide Netherworld.

*Say this line of strange words three times:*

PHORBA PHORBÓBAR BARÓ PHÓRPHÓR PHÓRBAI!

Then say:

Antiochia! Good Queen of Elfhame, Queen of Spirits Below, You who have power over all of the arts of Witchcraft, bless and make powerful my working here. Send forth thy serving ladies, the Brides from Below, the Fateful Women who weave Fates and Destinies, to aid me in this hour.

You Dark Mothers who fly through the night, in the name of the Elphen Queen I beg you to come forth and endow this talisman below my hands with the power to make my words and deeds known in the Unseen World.

Here I have poured out an offering of strong and vital substance for you. Rouse yourselves to come and aid me, as I ask! If ever I wear this talisman around my neck, wrist, or ankle, let my words and deeds echo into the Unseen while I wear it, so that any spirit or spirits I desire to reach will know all that I say or do.

**Empower this talisman as I have asked, by all the powerful words and names I have spoken here!**

*SISOCHÔR* is pronounced "see-sah-core". *PHORBA PHORBÓBAR BARÓ PHÓRPHÓR PHÓRBAI* is pronounced "par-buh, par-boh-bar, bah-roh, pore-pore, pore-bay"

Wait a good space of moments with your hands held over the talisman, then slowly gather it up. Blow three strong breaths directly onto it, and then place it between your cupped hands, and press your cupped hands against your chest. Close your eyes and take nine slow, easy breaths. After the ninth breath, put the talisman around your neck.

**From this day forward, *any* time you do *any* working of Witchery of any sort, wear this talisman.** Never let another person put it on. Keep it in a safe place when not being used. Close up your Gateway Ring as per the instructions, gather your things, and retire. Pour out the offerings you made onto the ground and take your bowls, too, of course.


## II. The Pact and the Cairn

You must now undertake to write out a message—called a **pact**—describing what it is you desire from one of the Great Powers in the Unseen who can bestow initiatory dreams, and what you will do for them if you obtain what you ask for. The pact will have to be delivered into the Unseen directly, by burying it in the earth along with a special ritual. After you begin this work, **do not tell any human person what you are doing**. You *have* to hide that you are doing this until it is over.

*If* you succeed, and gain the Witch Dreams, you should only ever tell about your success, along with any details of your dream or dreams if you choose, to *extremely* trusted people—the sorts of people you'd trust your life to. It's really best not to talk about it at all.

First decide which of the Great Powers you will approach and ask to be your Primary Empowerer, or Patron. You may decide to ask the Master of Spirits, whom men have called the Devil or (in other places) the *Fairy*

*King* to give you the boon of the initiatory dream, or you may ask the Good Lady of Elfhame to be the granter of your initiatory dream.

Whoever you decide, *if* they respond, they will always be your Patron and giver of power. If you succeed with one, there's no need to then try and obtain these dreams from the other. If you try with one, and don't succeed, you can try with the other. If you were to fail to again, you can try again with either, so long as you *limit your attempts* in accordance with the directions given later.

Only you can make the decision regarding which of these two Great Powers you will approach first, or at all, for you don't *have* to switch over and try the other if you fail your first attempt with one of them. You may feel that it's the Devil or nobody for you—or that you only desire the Good Lady of Elfhame's blessing in this regard. It's all a matter of how you feel in your own depths.

Once your heart or intuition has directed you to which of these Powerful Persons you will approach, take a piece of parchment or heavy paper, about the size of an ordinary sheet of paper, and with a nice ink-pen or charcoal pencil, draw a dividing line across the middle of it, from one side to the other. Note that I do not mean from top to bottom, I mean from side to side. Curve that line a good bit, making a somewhat shallow arch, so that it looks like you just drew a low hill right in the middle of the paper.

Below your hill, draw a primitive image (the best you can manage—it doesn't have to be pretty or good at all) of the Patron you are going to approach in your pact. If it is the Master of Spirits, draw an upper torso, neck, and a head with horns or antlers spreading from it. You can have simple arms at his side. Make two circles or ovals for eyes; put the curve of two brows over the eyes, and a nose-ridge between the eyes, and a simple mouth which need be nothing more than a sideways oval. He should take up most of the region under the hill you drew. If it is the Queen of Elfhame you will be reaching out to, draw a more feminine upper body, neck, head, and draw long flowing hair cascading down either side of her head. Make the same kind of face on her, but do your best to make the features more feminine, however you feel you can manage that. **Right above or below either figure (but still below "the** hill") draw the same four-armed symbol that you drew onto the cloth or parchment of your Breaching Talisman.

The image sits in the "Underworld" of your image, below the hill, below the ground. In the "Upperworld" of your image, above the hill, you will write your message—in your own handwriting—to this powerful entity.

First, you must address the Patron. If the Master of Spirits, you can use any of the names or titles given for him in this book. I suggest the format of the first line be like this:

*I write this message to Christsonday, the Master of Spirits, whom men call the Devil...* or: *I write this message to Robin, the Master of Spirits, whom men call the Devil...*

Or you can skip any formal name and just say *I write this message to the Master of Spirits, called by men the Devil,* or *I write this message to the Devil in Hell below* or *I write this message to the Master of Spirits, called by some the Fairy King* or *the King of Elfhame...*

It is up to your aesthetic sense and intuition what address you will use. If you will be approaching the Good Lady of Elfhame, address her this way:

*I write this message to Antiochia, the Good Queen of Elfhame and the Spirits Below, She who has power over all the arts of Witchcraft.*

After you write your opening line of address, you must **say who you are** and **write out what you are seeking.** This is where you ask for *empowerment,* the place where you ask to be endowed with a Familiar spirit or spirits, so that you can become capable of Witchcraft. But you have to ask for perhaps a touch more, too. I strongly suggest the following format, but you can alter this if you must, in accord with your own good judgment and sense of reality. Again, when stating who you are, you say your name, followed by "who was given life by" and then your biological mother's first and maiden surname.

*I am XX, who was given life by XX. I offer my allegiance to you, in this world and in the world to come, if you will endow me with the power to do Witchcraft in your name. Great One, send me dreams of initiatory power, and send forth a spirit or spirits to be my Familiars, ever ready to empower and aid my acts of Witchcraft. Send me dreams of guidance and instruction in the arts of sorcery.*

Next, you must write a **tangible thing you will do,** a direct and special thing you will give back—aside from the allegiance already mentioned—in exchange for this favor. This offer of a tangible return makes your pact or petition more likely to be accepted. I will give five examples here; I strongly urge you to choose **one** and write it in, but you can come up with one of your own, so long as it matches well with the amount of effort and "giving" that these five include.

*1. If you will empower me to be capable of Witchcraft as I have asked, I shall each year in the autumn create seven small images of human beings from twigs, straw, and cloth, carving human faces into them, and decorating them fairly, and hang them upon trees in a forest, or abandon them in a graveyard, as offerings to your spirit.*

*2. If you will empower me to be capable of Witchcraft as I have asked, I shall once per season make a great bonfire and around it pour out three large bottles or bowls full of strong liquors as an offering to your spirit.*

*3. If you will empower me to be capable of Witchcraft as I have asked, I shall once per year spend a whole day and night alone in a forest or some deserted place, neither eating nor sleeping, giving offerings to your spirit and keeping a vigil for signs from you.*

*4. If you will empower me to be capable of Witchcraft as I have asked, I shall twice per year create a great feast for you of many delicious foods, and half of all those foods will be put aside for you, and then burned in a great bonfire or buried in the earth.*

*5. If you will empower me to be capable of Witchcraft as I have asked, I shall once per year seek to discover a man or woman of power who harms the land or other people in or about my community, or a man or woman who abuses the minds and bodies of people in or about my community, and destroy them body and soul with Witchcraft, devoting their destruction to you.*

After you have written in your tangible extra offering, finish your pact-petition with one of these paragraphs:

If your petition is to the Master of Spirits:

*Good Master, if this offer be acceptable to you, let the first dream you send to me include a vision of a dog, a crow, a goat, a deer, a serpent, a man flying through the air, or let me see you in your great majesty, or allow me to see those powerful spirits who serve you. Be kind to me, Master, who wishes for your favors.*

If your petition is to the Good Lady of Elfhame:

*Good Lady, if this offer be acceptable to you, let the first dream you send to me include a vision of a dog, a deer, a serpent, a cat, a crow, or let me see you in your great majesty, or allow me see those powerful spirits who serve you. Be kind to me, Lady, who wishes for your favors.*

Once you have your whole pact-petition written in the "upper world" portion of your parchment or paper, prick any of the fingers on your left hand, and smear a streak of blood under the words you wrote. Then smear a streak of blood under the image of the Master or the Underworldly Lady that you drew. Put a lock of your hair, or pieces of hair from somewhere on your body (if you have no hair on your head) onto the parchment. Roll up the parchment or paper, fold the rolled-up paper in half, and tie that fold closed with a piece of string.

\* \* \*

You will be burying this pact in the earth under special conditions and with a special ritual. The place where you bury it will have to be remote, and not likely to be visited by other humans. The place where you bury it will be marked, too, by a **cairn of stones** you will erect over it. If you live in a place where the ground freezes for part of the year, you'll obviously have to do these workings at times when the ground is not frozen.

If you fear that your pact will be found by humans, you might want to write your petition in code. Any code can be used, such as the Theban alphabet, or literally any you like. Spirits, particularly the ones you're creating this petition for, can understand anything we write in this way, in any language or code.

The use of cairns and burying things in the earth is ages old in Witchcraft. The Witch Helen Rogie of Lumphanan is said to have possessed "a mould made of soft lead for making 'pictours'—and she was discovered by a neighbor "standing beside cairns she had erected for Devil-worship, casting earth and stones over her shoulder." The neighbor, it is recorded, was bewitched to death for his intrusion onto Helen's special working site. As an aside, if you wish to use a soft lead sheet, and mark all the needed images and write the needed words onto it with a metal stylus of some sort, you can. It can be blooded, given the lock of your hair, rolled up and buried just like any parchment petition.

It should go without saying, but if your pact is accepted, if the Witch Dreams you are asking for arrive, you **must** do what you *said you would do*. To fail to give or perform the tangible act you wrote down in the petition will *invalidate* your pact, and you will almost certainly lose the power you gained from it. And it's unlikely that you'll be able to restore it.

✳ ✳ ✳

You can bury your pact in the earth on a full moon, or a dark moon—you choose. Neither have any special advantage. You can do the burying ritual at twilight or any time at night. On the day that you bury the petition, a 28 day "count" begins. If you bury it on a full moon, your count is over on the next full moon. If you bury it on a dark moon, your count is over when the next dark moon arrives.

Collect at *least* 13 fist-sized stones, or more if the stones are smaller. If you have any trouble getting stones, even a very large double-handful of pebbles will work, but try to get stones. Journey to a secluded outdoors place, such as a clearing or spot in a forest a goodly ways from any trail, or some other such place. You can do this ritual at twilight or any time in the night of the day you choose.

Remember as much as you can about your journey to this secluded spot, and all the sights, sounds, smells, and feelings you encounter. Be present, pay attention to all that you feel and sense during the ritual itself. You will need these memories later.

Wearing your Breaching Talisman, make a Gateway Ring. Then, give an offering to the *Good Neighbors* just as you did in the creation of the Breaching Talisman. Then dig a hole somewhere in the northern side of your Gateway Ring, deep enough to take your petition. Place your petition in the hole. If your petition is for the Master of Spirits, you have to call upon the spirits who serve him *using the name or title and address you used for him in your pact*. Thus, if you called him "Christsonday, Master of Spirits, whom men call the Devil", you would say:

*I call upon the spirits who serve Christsonday, the Master of Spirits, whom men call the Devil. Take this petition marked with my own blood to your Master. Deliver it to his hands, and for this favor I will give you an offering of strong spirits, poured out here on a cairn of stones that I shall make. Mighty Earth, cover this secret petition and let it come into the possession of the one that I intend it for.*

If your petition is for the Good Lady of Elfhame, say:

*I call upon the spirits who serve Antiochia, the Queen of Spirits, the Good Lady of Elfhame below. Take this petition marked with my own blood to your Lady. Deliver it to her hands, and for this favor I will give you an offering of strong spirits, poured out here on a cairn of stones that I shall make. Mighty Earth, cover this secret petition and let it come into the possession of the one that I intend it for.*

Then bury the petition completely. Pack the earth back in good. Take your stones and make a cairn, a mound of stones, over the place where the petition-pact is buried. Then take a flask, jar, or bottle of whiskey or some strong distilled liquor and pour it directly onto the cairn. Close your Gateway Ring in the usual way, collect any extra things you brought in with you, such as the candles or lanterns or what have you, and depart.


### III. Dream Incubation

When you go to sleep on the night after you did the burial ritual, your dream *might* come—watch for it. **Sleep with your Breaching Talisman on**. Your dream has 28 days to arrive. If it does *not* arrive within the 28 days, the offer of pact you made has not been accepted. More on what to do about that later; let us deal now with the first three nights after the burial ritual.

On the first night, the dream might come. If it does not, then on the second night, you must use your hypnagogic state to *repeat your burial ritual*. This time, you're going to re-live the burial ritual in your mind. Lie down for sleep, and when you start to feel like you are shifting into the hypnagogic state, visualize the entire experience again. See yourself journeying out to the place where you made the cairn; remember how it felt, what you saw, what you did. Re-live the whole experience in your mind as you are falling asleep—and try not to fall asleep before you finish re-creating it. Once you "see" yourself pouring the final offering onto the cairn stones, you can fall asleep.

**Make sure you have your Breaching Talisman on for this night of sleep too, and on *any* night of sleep in which you are expecting or hoping for a Witch Dream.** Try to avoid going to sleep exhausted or over-tired on these nights.

Watch your dreams that second night. If the dream doesn't come, then on the next night, which is the third night, do this *again*—re-live your burial ritual again, right as you are falling asleep. If the dream doesn't come on the third night, then you must shift to the long final phase, in which you have 25 days left to receive the dream.

On the first night of this final phase, you will be using the Hypnagogic Prayer technique (given in the Appendix to this book) that you've read and understood already.

You will be doing the **full** Hypnagogic Prayer technique, using special information bequeathed to us in *Saducismus Triumphatus*. There, it is recorded how some Witches in the year 1664 worked a ritual to meet with preternatural beings or persons which led to the initiation of one of their number into Witchcraft. The passage reads:

"*The Examinant saith, That when she lived with Anne Bishop of Wincaunton, about Eleven or Twelve years ago, Anne Bishop persuaded her to go with her into the Church-yard in the night-time, and being come thither, to go backward round the Church, which they did three times. In their first round, **they met a Man in black Clothes**, who went round the second time with them, and then they met a **thing in the shape of a great black Toad**, which leapt up against the Examinants Apron. In their third round they met something **in the shape of a Rat**, which vanished away. After this, the Examinant and Anne Bishop went home... A few days after, Anne Bishop speaking about their going round the Church, told the Examinant, that now she might have her desire, and what she would wish for. And* *shortly after, the Devil appeared to her in the shape of a Man, promising that she should want for nothing..."*

This passage describes the *Thrice Backwards Ambulation* technique, and also provides you all you need to perform a Hypnagogic Prayer working that will open a spectral channel in your mind, allowing you to get messages to the Patron that you buried your petition for. This technique might be used hypnagogically to get messages to these Great Powers at *any* time, even when you aren't trying to obtain Witch Dreams.

**If your petition was to the Master of Spirits**, when you begin to slip into the hypnagogic state, visualize yourself walking at night towards an old church building in some rural place. Walk backwards around the church—starting at its front doors and going to the left. When you get back to the front doors, a tall man dressed in black clothing will be standing there, and he will then join you in walking backwards around the church for the next two rounds. He doesn't speak; he just walks backwards alongside you.

The next time you reach the doors, at the end of your second round, a large black toad is there. It leaps at you once and bumps into your body, and then hops away. At the end of your third round, when you reach the doors again, a large black rat is there, which looks at you long and hard before just vanishing. Then the Man in Black touches your shoulder and asks you to follow him. He leads you down a long dark road into a forest behind the church, to a clearing where a large bonfire is roaring. At that fire is a huge black dog, or a large black goat, or a large black or pale-colored deer—you choose which it is. This is the Master of Spirits.

Go to him and kneel on one knee before him, and begin your dialogue as explained in the Hypnagogic prayer technique. This beast can either speak to you in a dark voice, or project its words directly into your mind, to respond to you. After a short while into your dialogue—after you've exchanged polite openings and declared your reverence for Him—tell him that you have buried a petition in the earth for him, and beg him to be kind and accept it. Fall asleep dialoguing with him in this way.

**If your petition was for the Good Lady of Elfhame**, do the exact same "backwards walk" around the church, but this time, the Man in Black leads you into a dark meadow, and to a looming, steep hill. The hill opens—a doorway opens in its side—and a golden light pours out. He leads you into the golden light, down a steep ramp of earth, and into a vast underground feasting chamber with long tables, hearths cut into the ground, and pale, ghostly people sitting at the tables, eating lavish meals.

At the far end of the chamber, there is a throne, and on the throne sits the pale and beautiful form of the Queen of Elfhame. Go and take a knee before her, and begin the dialogue as it is elucidated in the Hypnagogic technique. Give your homage, converse, and finally mention to her your petition, and beg her to be kind in accepting it. Fall asleep in this dialogue.

If the dream comes that night, you have succeeded. If it does *not*, you have **24 more nights** in which you can do this Hypnagogic journey involving going around the church three times backwards.

You don't have to do it *every* night, and it would be a good idea not to. It would be better to do it every few nights, and allow the other nights to be free sleep/free dreaming. If your Witch Dream arrives at any point in these 25 days, congratulations. If it does not, then your petition was *not* accepted.

You can make a new petition and begin another 28 day cycle after **waiting two weeks**. Write a new petition, but change it—offer a *new* tangible offering; do not try the old one again. Repeat the whole process; go and bury your petition and create a cairn again in a **new** place. Do not *ever* return to the place where you buried an old petition.

If this second attempt fails, you can wait two weeks and then do one more full attempt—but you can **never** do more than three petitions a year. If you try three times and fail to get a response from any of them, wait 12 months before you try again. After a year has passed, you have three more tries you can make. If you try to make a fourth effort without waiting a year, it **will harm you, immensely**. For your own sake, do not *ever* do this. Wait the 12 months, and then you can try again safely another three times.

Sometimes, the petitions are not accepted because a better tangible offering is needed, one more suited to you. Sometimes, they are not accepted because the Unseen might wish to test your resolve, or because it's not the right time for you. And sometimes, they aren't accepted because you are simply not meant in this breathing life to be *Witched*. You can never know until you try, and see what happens. Success here **cannot** be forced. These Great Powers can endow whom they please with their strength for Witching. You can only sincerely present yourself, and hope in gratitude to *receive*.

If your *Witch Dreams* come, you will learn certain things than no book can show you, and you will understand things about your own empowerment that no one else can or ever will. Record every initiatory dream you get, for you may get more than one; pay *special attention* to the dreams you have in the week following your initial Witch Dream.

Alongside precious visions of the Master or the Good Lady revealing themselves to you in any of the *many* forms they can appear—which they sometimes will—you may see familiar spirits, who will usually either make themselves known, or you will have no doubts upon waking about who they were. Familiars can appear as humans, as animals, or as even stranger creatures: non-recognizable beasts, hybrids of humans and beasts, beasts larger or smaller than they should be, humans smaller than they should be, and so forth.

If they appear as human, they can be obviously dead humans (strangers, or those known to you), or they might even *seem* to be the doubles of living humans—all are metaphysically in the range of possibility.

Familiars might appear in countless ways. Any of these Dreams (whether or not familiars appear in them) can be mind-bendingly strange. What you must do—so long as you have seen a sign of verification that you asked for, proving that you are indeed having a Witch Dream—is **trust yourself fully** upon waking from the dream to understand what it meant, and who these beings were that you met or saw in the dream. Let your intuition tell you, as soon as you wake, what just happened.

If you wait too long, thinking too much about your dream after waking, your chances of accurately understanding what happened go down; always record or remember your first impressions upon waking and take those first impressions seriously.

One thing is **certain**: if you have a dream showing you the things you asked to see (the *signs of verification* such as the crow, the deer, the serpent, etc.) **do not doubt** that you obtained a Witch dream. From that day forward, you are *bound* to do what you said you'd do in the petition, and if you perform any acts of sorcery or Witchcraft in the name of your Patron—and you should always do these works in their names—assume that familiar spirits are assisting and empowering you *even* if you don't believe you've seen them in a dream or vision yet.

Upon obtaining these dreams, the Workings in this book are now open to you in their full strength. So are many others, in fact; but you will have to negotiate this and assay these and any other workings utilizing the special dimensions of relationship that you will learn about in these special initiatory dreams—things mysterious and unique to you and your situation.

* * *

The kind of pact and petition you were guided to make here was a very general sort: a petition for general sorcerous empowerment or empowerment to capability in Witchcraft generally considered. This covers all manner of workings from the most benevolent to the most cruel; but being a *general* access to empowerment, as it were, it spreads its strength out for all workings.

Petitions and pacts can be customized beyond what was explained and suggested here. A general request for Witching and the power to do Witchcraft is an all-around good thing to obtain, but you might wish to forego that and **specialize** instead. You may wish to ask **only** for a certain ability—such as the sole power to heal, or only the power to divine, to hex, curse, or do *eyebiting*—another name for *maleficia* or hexing. You can ask for such a thing merely by re-wording the petition/pact you will bury in the earth. Example: "*I am XX, who was given life by XX. I offer my allegiance to you, in this world and in the world to come, if you will endow me with the power to heal with Witchcraft in your name.*"

To *specialize* means that you won't have effectiveness in other arts and goals of sorcery beyond your specialty; the familiars who come to you (assuming you succeed in gaining the Witch Dreams) will be familiars oriented around that focus you requested. If you asked specifically for works of healing to be empowered when you do them in your Patron's name, then familiars attracted or sent to you will be the sorts of spirits who heal people. They won't typically be capable of empowering other sorts of workings. But because they (like you) are specialized, they (and you) will ordinarily be *better* at the thing you specialize in, compared to those who do similar workings. So, the power is much the same: a Witch who can only do healings does healings at much stronger level than one who is not specialized in the sorcerous healing arts. What they lose in range, they gain in focus and strength on their chosen specialty.

Aside from specializing in a particular art (which doesn't require you to alter your pact at all beyond a simple re-wording) there is another permutation on the pact you might wish to look into. When making your pact, you can ask for *more* than just empowerment in Witchcraft; you can ask for **special favors**. But if you choose to do so, things can change rather dramatically. You can make a request for general empowerment in Witchcraft, just as this chapter teaches, but alongside that add in other favors you want. You might *also* request freedom from serious illnesses or injuries for the space of ten or twenty years. You might also request that your power of persuasion with other human beings increases such that you have the power to gain what you desire from them if you attempt to bend them to your will. You might ask for complete protection from the attacks of wild animals for the rest of your breathing days.

There's no limit to the other special favors you might ask for—bearing in mind that you have to ask for things that are within the range of human and worldly reality. There's no limit to what favors you might ask, and you should **never** ask for more than one or two in your pact. I think you should consider *not* asking for special favors at all; the gift of general empowerment in Witchcraft, or some specialty empowerment to perform a craft-related wonder or transformation with the help of good familiars, should be enough. But if you really *must* ask, for reasons of your own, then asking for one favor won't require you to do anything but write it into to your pact—being very careful and precise in your wording.

After you write the line *"Send me dreams of guidance and instruction in the arts of sorcery."* add *"Also, grant me the favor of X".* Later, when you write *"If you will empower me to be capable of Witchcraft as I have asked",* add *"and if you will grant the favors I have asked,"* Very easy adjustments.

**If you ask for more than one extra favor, you *have* to increase your tangible offerings**. Instead of offering one tangible offering, now you have to offer two. You *have* to give back for what you're trying get. If your pact isn't being accepted, and you've asked for extra favors, it's possible that you've asked for something too much in that favor or those favors, or you're not offering enough back tangibly.

### Fairyism, Witchcraft, and a Final Note

Those wishing to actualize the ancient *Fairyist* folkloric emanation of Witchcraft have many options with regards to the complex figures of both the Fairy King and the Fairy Queen. As has been mentioned, the overlap between the Devil and the Fairy King is enormous in folklore, but the line can be blurry. Falling on the *Fairy* side of the line may represent a calling in some modern people, and it may be an effective calling that can unlock the Hidden space of the Unseen *if* one comprehends the darker truth behind the term "fairy", which has been subjected to so much diminishment of its seriousness in modern times.

In 1647, Margaret Alexander confessed that she had renounced her baptism to the King of Fairies—a pact that her interrogators certainly would have thought diabolical or hatefully demonic, though they happily did record her confession without substituting *Devil* for "king of fairies." More confessions like this may have existed that simply got lost under substitution.

The names **Oberion** or **Oberyon** for the Fairy King can be used by those seeking pact with the Fairy King, for the discovery of the 16th century fairy-related material in the V.b.26 grimoire manuscript in the Folger Shakespeare Library proved that the famous name *Oberon*, used by Shakespeare in his famous play, was *not* his invention; it is a name for the Fairy King from folk tradition. The powerful name **Ouragus**, a form of *Orcus*, the "Old God of Death", is suitable for the Fairy King and the Devil alike, due to Orcus being a widespread name for the King of the Underworld in Pagan times.

That same collection of magical operations and folklore revealed two folkloric names for the Fairy Queen: **Tytam** and **Mycob**. Those names, along with certain other names that emerge from British folk-tradition—such as *Mab* and *Nicneven*—are pregnant with much power. The somewhat broader myth-tradition related to the Fairy Queen as empowerer of Witches yields the powerful (and presently popular) name *Hecate*. The ancient names *Herodias* and *Abundia* are likewise powerful names for the *Witch Queen* as she intersects with the Fairy Queen. All of these names can be used to address the Good Lady of Elfhame in the seeking of pacts, though the name *Antiochia*, which I have focused on in this work, should not be overlooked.

Some may wonder what it would mean if their Witch Dream came on the night right after their 28th night. Is it a sign that the Pact is good, if the dream appears on the night *immediately following* the end of the 28 night period in which the dream was hoped for, but failed to appear? What about a dream that happens at some point during the two week wait-period between having made one unsuccessful attempt at a Pact, and the attempt at another?

I say that the Witch Dreams should only be considered valid if they appear within the 28 day/night allotted time. The deeper powers naturally know full well that you have established a 28 day period of vigil in which you will be watching for a dream—you don't even have to say it; if it lives inside you as an expectation, as a dimension of your work, they *know*.

In the end, this is a personal matter between you and your dreams, but for the sake of all belief, consistency, and metaphysical cleanliness (as the case may be) I would ignore a dream that happened "out of sequence"—as painful as that might be if the dream seemed powerful. If it *was* a precious Witch Dream, the deeper powers might understand why you're not trusting it, and surely it won't put them out to send another within the time-frame you expect. Or the dream may be so compelling that you, in your best discernment and honesty, will be unable to ignore it; this is again up to you and your own conscience. I would strive to avoid such a thing and hope that the Good Powers understood why I was repeating the process, even after such a tantalizing dream.

Take note that the **signs of verification** you asked for so that you would know you were having the Witch Dream you petitioned for—the different animals, particularly—are just that, signals to you that your dream is happening. Do not automatically assume that those animals are intended to be forms of a familiar or familiars that will work with you, but sometimes they might be. The first dream (or dreams that follow it) will reveal what is the case.

**The Moon Sign**

If you succeed at gaining Witch Dreams, it would be powerful (though of course not necessary) to mark the occasion by obtaining a particular piece of jewelry, or getting certain tattooed markings on your body, to symbolize what you obtained. There are three signs or symbols/images that most perfectly embody the reality of Witching: the **moon**, **owls**, and **toads**. Obtaining charms or talismans of them, or getting tattoos of them, would cement your achievement greatly, and act as ongoing reminders of *who* and *what* you have transformed into.

The *Moon Sign* is (spiritually-aesthetically speaking) the most potent sign of Witchery because the moon is the *Lamp of Night*, the light in the darkness, which in symbolic language refers to the spirits who hover in the darkness of the Unseen, but also to the hidden realities of the world and the "Nighted" or Unseen side of the world to which any *Witched* man or woman truly belongs. The people of the sun—representing the obvious, ordinary world of rational entanglements—have done enough damage. To embrace the moon sign is to reject the many falsehoods of the countless lives lived on the sunlit surface level of the world only. The moon is *the Other*.

The image of the Owl is associated with Witchery because the Owl itself is a nigh-universal messenger, in myth and folklore, of darker or more occult powers. It is a herald of death, of hidden things, and Witchcraft. The Owl seems to have the power to navigate through the darkness, flying silently and striking at prey silently—and they have a disturbing habit of sitting very still and watching everything. Their stillness endows them with a kind of invisibility; they might not be noticed until they move. This bird may be a thing of ill-omen to non-Witched people, but for those who have obtained the blessing of the Unseen, the owl is a kindred spirit. The Witch and the owl both belong to the dark forest Unseen.

The image of the Toad is folklorically deeply associated with Witchcraft and sorcery all over Europe, but particularly in Britain, where *Tudders* or Toad-men are a fixture in occult folklore. The toad, aside from being one of the Witch Familiar forms *par excellence*, is a powerful creature for many reasons, and it takes a Witch to really understand them. Toads sit in the dark, boggy waters of our world, communing with the watery passageways between above and below. They croak and sing strange songs in the night. They can plunge deep down into the Unseen, and surface again elsewhere—an important talent, as both going *and* returning are critical. The toad or frog is a creature of the *nightside* of the world, just as much as the owl or the Witch.

# THE WORKINGS

# THE GATEWAY RING

To create the Gateway Ring, surround yourself with a circle of any size—a circle made from flour, sand, stones, twigs, branches, or drawn upon a floor with charcoal or chalk. You can also mark the circle upon the ground with a stick or a blade. Then go to the Eastern edge of the circle, and facing east, cast a small pinch or palm-full of earth to the east three times, saying the word **NURTANUMO** each time you throw it.

Next move to the Southern edge, and cast the three measures of earth to the south, saying **NURTANUMO** each time. Then move to the Western edge doing the same, then to the Northern edge where you do the same.

Go to the center of the circle, and allow a final pinch or handful of earth to trickle from your hand down onto the center. Bend forward and whisper **NURTANUMO** once to the ground at the center. This creates the Gateway Ring.

The interior of a Gateway Ring becomes open to the Unseen World; the metaphysical barriers that ordinarily exist in or about most places are thinned or weakened by the Ring. Any spirit or spirits that you call upon while inside the Ring will be more able to sense you and hear you; they will be aware of all your words and deeds inside that circle.

Further, the Word of Power used to enliven and open this Ring will endow you *and* any person who took part in its creation by also casting the earth to the four directions and then the center, saying the word each time, with an **aura of sympathy** to the spirits in the Unseen World. This means that if you ask Spirits for favors or aid, or help in a sorcerous act, your aims will seem sympathetic to them; they will be more inclined to lend their aid. You will seem more kindly disposed; you will seem a friend to them.

But to be certain of their aid you *must* give them an offering of any of the following: blood, strong liquor, tobacco, meat, milk, cheese, or butter. You must make this offering at the time of your asking for their help or favors. The Word of Power you have said will encourage any spirit you call to come to your Ring, and will dissuade them from harming you.

To close the Gateway Ring, you only have to strike the ground seven times in rapid succession at the center, and it is done. Anything you said or did within the Ring, any request for help you made, will remain good and powerful even after the Ring is banished in this manner.

While the Gateway Ring is active, anyone can leave it and return to its interior without disrupting its effectiveness. It should never be left established and active for days at a time; it should always be closed within a few hours of its creation, or a reasonable length of time otherwise.

**Analysis and Further Elucidations**

The Word of Power **NURTANUMO** is pronounced as such: *Ner-tah-noo-moh*. The "moh" sounds like "mow" as in "to mow the grass." Stress is divided evenly among all four syllables.

If one uses stones to create a Gateway Ring, the stones don't have to touch; they can be spaced out from one another, so long as they show a clear circular boundary. It very much helps to mark the Northern direction of the Ring somehow—even with a simple candle, a skull, or something of that nature.

There is an addition that can be made to a Gateway Ring which, though not necessary, can aid to strengthen the operation. A stone or stake of wood can be made, and etched, carved, or somehow marked with a sigil which is the word **NURTANUMO** transformed into a visual symbol. This sigil has two forms, a rectilinear or angular form and a curvilinear form.

Either can be chosen to be etched or carved, and this stone or stake of wood can be set up or driven into the earth at the North of the Ring, making a more formal "Northern marker". The two forms of the **NURTANUMO** sigil are given on the next page.

**NURTANUMO** sigil, *rectilinear*

**NURTANUMO** sigil, *curvilinear*

Gateway Rings render the basic operations of Sorcery, or spirit-aided workings, possible. And it does this even for men and women who are not *Witched* or otherwise in special union or relationship with Unseen powers. By simply making a Gateway Ring, and calling out to the nearby spirits of the Land one is upon, or the spirits of the area, one can obtain their attentions and sympathy towards many things one might need. Understand that local land-based spirits may not be able to cause changes or bring about needs that involve faraway places or persons. But they can have *enormous* influence in and around their own area.

A Gateway Ring created alongside or within a cemetery will allow for the wandering souls of those whose bones or remains lie in the ground there to be contacted, assuming they are in a metaphysical place in which they can be responsive. One's own Familiar Spirits can be directly communicated with or conjured via the Gateway Ring, and asked for special favors or help. But no matter who you may call, you must either *know their names*, or be able to describe them in such a way as your description can *only* refer to them.

If, for instance, you do not know the name of a person buried in an unmarked grave, you can still call upon them by referring to them as "the wandering soul of that man, woman, or child whose remains lie in the earth in (describe the place specifically) or "whose remains lie in the earth in the unmarked grave before me."

Never forget that no basic sorcery of this kind is possible without giving the offerings mentioned in the description of the working. I carry a flask of whiskey with me everywhere I go, simply because few offerings in my experience have excited spirits more, or drawn them to help me more eagerly. As ironic as it may seem to some, a flask of strong spirits may be among the most useful sorcerous tools there is. One way to increase the certainty of aid from spirits is to promise them that you will give them more offerings *after* they accomplish the requests you make of them, or lend their aid somehow.

That means you will return to the same place (if you can) where you made your Ring and call to them again, and give them another cup, bowl, or flask of whiskey if that's what you used to gain their aid the first time, or whatever offering you made. Failure to keep your promise of more offerings in return for their aid will be a poor showing that will degrade your power to get spirits to trust you in the future. Never fail to give what you said you would.

A Gateway Ring is easy to make, even on the spot when you weren't prepared to make one. Anyone can find twigs or stones and take some earth from the ground to use as the casting earth. It is the most practical technique of sorcery that I am privileged to know and use. You can use candles or lanterns—as many as you need, if you are working at night—or build a fire inside a Gateway Ring, all without disrupting it in any way. You can bring other implements or items into it, or put them all around it, without disrupting it. There is never a bad time to make a Gateway Ring, whether indoors or out, if you are doing an act of sorcery or Witchcraft that will be calling upon spirits in the unseen for aid; and *all* genuine acts of sorcery and Witchcraft must do so. Not all acts require a Gateway Ring, but it can't hurt any. Wearing a Breaching Talisman while creating and using a Gateway Ring only makes the work ten times more powerful, and your words and deeds that much easier for the Unseen World to comprehend while you are in the Ring.

I find that it is quite powerful to use the Gateway Ring to ask local spirits for dream meetings—just as you can ask Familiars or *any* other spirits whom you can name or describe for dream meetings. If you're going to be doing works of Witchcraft within a certain area for a long period of time, it's quite polite to show yourself to the local spirits in this way, and give them offerings, and get them to appear to you in your dreams so that you can verify that a relationship of some warmth or knowledge has been established.

Near my home, in a clearing near to the edge of our forest, I have a circle of twigs whose northern edge is marked with a stag's skull, which I sometimes use for my sorcerous workings. I transform it into a Gateway Ring quite often. I first set about to meet the Spirits of the forest here by creating a Gateway Ring and calling upon them, introducing myself and asking them if they would reveal themselves to me in my dreams that night.

I naturally told them how much I desired their friendship. I asked that they would make it so I recognized them in my dreams. I gave them a whole wooden bowl of whiskey and told them I'd bring another if they satisfied my request and appeared to me.

That night, I broke one of the cardinal rules of dream-work, and went to bed a bit too tired. And yet, just as I slipped into the full sleep state, I had a short dream of a dark man walking out of the edge of the forest near where my working spot is, and stopping to look at me. That was all for that night, and since I'm cautious, I returned to my working place, created a Gateway Ring again, and told the spirits of that forest that I wasn't sure if they had come to me or not, but on the off-chance they had, I was making good on my word and giving them another bowl of whiskey. And so I did. I then asked them to come to my dreams again that night, with promises of more offering.

That night, a strange dream descended upon me, a dream of odd clarity— always a sign of something from the outside of one's soul bringing a subtle influence to bear. I found myself in a dark forest where a great bonfire was blazing, and all around me were crowds of wild, strange beasts. Some were goats, some were deer, some were animals that I could not recognize, but I accepted them in the moment of the dream, as dreamers do. I knew we were here to dance, so I ran towards the fire to dance—and out of the darkness around me, a baby goat came sailing and landed in my arms softly. Holding the goat, I danced, and danced, while these strange beasts hopped and pranced around me, dancing in their own way. I woke up from the dream overjoyed, for I knew it was *Them*. They had revealed themselves to me as I asked. The next day, I went again to my working place, created a Gateway Ring and gratefully gave them another bowl.

This was not the only time their presence and friendship was affirmed to me so tangibly; a few weeks later, while asleep, I began to slip into a bad dream, for I had been ruminating on woeful matters as I slipped into sleep. As this nightmare began, I suddenly found my dream-space invaded by hoofed and horned crowds of beasts—and one of them bumped into my leg, hard, shocking me into a kind of clarity. The nightmare faded. My friends in the Forest right outside had sensed what was happening to me and come to protect me.

If they can be so friendly and protective to we who live here, what might they be asked to do to intruders, or people whose presence is obnoxious here? In this, we see the spiritual-ecological heart of true Witchcraft, and the local spirit-contact principle that also lives at that dark heart, from ancient times to Early Modern times, to right now.

One must never get carried away with conjuring spirits from within an empowered Gateway Ring. The Great Powers themselves—the Master of Spirits, the Good Lady of Elfhame—these are *not* the sorts of beings you "conjure" in any sense beyond a reverential one. They are not to be called upon in a spirit of trying to coax them to do something for you in exchange for a big bowl of milk or whiskey. Even the powerful act of giving of blood as an offering to spirits—which is *always* done by getting a twig, peeling it smooth, putting nine drops of your own blood on it by pricking your own fingers and offering them the *blood twig* as soon as you put the blood on, is not enough to justify taking some kind of haughty or demanding tone with the Great Master or the powerful Lady of the Fayerie Underworld.

It's best, if you call upon them, to ask for their blessings on your work, whatever it is. Give them offerings out of respect. Offerings given in an Gateway Ring don't all have to go into bowls or plates; you can pour or place them directly on the ground if you need. **It's the spirits who serve the Master or the Elphen Queen** who are in the range of practical conjuration and most appeals for aid. So call upon them—"*You who fly in the aerial host of the Master of Spirits...*" "*You who serve the Elphen Queen below...*" and give *them* offerings and ask them for help with practical matters you have on your mind.

Aside from general invocations to *Those Who Serve* the Great Master of Spirits/Devil, or the Fairy King, or general invocations (such as the one used in the creation of the Breaching Talisman) to the *Brides from Below* or the *Dark Mothers* who serve the Queen of Elfhame, the V.b.26 collection gives the names and sigils of *specific* spirits connected directly to the Fairy King/Master of Spirits and the Fairy Queen. I will give them now for those who wish to attempt to contact them or bargain with them for powerful outcomes. This may fall under a kind of occult experimentation, but it's true that you never can quite tell what relationships might be possible if luck is with you, and if you show the right kind of respect and reverence.

I would suggest that before attempting to invoke any of these individual spirits for aid in Witchcraft or sorcery, a man or woman create a Gateway Ring, draw their sigil on the ground or on a piece of parchment or paper (or create it somehow otherwise), and call upon them to ask (in the name of their Master or their Queen, as is appropriate) that they will **appear to you first in a dream.** Of *course* you'll give them the expected offering that you give any spirit you ask a favor of, when you make this request. You can make this request multiple times until you gain the dream, but space out your requests; don't badger these beings. If the dream won't come after a while, don't press the issue. Wait a few moons before asking again.

Only after you have a dream of them (and they can appear in many forms, human or animal) should you then interact with them further. More advanced workings given later in this book—such as the **Spirit Audience** working—can be used to contact them too, asking them to appear in the dark glass of a scrying mirror or in the dark, still surface of a vessel of water. But getting them into an initial dream-meeting is important still.

It is recorded that the **Seven Fairy Sisters**—a group of powerful spirits who serve the Good Lady of Elfhame—are named **Lillia** (LILL-ee-uh), **Afryca** (uh-FRICK-uh), **Fata** (FAH-tah), **Folla** (FOH-luh), **Iulia** (YOO-lee-uh), **Restillia** (res-TILL-ee-uh), and **Venulla** (ven-OO-luh). Iulia I know can appear as a wolf; it may be that all her sisters can, among other shapes.

It is recorded that the Fairy King has four special Serving-Men, four *counselors* that have his ear, or huntsmen who are intimately-connected agents of his power. They are named **Caberyon** (kuh-BARE-ee-on), **Carmelyon** (kar-MELL-ee-on), **Severyon** (suh-VARE-ee-on) and **Storax** (STORE-acks).

The sigils for all these spirits are given on the next page. Only one sigil associated with each of these 'Serving Men' is given in this book; others are known. Almost all of them incorporate the symbol of a stylized *arrow*, hinting that these spirits have the power to kill or harm at will. They are officers or sub-leaders in the *Wild Hunt* or Spirit-Host that is folklorically depicted as following the Master in a timeless or cyclical

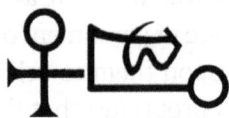

LILLIA

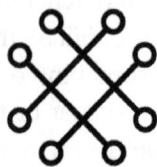

AFRYCA

FATA

FOLLA

IULIA

RESTILLIA

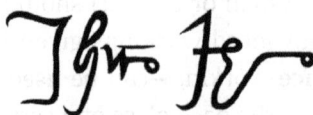

VENULLA

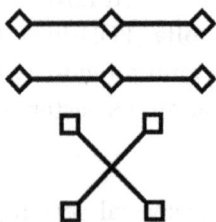

CABERYON

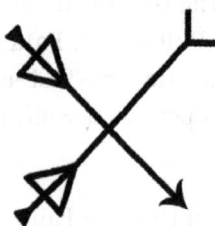

CARMELYON

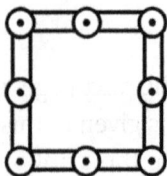

SEVERYON

STORAX

hunt for spirits, and perhaps for the souls of those humans and beasts whose "hour has caught them"—whose time has come to die.

When invoking one of these spirits, always call their names at *least* three times. Contemplate their sigil for a while before you make the call. *Always* ask them to come and be well-inclined to you in the name of their Queen (or King, in the case of the four Serving Men); any name for the Elphen Queen will suffice for this call; *Oberion* is what you should call the King when invoking the four Serving Men. Give offerings to them into a bowl or bowls next to the sigil you created, or, if it's drawn on the earth, you can pour or place offerings directly onto the sigil.

✶ ✶ ✶

Gateway Rings are useful for many reasons beyond the ones already mentioned. Acts of divination are rendered more possible through them; merely surrounding yourself with a Ring and invoking the aid of one of the Great Powers on an act of divination you are about to perform, and asking them to send one of their serving entities to you to guide your hands, your mind, and your method that you will discover the truth (through your device of divination) of anything that you are about to ask, and *then* giving an offering to them will magnify the accuracy and power of any divinatory act done thereafter. And this assumes that you *don't* have individual spirits as familiars who empower you in such acts, to whom you can appeal.

# YIELDING THE GREEN OYL

Within the pages of *Saducismus Triumphatus*, we find the following account:

*"Further she (Alice Duke) confesseth, That she hath been at several meetings in Lie Common, and other places in the night, and that her Forehead being first anointed with a Feather dip't in Oyl, she hath been suddenly carried to the place of their meeting... in the said Common in the night, were present Anne Bishop, Mary Penny of Wincaunton, Elizabeth Style of Bayford, and a Man in black Clothes with a little Band, whom she supposeth to have been the Devil. At the meeting there was a Picture in Wax, which the Man in black took in his Arms, and having anointed its Forehead with a little greenish Oyl, and using a few words, Baptized it by the name of Elizabeth or Bess Hill, for the Daughter of Richard Hill. Then the Devil, this Examinant, Anne Bishop, and Elizabeth Style stuck Thorns in the Neck, Head, Hand-wrists, Fingers and other parts of the Picture, Saying,* **a Pox on thee, I'll spite thee.**"

The mysterious *Green Oyl* mentioned in these passages—and in others in which it is found—appears to have been a talismanic oil that endowed those persons or things it touched with some kind of heightened vitality or power. In the case of living people, it exerted some kind of vivifying or even visionary impact—a hint that it may have contained entheogenic or psychotropic substances.

In the case of those not-yet-living—the images created of living persons that were later endowed with preternatural life and *connection* to the human being they intended to mimic—the potent Green Oyl acted as a **facilitator of sympathetic sorcery**—the most storied and legendary Art of Witchcraft since time immemorial.

The power that the Green Oyl channels is the power of the Underworld: the place from whence the raw force of life comes and to which it returns. It is *green* because the spirits of nine plants aid in its creation, and they are children of the *Green World*, of the enormous and ancient family of green and growing entities which is one of the primary manifestations of the dark surge of life from the Unseen into the visible world. The roots of plants sink into the dark womb-world below, and mediate its power into the airy world above. Without their help, the Oyl cannot be crafted.

Every Witched soul ought to strive to make a jar or bottle of the *Green Oyl*, for it opens the doorway to workings of immense power and effectiveness; it is a master-tool of practical Witchcraft, a mighty facilitator of strength and healing for those who need it, and a sharp sword of wrath against those whose foul deeds have marked them out as deserving.

The process of *Yielding the Green Oyl* always begins in late spring, summer, or very early autumn, when you seek out the nine plant-helpers whose leaves or flowers will be gathered to create your Oyl. In later autumn or winter, the life-force of these beings is withdrawn to their roots and they enter their winter trances, and thus asking them for donations of their power and vitality becomes largely unworkable. Evergreen plants might be appealed to for their aid in the midst of a winter, but their power is of another, stranger sort.

You will approach nine different plants and give them an offering of drops of your own blood, of whole cream, or strong spirits in exchange for one of their leaves or flowers. You will kneel or sit before them with your Breaching Talisman on, and say the following words:

**Lyacham, Lyalgema, Lyafaran, Lialfarab, Lebara, Lebarosin, Layararalus**

Pronounce them to the best of your ability. You must now address the plant by its name—and aside from knowledge of plants learned from others, or any of the excellent field guides that are available for any region, technology has provided many means of identifying plants. Tell the plant:

*"I greet you, (name of plant), and wish the blessings of the King of Spirits and his Queen upon you and your kin. I come as a friend to ask a favor of you, and to pay for that favor with good offerings that you will desire. Give to me a small portion of your body, and preserve within it a measure of your power to support my sorcerous work. I wish to craft an oil that will act as a medium for the power of the Underworld—that dark place to which your roots forever reach. Take this offering, and may it delight you and make you stronger, and forgive me any pain I cause when I take from your goodly shape."*

Give your offering to the area around where the plant meets the ground, and then quickly take the portion you are there to get—a leaf or a flower. Cut it away quickly, and use your intuition—never take a portion of a plant that feels too potent or precious to the plant. Collect the leaves or flowers in a bowl as you go through the woods or meadows.

**Do not** collect portions from poisonous plants. The Green Oyl will be used to anoint yourself and potentially others upon whom you wish to confer its blessings, and that could be quite disastrous—for obvious reasons—if you choose dangerous plant helpers.

Get a smallish clear jar or bottle that can be corked very firmly or perfectly sealed, and fill it with a base oil—olive oil is the obvious and easiest choice for most, but any neutral plant-based oil will work as a carrier or base. Put all nine of your plant-portions inside it and let them sink into it. This bottle will now undergo the lengthy, powerful treatment that will transform its contents into *Green Oyl*.

On **Thirteen different nights**, you will create a fire and boil water or heat the water to scalding hot in a cauldron or pot over that fire. This is best done over a fire built outside, with the cauldron or pot hanging from a tripod, but truly, if the situation required it, you could do this without a tripod, or simply over the fire of a stove indoors with a pot boiling/simmering on the eye, so long as you worked only by candlelight.

You must undertake the *scald* the bottle holding your base oil and the nine different plant-portions in the boiling water. This means submerging or suspending the bottle in the boiling or scalding hot water, so that it heats up. It only needs to be scalded for a few minutes. While it is scalding, you must say a special Word of Power **nine times** over the bottle, and that word is **ABANHOU**. After you have said the word nine times (with a small pause each time you say the word), remove the bottle and set it aside. After it cools a bit, open it, and speak **ABANHOU** into the bottle nine times.

That represents one successful scalding work, of *thirteen* that you must perform. This must always be done at night. At least three of the nights must be *waning moons*. At least three of the nights must be *waxing moons*. And at least three of the nights must be *full moons*—the other four nights can be with any moon phase. This work will necessarily take three months to accomplish, if done as quickly as possible. After your thirteenth scalding session, if you have met the necessary lunar criteria for the nights, the Green Oyl is activated. If you were to anoint your forehead with this Oyl and say the word **ABANHOU**, it will make strong your body and soul; it will also endow you with protection from harm and make spirits well-inclined to you. If you were to anoint the head of any other person with the oil and say the word **ABANHOU**, it will do the same for them.

Further, the Green Oyl will greatly empower sympathetic works of sorcery, which is to say workings done upon images made of living humans or other beings. If ever you take an image of clay, wax, or wood made of any person, and anoint that image with the Oyl, saying the word **ABANHOU** as you do, and then baptize that image with water in the name of the King and Queen of Spirits, giving the image the name of the person it is intended to represent, **the Oyl will connect that image to the soul and vitality of that person**. This will allow the holder of the image to harm that person, or help them as they desire, by speaking charms to the image, anointing it with empowered oils or bathing it in empowered waters, or damaging it with pins, nails, needles, stones, fires, hot coals, bones, or blades.

## Analysis and Further Elucidation

The Word of Power **ABANHOU** is pronounced "ah-bonn-hoo", with "bonn" sounding like the "bonn" in "bonnet." Emphasis is spread out evenly among its three syllables.

The first bottle of Green Oyl created in line with this criterion and understanding was made from Horseweed, Garden Phlox, Blue Wood-Aster, Musk Mallow, Lady Fern, Hedge Bedstraw, Wrinkleleaf Goldenrod, Yellow Avens, and Fleabane, all found and allied with on the grounds of Ledgewood. The clear glass jar containing the oil had two small handles on either side of it, so I ran two sturdy wires on either side of the jar, which easily suspended it over the cauldron of boiling water, allowing the jar to sit largely submerged in the scalding liquid as I did the needed recitations of the word of power over the nights of its creation.

Anointing yourself or another with the Green Oyl after its creation is easy enough to understand. The metaphysical benefits of doing so are likewise easy enough to grasp. Utilizing it as an empowerer of sympathetic sorcery must be elucidated further.

This will eventually carry us away from the topic of the sympathetic sorceries empowered by the Green Oyl and at length into the **Arts of ensorceling and enchantments** generally speaking.

**ABANHOU Sigil**

The **ABANHOU** Sigil is a means of representing the Word of Power in a different shape, but it still directly carries or mediates the power living within the sounds of the word. You don't have to use it if you choose not to, but there are ways it can be utilized to add extra power to the act of scalding the bottle of Oyl, in its creation. You can carve it or otherwise mark it onto the pieces of wood or firewood that you'll be using to make the fire that boils the water, and this will increase the strength of the work. If possible, label or mark any jar containing the Green Oyl—or any box storing jars of Green Oyl—with this sigil.

When you empower an image of another person with the Green Oyl, the image *must* be made from clay, wax, or wood. The image must be baptized "in the name of the King and Queen of spirits" after you anoint it and say **ABANHOU** over it once. Technically, a simple bowl of water will suffice for this baptism. Hold the image cradled in the crook of your arm, as though it were a baby, while you are anointing it and baptizing it.

To add great strength to this "baptism", this *initiation* of the Green Oyl-empowered image through the power of water, I strongly suggest that the water used in the Baptism be created in the following way:

Put a pinch of earth into a bowl of water. Light a long, thin candle (or a twig) aflame and lower the flame into the water, extinguishing it. Then say, over the water, the following incantations:

**ABRAT ABRASAX SESENGENBARPHARANGÊS
SISOCHÔR SESENGENBARPHARANGÊS SABAOTH**
*(say these two lines of strange words aloud three times)*

**Dark King of the World Below, let your power rise up and bless this water, making it a water able to bestow the power of life.**

Then blow three times upon the surface of the water.

**PHORBA PHORBÓBAR BARÓ PHÓRPHÓR PHÓRBAI**
*(say this line of strange words aloud three times)*

**Horned Queen of the Netherworld, Good Lady Below, let your power rise up and bless this water, making it a water able to be-stow the power of life.**

Then blow three times upon the surface of the water, and it is done; the water will now act as a true Underworldly baptismal fluid that will endow metaphysical life-force further into any image baptized with it. When you dribble some of the water over the head of the image, say *I baptize you in the name of the King of Spirits and his Queen—and I name you XX, who was given life by XX.*

This naming convention you should be familiar with by now. It requires you to know the first and maiden names of the mother of the person you are attempting to connect the image to. If you do not have the mother's information, or if you are making an image of some other-than-human person, you can try to get around this by stating a fact about the person that **can only be true about them**. In other words, you may say *I name you John Smith, who lives at 145 Eckhart Street in Orrington, Maine.* Or *I name you Erin Johnson, who is sister to Renee Johnson, who lives at X place.* This is not as powerful or effective as knowing the mother's maiden name, but it can sometimes suffice.

When you make your wax, clay, or wood image, do your best to make it resemble—as far as you can—the person it is intended to represent. If you can at all get material links to the person—their hair, scraps of their clothing, and the like, **incorporate those things however you can** into the image. They can and *will* endow such an operation as this with high effectiveness. The crude face you carve or etch or shape onto the image doesn't have to look like the person at all; but you have to have a face with eyes and some attempt at a mouth. Anything else you can do should be done; if the target of your work is very tall or has long legs, reflect that into the image. Try to get their body shape captured as best you can always remembering that this doesn't have to be a work of (ordinary) art.

Once it is anointed and baptized as described here, it is metaphysically connected to the soul and vitality of the person. This means that workings done upon the image—whether they are for good or for ill—are delivering their power **directly to the soul of the person that the image represents**. If the soul is *helped* or *harmed* too strongly—empowered or disempowered too much—that will have a sympathetic tangible impact on the physical, breathing life of the person, in some form or fashion.

The Word of Power **ABANHOU** allows you to do **helpful** works on these enlivened images by using spoken charms, anointing the image with benevolently empowered oils, or bathing it in benevolently empowered waters. It also allows you to do **harmful** works on these enlivened images (again) through using chants or spoken charms, anointing the image with banefully empowered oils, bathing it in banefully empowered waters, or damaging it with pins, nails, needles, stones, fires, hot coals, bones, or blades.

A *spoken charm* is just that: a few verses you compose yourself, saying what you want the soul of the person to "hear". Speaking directly to the image, with your mouth close to its head, urging it with peaceful and beautiful words to arise in strength, to be calm, to be soothed, to be healed, all in the names of the Good Master *or* the Lady of Elfhame, will begin to have a good impact on the person (depending on their need and your aim) if you do it enough. Repetition is the key here—speaking such things to the image over and over again, every day.

Hateful verses, packed with insults and wishes for all manner of horrors to befall the person, or, more to the point, *commands* for such horrors or misfortunes to befall them (again in the name of the Good Master or the Lady of Elfhame) will *disempower* the person over time. It will begin to exert a grim or troubling effect in their lives. Hypnotically speaking these terrible things into their soul will disturb their unconscious minds and sleep after a point, and begin to spill over into their waking lives, potentially exposing them to woeful situations, accidents, or declining mental or physical health.

In the same way you empowered the Baptism Water with the incantation-charms above, you can empower oils—of any sort—or containers of water to become healing or soothing oils or waters, or hateful, baneful oils or waters used in hexing or cursing. The only difference is you don't have to put the pinch of earth into oils or waters that you make for these ends, nor douse a candle in them.

Wearing your Breaching Talisman, and ideally standing in a Gateway Ring, you just have to put the oil or water in a bowl, jar, or cup, place that in a triangle made from three wooden branches or sticks, and then say **one** of the incantation-charm formulas over them **three times**.

Don't say both formulas, choose one. And if you choose the first (**Abrat, Abrasax...**) then you'll ask the Devil or the Master of Spirits (by whatever name you use for him) to send forth his serving beings to empower your oil or water with the power to do what you need—to heal someone? To harm them? Ask for it. Explain what you want. When you're done asking, **blow onto the surface of the oil or water three times**.

Give the servants of the Master their due in offerings for helping you, and then you can use your ensorcelled oil or water on the image, by simply anointing the image, or pouring the water over it, or setting it in the bowl or container of water and letting it soak. Such enchanted waters don't have to be used *only* on images; you can apply them directly to others, or yourself in any manner.

If you instead choose the formula that begins "**Phorba...**" then you'll be asking the Good Lady of Elfhame to send forth her Serving Ladies to attend you and empower your oil or water, but it's just the same as explained before. Always blow on the surface of the oil or water three times after you're done asking for what you wanted.

It is critical that you understand what you are doing here—this is the **basic act of ensorceling or enchanting** things. The extremely potent formula "**ABRAT ABRASAX, etc.**" is pronounced

*Ah-braht  ah-bruh-socks  sess-in-gen-bar-par-ahng-ays*

*See-sah-core  sess-in-gen-bar-par-ahng-ays  sah-bah-oat*

("gen" is pronounced with a hard g, "ahng" sounds like "ankh" but it ends with a hard g; "oat" sounds like the "oat" in "oatmeal.)

This formula—which is always to be chanted three times—is a **direct conjuration formula that gains the attention of the Underworldly King**, whether you understand him to be none other than the Devil, a powerful ruling spirit below of some other sort, or the King of Fairy. The other formula, beginning with "**PHORBA...**" already had its pronunciation given earlier in this work. It is always to be said three times as well when used, and it is a **direct conjuration formula that obtains the attention of the Underworldly Queen**—no matter who you understand her to be.

You don't ever have to use these two formulas together, outside of making the Baptism water. They work perfectly fine used alone. And it must be made clear that if you are *Witched*, it doesn't matter who your patron-empowerer is; you can use either of these formulas anytime you need them. And there's *no end* to what kinds of works they can empower. Instead of empowering oils or waters to use on Images, you can put talismans or jewelry (or what have you) inside those triangles, and ask for various special benefits *or* malefic things to be endowed upon them— **just as you did when you made your Breaching Talisman**.

You can (temporarily) steal objects from enemies and *curse* the objects in this manner, before returning them (hopefully before they are noticed missing)—and leaving the deserving enemy to suffer under this cursed object now exerting its baneful power upon them every day from within their homes or worn right on their bodies. This was apparently not an uncommon form of Hexing; the Witch Alice Duke, whose confession we read so much of in *Saducismus Triumphatus*, was recorded as causing a "hurt (to) Dorothy the Wife of George Vining, by giving an Iron slate to put into her steeling Box." Alice also laid a man and his daughter low by giving them a "pewter dish" which she said she had "from the Devil"— but it's clear from the description that it was a cursed dish—perhaps bearing a curse *empowered* by Alice's master, the Devil, whom she called *Robin*.

Another witch, Isobel Strachan, who was said to have learned her skills from an "elf man", was a match-maker of types; she would sew a penny into a piece of cloth that was hung around the necks of her clients, and they were told to make sure the one they wanted simply touched the cloth packet—or to just strike them with it. This is another example of many given in historical records of a common object being enchanted to cause a simple lust or desire effect.

Alternatively, one might take a knotted cord of twine that's tied into a loop large enough to fit over a person's body and enchant it with the power to capture any powers of sickness or illness within the body of a man or woman that it is passed over and around three times, and then keep that cord tucked away. If you (or another) get a wretched cold or flu, you should drop it over your head and let it fall to your feet, or do the same to them, and then repeat this twice more, before **burning the knotted cord**. When you're sick, you have everything to gain from the potential help that can be had from an ancient healing work like this. I believe that this work, if rightly done, will greatly speed recovery time.

This is, after all, quite an old practice. Edward J. Cowan mentions that a witch named Isobel Cockie "was forced to un-witch a man when his son threatened to burn her. On another occasion, she relieved a millwright, a victim of the evil eye, who was consumed with fever... the cure consisted of three draughts of a herbal drink mixed with butter and saffron, as well as an elaborate ritual involving the knotting of green threads **upon which the witch blew**. When the patient inquired why, she replied that no one knew the answer. She then passed the thread around the man's body, under his oxters, and threw it in the fire, while leaving another thread around his waist for 24 hours; when it broke, she had his wife burn it. His wife fetched water from a south-running stream, washed him with it, and returned it to the stream."

The logic behind these workings is of an extremely old and potent sort. More than just the knotted cord taking away sickness once it is empowered to do so, the water from the stream "gained the sickness" from the man, and carrying it away and throwing *back* in the stream was healing. You must comprehend this *law of contagion* when you consider your own works, particularly healing works. You can be sure that Isobel Cockie's "herbal brew" with butter and saffron was enchanted to be a healing draught, a thing you can easily accomplish on any herbal mix you can create yourself.

One's imagination is truly the limit, so long as the basic rules are followed as written here: saying one of the formulas thrice aloud; calling upon the Master (or the Lady, depending on the formula you used) by the name you know them under, or by titles referring to them; asking them respectfully for blessings on your work; asking them to send forth their serving spirits to accomplish a specific need or desire, having any substance or object you want ensorcelled in a triangle of wood; blowing on the objects or fluids (or whatever) three times after you're done asking; and paying the beings you asked to help do this with real offerings.

When it comes to damaging images with pins, nails, needles, stones, fires, hot coals, bones or blades (and these are the only things **ABANHOU** will allow you to use on the images it empowers) that process is easy. You don't actually have to do anything special to the implement you will use to damage the image; simply taking a nail and a hammer, and driving the nail into the body of a wooden image, while saying **A POX ON THEE, I'LL SPITE THEE**, will deliver a burst of metaphysical harm directly to the soul of the victim.

The same is true of needles, pins, or nails heated in a candle flame and stabbed into a wax image, or needles or pins or nails sunk into a clay image. Stones used to beat these images (always saying the *Pox* phrase), bones used to beat them, or blades used to stab them: it's all the same effect. You have to *intend to harm*—feel hatefully and malicefully inclined to harm the person when you damage the image with these things, and while you say the *Pox* phrase. This is critical.

If you make a glowing bed of coals, you can roast a clay image in the coals, growling the *Pox* phrase at it over and over. You can burn up a wooden image in fire, or melt a waxen one completely in coals. You can use a flame—like a candle flame—to scorch or warp any image over and over again, harming it (again using the *Pox* phrase).

But to **increase the metaphysical power** of this kind of aggressive sorcery, you would perform an act of **basic enchantment**—just as I finished describing—on the nails, pins, needles, stones, blades, bones, candles, or coals that you'll be using to harm the image *before* you use them to harm the image.

Asking the Devil's very devious servitors (or the malicious spirit-forces of the Underworld otherwise) to come up by the authority of one of those special formulas I've already explained, and endow upon a bowl of needles or nails or a blade sitting in a triangle some specific horrible power, and then *driving those* into an image, turns an ordinary working of spite into a masterpiece of malicious sorcery. *A pox on thee, I'll spite thee* might not sum it up, if the darkest corners of your mind really engage.

I trust the moral sense of the people reading this work when it comes to harmful workings. Mature people do not inflict vicious harm on others that don't richly deserve it. And people who are just irritating, or not as smart as you, or who ignorantly express pedestrian stupidity or make childish insults to you on social media (and suchlike) do *not* deserve hot nails boiling with the power of the Underworld driven through the hearts of their own souls. Save baneful workings for the people you *know* have it coming—and yes, you have to decide that. And when the time comes, you *will* know.

And there will be severe consequences for deciding that someone "deserves" something, only later to discover that they *didn't* deserve it. So take care to make these sorts of grave decisions very impeccably. Sometimes, vengeance is something due to you or to another, but you are a fool indeed if you allow vengeance to consume you and become a regular or constant motivation for the works you are doing. And you're walking on very dangerous ground if you ever find that this has become the case.

Witchcraft can and *should* be used to give justice to those who truly need it, but cannot seek justice through any ordinary social system or institution. Contemplate, if you can, the subtle yet real distinctions to be found between fair justice and vengeance.

Some astute readers may have noticed that when the "Baptism Water" operation was described, it called for the use of both of the incantation-formulas. The attentions of *two* of the Great Powers themselves is to be gained by the recitation of those special formulas three times, but a request for them to send forth their special serving-spirits to endow the water with the power to grant life **wasn't** part of the instructions. This is because the two formulas given (these incantations that potently obtain the attentions of the Underworldly King and the Queen of Spirits respectively) have the ability to enchant things on their own—but it is a very special or particular sort of enchantment.

You can use one of these formulas, saying it three times (always wearing your Breaching Talisman!) and then ask the Netherworldly King or Queen to grant some kind of empowerment upon a thing—like a container of water, or upon an object, or suchlike—and it can of course be an empowerment that ranges from baneful to beneficial. Then, blowing thrice upon the thing to be enchanted, it will gain a "charge". But this charge is a short-duration empowerment. It will *not* endure anywhere as long as enchantments woven by the serving spirits of these Great Powers: the enchantments paid for with offerings and accomplished by spirits dispatched to your working area to perform a task.

This "short duration" enchantment can still accomplish many things, and is a good alternative to have if you find yourself in an emergency or surprise situation. You don't have to do it inside of a Gateway Ring, and you need no triangle of wood to accomplish this. It's all very easy.

## Practical Witchcraft

Much has been spoken by others on the topic of *Practical Witchcraft*, but the accumulation of ideas on the subject has not yet yielded a very clear view. I will now undertake to condense the subject down to a bare essence that shall lead readers of this work a-right when situations press down upon them that call out for practical applications of Witchery.

Witchcraft must be practical; it has to accomplish things that people need in the breathing world of our ordinary experience. If it doesn't, it's not worth having. Practical Witchcraft is Witchcraft that **solves problems**.

You have a *problem* if a person, a place, a thing, or some situation is **harming** you, harming people you care about, or people you have been hired to help.

**Harm** means that a person, a place, a thing, or a situation is hindering you or another; that person, place, thing, or situation is unfairly forcing you (or another) to *do something that you don't want to do*, or *stopping you* from *doing something that you **do** want to do*—or it is stealing, diminishing, or taking vitality, health, power, one's means of surviving, or straining one's relationships with others.

A problematic situation that is now over—even one that has been over for a long time—can *still* be a harmful one if it inflicts you or another person with persistent left-over depression, trauma, or a desire for revenge, even. That is another kind of problem and harm: a situation that exists right now which stops you or others from having peace.

A problem is thought **solved** when the element of *harm* is diminished or gone completely. What I am about to say regarding problems is something you ought to burn into the pages of your mind. Don't ever forget it, and meditate upon it until it becomes a part of you.

**There is no such thing as a small problem**. Small problems either multiply into *many* small problems, or they grow stronger until they become *big* problems. You have to treat *every* small problem as though it were a big problem. And you must destroy or diminish every small problem you can, with great force and cunning.

By the time a big problem exists, it becomes doubtful—and usually unlikely—that Witchcraft (or anything else) can substantially impact it or solve it. *Every* big problem was once just a small problem, or a group of small problems. Remember this always: a single mangy dog might not seem threatening, but **twelve mangy dogs can kill a lion**. A single pebble, really no matter how small, will make it impossible to walk very far if it gets into your boot.

People may wonder at this attitude, thinking that it must be stressful to have to be so alert or alarmed about small problems. To them I say "Any stress I pay out on solving small problems *can't* compare to the stress I will face if a big problem—or a group of those—overwhelms my life." Big problems kill people. They lay savage waste to lives, to relationships, and finally to the possibility of peace or happiness in this world.

If you are facing a problematic situation that you will use Witchcraft to attempt to solve, make certain that at least a few legal, normal, safe, or socially-acceptable means of solving it have been tried or at the very least honestly thought about. Witchcraft does not exempt us from being relational human beings in a human world. We *have* to talk to people, live with people, co-create needful things with people, and work together with them to solve problems affecting everyone.

It's when those very *human* things have failed for some reason, or become unsafe, or need an extra dimension of influence that Witchcraft becomes a powerful means of help. To fail to try and address problems in a sensible human way is an arrogance of sorts; a declaration that one feels that the basic natural rules of *humanness* do not apply to them anymore. Witchcraft need not be a "last resort"—but it shouldn't be one's *only* resort as a rule.

When you're going to use Witchcraft to attack a problem, **try to simplify the problematic situation in your mind**. Identify the harm and the agents of the harm. Figure out what the **easiest possible way** would be to change, distract, transform, or destroy the harmful persons, places, things, or situations, and start there.

If you regularly find and eliminate small problems—which you (particularly as a Witched person) can usually easily do—you'll have *less* big problems in the future, as will those you find yourself working on behalf of.

Some may have taken note that all the Witching methods I have discussed so far have centered around the themes of harm and help—they have been focused on the idea of healing or soothing, or outright harm. If this seemed a bit polarized, it *should* because it is. There are some things that can't really be taught—they have to be understood and figured out by people's deeper and more creative minds. There is a very wide excluded center of Witchcraft that lies between acts of blessing and healing on the one end, and terrible harm on the other. And in that space, we find the works of **Delusion** and **Manipulation.**

And when it comes to Practical Witchcraft, manipulation workings find their *true* home ground. Often, our foes within problematic or harmful situations will be other human beings who are doing cruel, selfish, or otherwise unacceptable things. There's usually (owing to the social realities of our cursed modern day) *no* chance that anyone will be able to talk these people out of their selfishness or evil.

You can't appeal to the better angels of a person's nature when they simply don't have better angels—and we are **naïve** indeed if we think that *everyone* has to have some hidden "good" underside to their character. It is certain that not all people do, again such is the nature of our diseased social world. Our fallen society produces warped, diseased people. They may not be the majority of people, but they *are* there, and you will encounter them many times before you breathe your last.

So when facing a problematic human person, it may be that the fastest or best way to eliminate their problematic influence is to destroy them, and if you are ever in such a situation you may feel that this is needful. But what about the times when you *don't* think something so extreme is the best way forward? That's when the works of delusion or manipulation are useful.

A work of manipulation—in this case using an empowered image of another person—can be accomplished just as you might expect, but with a few notable changes.

You can hypnotically whisper your spoken charms into the "ear" or head of the image itself—daily and nightly **commanding** the person that the image represents, in the name of the King and/or Queen of Spirits, (or the *Devil*, or the *Good Lady of Elfhame*, whichever conventions you use) to **alter their course of action** regarding a certain situation.

You can tell them how they feel: "you, *X* person, now feel as though you no longer wish to pursue *X* course of action or remain in *X* place." "You, *X* person, no longer feel attraction for *X* person." The key to success here is constantly "speaking" to the image with your charm. Doing it ten times a day and night might be good, or even more. It can't be done enough.

But you can also (as I hope you've guessed already) use the ensorcelled waters or oils: use your method of basic enchantment to endow oils or waters with the power to **cause X. person to feel differently about someone else, or to decide to take some other course of action, or behave differently**—and then anoint their image with the oil, or sprinkle the image with the water, or soak the image in the water.

The sharp implements that were used, in our original discussion, to harm empowered images (the pins, the needles, the nails, the blades, and so forth) can be turned to the causes of manipulation *very* easily. The pins, nails, and needles are especially quite useful in manipulation workings, because they can **each be enchanted to carry some feeling or idea into the head, mind, or heart of a person**—and after they are enchanted so, they can be driven into the literal head of the image to put those kinds of thoughts into the mind of the person the image represents, *or* they can be driven into the *heart* of the image to put the sorts of feelings they were enchanted to carry into the person's being.

As was stated before (but perhaps not strongly enough) these enchanted substances—particularly the enchanted waters—don't have to only be used on empowered images. If you enchant water to cause a person to feel a certain way, and take a vial of it away, you can drop some of that water into a drink you give the person and enjoy the results of a direct burst of that enchantment taken by them internally. *Any* enchanted substance that you pass into the food or drink of your clients (or victims) will deliver their metaphysical punch most directly.

This of course implies that you are manipulating a person unawares who trusts you enough to take a glass of water or food from you. It's not always about manipulation and secrecy; you might have clients who come to you for help and want you to enchant up healing water for them, or some other such thing, and they'll drink it quite eagerly when offered. It's important to remember all of the possibilities for practical workings.

Speaking of practical workings, I have mentioned little or nothing about **protection** workings, which are also found in the "middle range" of workings between helping and harming. Anyone possessing a keen mind for Witchcraft wouldn't need me to mention these works; by now an astute person ought to have realized how useful it would be to enchant objects or even certain substances to act as **protectors** of the body and soul from harmful or hostile spirits, from the baleful Witchcraft of other human or spirit-enemies, and suchlike. These objects or substances can protect not just humans or other creatures, but places, too. And if you haven't yet laid plans to create such things, I advise you to begin.

### Familiars and Enchantments

To your acts of ensorceling or enchanting, the power of any familiars you obtained through your Witch Dreams is likely already being added anytime you work. You don't *have* to call upon familiars individually by any names you might have received for them, or call upon them by describing them as you saw them, to ask for their help. It's possible that your act of asking the Master of Spirits or the Good Lady of Elfhame to send their serving spirits to accomplish things for you *automatically arouses* and tasks familiars attached to your soul into action.

Even if your Witch Dreams did not reveal spirits that you surmised to be your familiars, you *did* ask to have them granted to you, and so if you gained the Dreams, then you *do* have one or more. And they will empower you when you work.

However, you may wish to invoke known familiars individually or collectively; it comes down to your own feelings on the matter. Doing so is easy; at the point when you ask the Master or the Good Lady to send forth their servants to your aid, say (right after you are finished asking those spirits for what you need): ***"Spirits familiar to me, be you roused and come to my aid in this work. Accomplish here all that I intend!"*** And that should be quite sufficient. When doing other kinds of workings that aren't enchantments, you can call on your familiars for aid in your success in just the same manner.

# THE GREAT AND TERRIBLE NAME

What follows is a brief discussion of a very advanced form of Witchcraft, and its power cannot be understated. At this point we will explore something that is both powerful *and* dangerous to a deep degree. Only *Witched* men and women with extensive experience will be able to embody or utilize the metaphysical matters we will be discussing here. There is no compelling reason to attempt the workings described here, when basic enchantments and workings of the sort we have already discussed *will* suffice—and they almost always will.

There is a Name, many ages old, which channels, stirs, and moves the great power of Nature itself—and for a man or woman to utilize it, they have to understand what it was I spoke about earlier in this book when I described *The Dark Ecology of the Devil.* I talked about the figure of the Devil as the famed *Lord of this World*, and how his mysterious person can be grasped (in a way) as not *just* a person, but an **ecology of powers**. There is a perceptual place, a metaphysical point, in which the Person of the Great Master of Spirits begins to give way to a less personal rhizome of Natural Forces and to the very fundamental force of Nature or Life itself.

And this metaphysical point takes us beyond rational understandings of persons versus non-persons, beyond rational understandings of any sort and into the emotional and intuitive encounters that we might have with the great and vital powers that animate our world. The closest that we may ever get to really facing these powers with our eyes, our senses, and our bodies will be when we stand under the open sky while a thunderstorm is raging and roaring above us, feeling and hearing the rush of rain pounding down, seeing the sudden flash of lightning, and hearing the mighty roar of thunder that seems it might split the sky asunder. If we witness with our own eyes the mighty destructive power of Nature in any form, we are truly *seeing* what the Ancient Name is an expression of.

Only a *Witched* soul can hope to call upon this Name, and receive of its strength, and thence mediate that strength into the end of a practical work of Witchery. And even those who are *Witched* and experienced enough will have to spend time pondering the name, and the great powers to which it connects, before they can hope to utilize it.

Below, I will give the three forms of the Name, and notes to their pronunciations. These are *not* Names that you ever use outside of a ritual of Witchcraft. You *never* say them aloud outside of a working, except in one special circumstance: if you are **outdoors** and **alone from human company**, you can say them aloud as a means of practicing saying them and internalizing them perfectly.

I will not write the Names formally; I will *only* give them phonetically so that you can learn to say them properly. I don't think they should be written down.

**The Great and Terrible Name, short form:**

**ABERAMEN-TOW-OO**

This is pronounced just as it looks; "Tow" is pronounced like a "toe" on your foot. "OO" is just a long O, like the "oo" in "hoot". TOW is underlined because that's where the stress should be put.

**The Great and Terrible Name, long form:**

**ABERAMEN-TOW-OO  LERTECKSANOCKS**

This is pronounced just as it looks.

**The Great and Terrible Name, palindromic Form:**

**ABERAMEN-TOW-OO LERTECKS ANOCKSETREL**

**OO-OWT-NEMAREBA**

This is again pronounced just as it looks—it's all one line, all one flow of sounds, and the final portion (OO-OWT-NEMAREBA) is "ABERAMEN-TOW-OO" except arranged backwards. "OWT" sounds like the "oat" in "oatmeal". This is a *palindrome*, and **the most powerful form of the name**. The stress in the palindromic form of this name is spread out equally among all syllables.

Any time you use one of these forms of the Great and Terrible Name, you must say it aloud—**in a loud, clear tone of voice, if not a shout**—and you have to say it *three* times. For the *most* potent workings, it's the *Palindromic Form* you will always use (again, said clearly and loudly three times).

These are the sounds of the Lord of this World, the *Lord of Gods*—they cause forces belonging to a profound and fundamental substratum of the soul, the mind, and of Nature to begin moving by their recitation, or perhaps in more mysterious ways. Neither you nor I have the full wisdom to engage this; I don't believe any human does. But we can hope that by these special sounds, a certain empowerment will come upon works done that will lend to them great effectiveness.

∗ ∗ ∗

Instead of using the **ABRAT** formula or the **PHORBA** formula to accomplish some enchantment, one *might* instead utilize the Great and Terrible name—if one has a very suddenly serious, alarming, or emergency situation on hand that requires special power.

To use the Great and Terrible name in this way, to power enchantments in the place of the **ABRAT** or **PHORBA** formulas, you would **say either the short form of the Name or the long form** *three times*, and follow it with this passage:

> **Great and Terrible Lord who Disturbeth the Night,**
> **Who Blasts the Sky with Thunder,**
> **Who Unleashes Storms upon the World,**
> **Who Exhales Withering Heat and Chilling Cold,**
> **Breaker of Stones, Who Causes the Waters to Boil,**
> **You Who stirs up the Mighty Deep!**
> **By the Powerful Words I have said here,**
> **Let spirits and powers move as I require them;**
> **Let them endow** (*X substance or thing in X way*)
>
> **IO ERBAYT, Let it be so.**

*Then blow on the substance/thing three times.* IO ERBAYT is to be pronounced exactly as it looks—"*ee-oh er-bait*".

Nine outlines of specific workings empowered by the Palindromic form of the Name will now be given, along with notes to their operation. These are the most powerful operations because they utilize the most powerful form of the name. If you manage to *become* the sort of person who can do them, do them **sparingly**.

# Healing Injuries By the Great and Terrible Name

*(The Palindromic Name is said Three Times)*

Great and Terrible Lord who Disturbeth the Night,
Who Blasts the Sky with Thunder,
Who Unleashes Storms upon the World,
Who Exhales Withering Heat and Chilling Cold,
Breaker of Stones, Who Causes the Waters to Boil,
You Who stirs up the Mighty Deep!


By the Powerful Words I have said here
Let me receive a portion of the Power
That Moves the Sky, Stirs the Depths,
And Drives the blossom to bloom!
Arouse, move, and compel the forces that
Heal injuries inflicted upon the bodies of men and Women (or beasts),
leaving them healthy and whole

*If you are using water:*

Sending them upon this water!
Let this water that seethes with the heat of fire
Receive them and harbor them,
Becoming a water of healing.
IO ERBAYT, Let it be so!

*If you are using burning coals:*

Sending them upon these burning coals!
Let these coals that seethe with the heat of fire
Receive them and harbor them,
Becoming a burning field of healing.
IO ERBAYT, Let it be so!

*If you are using a container of oil:*

Sending them upon the oil that is in this (jar)!
Let this oil drink them in, receive them
And harbor them,
Becoming rich and dark with the power of healing.
IO ERBAYT, Let it be so!

*If you are enchanting an object:*

**Sending them upon this (cord, talisman, etc)**
**Let this (thing) receive them and harbor them,**
**Becoming a House for the Power of Healing!**
**If a man or woman wears this (or bears it upon their person), let it**
**bless them with its boon!**
**IO ERBAYT, Let it be so!**

✳ ✳ ✳

Regardless of what vehicle you were enchanting, you *blow on it three times* after you have spoken. How would a bed of hot coals be used to heal? You would heat a clay image of a person in the bed of coals, permeating their body and soul with the force of the healing power. It is best to use boiling water for this spell, but not strictly necessary; you *will* have to change the wording if you don't. Giving an injured person the water you might have enchanted this way, having them drink it or washing their wound with it, will rapidly speed healing time. Anointing them with the oil will do the same. A knotted cord you enchanted, that they can wear as a bracelet, will do the same.

# Banishing Disease
## By the Great and Terrible Name

*(The Palindromic Name is said Three Times)*

Great and Terrible Lord who Disturbeth the Night,
Who Blasts the Sky with Thunder,
Who Unleashes Storms upon the World,
Who Exhales Withering Heat and Chilling Cold,
Breaker of Stones, Who Causes the Waters to Boil,
You Who stirs up the Mighty Deep!

By the Powerful Words I have said here
Let me receive a portion of the Power
That Moves the Sky, Stirs the Depths,
And Drives the blossom to bloom!
Arouse, move, and compel the forces that
Preserve the bodies of men and women (or beasts)
From perilous diseases, which cast out
The those powers of disease,
Leaving bodies healthy and whole,

*If you are using water:*

Sending them upon this water!
Let this water that seethes with the heat of fire
Receive them and harbor them,
Becoming a water of healing.
IO ERBAYT, Let it be so!

*If you are using burning coals:*

Sending them upon these burning coals!
Let these coals that seethe with the heat of fire
Receive them and harbor them,
Becoming a burning field of healing.
IO ERBAYT, Let it be so!

*If you are using a container of oil:*

**Sending them upon the oil that is in this (jar)!**
**Let this oil drink them in, receive them**
**And harbor them,**
**Becoming rich and dark with the power of healing.**
**IO ERBAYT, Let it be so!**

*If you are enchanting an object:*

**Sending them upon this (cord, talisman, etc)**
**Let this (thing) receive them and harbor them,**
**Becoming a House for the Power of Healing!**
**If a man or woman wears this (or bears it upon their person), let it**
**bless them with its boon!**
**IO ERBAYT, Let it be so!**

✳ ✳ ✳

As always, you must blow three times upon the object or substance of your enchantment after saying the final words. Read the note in the previous working regarding boiling water for healing works.

# Inflicting the Consuming Fever
## By the Great and Terrible Name

*(The Palindromic Name is said Three Times)*

Great and Terrible Lord who Disturbeth the Night,
Who Blasts the Sky with Thunder,
Who Unleashes Storms upon the World,
Who Exhales Withering Heat and Chilling Cold,
Breaker of Stones, Who Causes the Waters to Boil,
You Who stirs up the Mighty Deep!

By the Powerful Words I have said here
Let me receive a portion of the Power
That Moves the Sky, Stirs the Depths,
And Drives the blossom to bloom!

Arouse, move, and compel the forces that
Consume the flesh of men and women (or beasts)
With burning fever,

*If you are using water:*

Sending them upon this water!
Let this water that seethes with the heat of fire
Receive them and harbor them,
Becoming a water of consuming fever.
Let the powers conjured here harm me not!
IO ERBAYT, Let it be so!

*If you are using burning coals:*

Sending them upon these burning coals!
Let these coals that seethe with the heat of fire
Receive them and harbor them,
Becoming a burning field of consuming fever.
Let the powers conjured here harm me not!
IO ERBAYT, Let it be so!

*If you are using a container of oil:*

**Sending them upon the oil that is in this (jar)!**
**Let this oil drink them in, receive them**
**And harbor them,**
**Becoming rich and dark with the consuming fever.**
**Let the powers conjured here harm me not!**
**IO ERBAYT, Let it be so!**

*If you are enchanting an object:*

**Sending them upon this (cord, talisman, etc)**
**Let this (thing) receive them and harbor them,**
**Becoming a House for the Consuming Fever!**
**If a man or woman wears this (or bears it upon their person), let it**
**drag them down to death!**
**Let the powers conjured here harm me not!**
**IO ERBAYT, Let it be so!**

✳ ✳ ✳

As always, you must blow three times upon the object or substance of your enchantment after saying the final words. The creation of this baneful water always must be done with *boiling* water. **Always** make yourself immune to these baneful things conjured with the insertion of the immunity line, given above. Then you can handle them without harming yourself.

# Bestowing Peace by the Great and Terrible Name

*(The Palindromic Name is said Three Times)*
Great and Terrible Lord who Disturbeth the Night,

Who Blasts the Sky with Thunder,
Who Unleashes Storms upon the World,
Who Exhales Withering Heat and Chilling Cold,
Breaker of Stones, Who Causes the Waters to Boil,
You Who stirs up the Mighty Deep!

By the Powerful Words I have said here
Let me receive a portion of the Power
That Moves the Sky, Stirs the Depths,
And Drives the blossom to bloom!
Arouse, move, and compel the forces that
Bring peace to the minds and souls
Or men or women ravaged by Madness
(or Grief, or Fear, or Torment),

*If you are using water:*

Sending them upon this water!
Let this water that seethes with the heat of fire
Receive them and harbor them,
Becoming a water of Peace.
IO ERBAYT, Let it be so!

*If you are using burning coals:*

Sending them upon these burning coals!
Let these coals that seethe with the heat of fire
Receive them and harbor them,
Becoming a burning field of Peace.
IO ERBAYT, Let it be so!

*If you are using a container of oil:*

Sending them upon the oil that is in this (jar)!
Let this oil drink them in, receive them
And harbor them,
Becoming rich and dark with the power of Peace.
IO ERBAYT, Let it be so!

*If you are enchanting an object:*

**Sending them upon this (cord, talisman, etc)**
**Let this (thing) receive them and harbor them,**
**Becoming a House for the power of Peace!**
**If a man or woman wears this (or bears it upon their person), let it**
**bless them with its boon!**
**IO ERBAYT, Let it be so!**

\* \* \*

As always, you must blow three times upon the object or substance of your enchantment after saying the final words. And the water doesn't *have* to be boiling; boiling is needful for baneful workings, but healing works and other works can use cool or warm water. Adjust the wording accordingly if you won't be working over a scalding container or cauldron of water—simply say *"Let this water receive them and harbor them..."*

## Inflicting Madness
## By the Great and Terrible Name

*(The Palindromic Name is said Three Times)*

Great and Terrible Lord who Disturbeth the Night,
Who Blasts the Sky with Thunder,
Who Unleashes Storms upon the World,
Who Exhales Withering Heat and Chilling Cold,
Breaker of Stones, Who Causes the Waters to Boil,
You Who stirs up the Mighty Deep!

By the Powerful Words I have said here
Let me receive a portion of the Power
That Moves the Sky, Stirs the Depths,
And Drives the blossom to bloom!
Arouse, move, and compel the forces that
Wrack the minds and souls of men and women
(or beasts) with Madness,

*If you are using water:*

Sending them upon this water!
Let this water that seethes with the heat of fire
Receive them and harbor them,
Becoming a water of Madness.
Let the powers conjured here harm me not!
IO ERBAYT, Let it be so!

*If you are using burning coals:*

Sending them upon these burning coals!
Let these coals that seethe with the heat of fire
Receive them and harbor them,
Becoming a burning field of Madness.
Let the powers conjured here harm me not!
IO ERBAYT, Let it be so!

*If you are using a container of oil:*

**Sending them upon the oil that is in this (jar)!**
**Let this oil drink them in, receive them**
**And harbor them,**
**Becoming rich and dark with the power of Madness.**
**Let the powers conjured here harm me not!**
**IO ERBAYT, Let it be so!**

*If you are enchanting an object:*

**Sending them upon this (cord, talisman, etc)**
**Let this (thing) receive them and harbor them,**
**Becoming a House for Madness!**
**If a man or woman wears this (or bears it upon their person), let it**
**drag them down to misery!**
**Let the powers conjured here harm me not!**
**IO ERBAYT, Let it be so!**

✳ ✳ ✳

As always, you must blow three times upon the object or substance of your enchantment after saying the final words. The creation of this baneful water always must be done with *boiling* water. **Always** make yourself immune to these baneful things created with the insertion of the immunity line, given above. Then you can handle them without harming yourself.

# Inflicting Disease by the Great and Terrible Name

*(The Palindromic Name is said Three Times)*

Great and Terrible Lord who Disturbeth the Night,
Who Blasts the Sky with Thunder,
Who Unleashes Storms upon the World,
Who Exhales Withering Heat and Chilling Cold,
Breaker of Stones, Who Causes the Waters to Boil,
You Who stirs up the Mighty Deep!

By the Powerful Words I have said here
Let me receive a portion of the Power
That Moves the Sky, Stirs the Depths,
And Drives the blossom to bloom!
Arouse, move, and compel the forces that
Feast upon the flesh of men and women
(or beasts) in the shape of dread Disease,

*If you are using water:*

Sending them upon this water!
Let this water that seethes with the heat of fire
Receive them and harbor them,
Becoming a water of Disease.
Let the powers conjured here harm me not!
IO ERBAYT, Let it be so!

*If you are using burning coals:*

Sending them upon these burning coals!
Let these coals that seethe with the heat of fire
Receive them and harbor them,
Becoming a burning field of Disease.
Let the powers conjured here harm me not!
IO ERBAYT, Let it be so!

*If you are using a container of oil:*

**Sending them upon the oil that is in this (jar)!**
**Let this oil drink them in, receive them**
**And harbor them,**
**Becoming rich and dark with the power of Disease.**
**Let the powers conjured here harm me not!**
**IO ERBAYT, Let it be so!**

*If you are enchanting an object:*

**Sending them upon this (cord, talisman, etc)**
**Let this (thing) receive them and harbor them,**
**Becoming a House for Disease!**
**If a man or woman wears this (or bears it upon their person), let it**
**drag them down to death!**
**Let the powers conjured here harm me not!**
**IO ERBAYT, Let it be so!**

✶✶✶

As always, you must blow three times upon the object or substance of your enchantment after saying the final words. The creation of this baneful water always must be done with *boiling* water. **Always** make yourself immune to these baneful things created with the insertion of the immunity line, given above. Then you can handle them without harming yourself.

# Withering by the Great and Terrible Name

*(The Palindromic Name is said Three Times)*

Great and Terrible Lord who Disturbeth the Night,
Who Blasts the Sky with Thunder,
Who Unleashes Storms upon the World,
Who Exhales Withering Heat and Chilling Cold,
Breaker of Stones, Who Causes the Waters to Boil,
You Who stirs up the Mighty Deep!

By the Powerful Words I have said here
Let me receive a portion of the Power
That Moves the Sky, Stirs the Depths,
And Drives the blossom to bloom!
Arouse, move, and compel the forces that
Rob vitality from the flesh of men and women
(or beasts), **Leaving them listless and fading
From this life,**

*If you are using water:*

Sending them upon this water!
Let this water that seethes with the heat of fire
Receive them and harbor them,
Becoming a water of Withering.
Let the powers conjured here harm me not!
IO ERBAYT, Let it be so!

*If you are using burning coals:*

Sending them upon these burning coals!
Let these coals that seethe with the heat of fire
Receive them and harbor them,
Becoming a burning field of Withering.
Let the powers conjured here harm me not!
IO ERBAYT, Let it be so!

**Sending them upon the oil that is in this (jar)!**
**Let this oil drink them in, receive them**
**And harbor them,**
**Becoming rich and dark with the power of Withering.**
**Let the powers conjured here harm me not!**
**IO ERBAYT, Let it be so!**

*If you are enchanting an object:*

**Sending them upon this (cord, talisman, etc)**
**Let this (thing) receive them and harbor them,**
**Becoming a House for Withering!**
**If a man or woman wears this (or bears it upon their person), let it**
**drag them down to misery!**
**Let the powers conjured here harm me not!**
**IO ERBAYT, Let it be so!**

✳ ✳ ✳

As always, you must blow three times upon the object or substance of your enchantment after saying the final words. The creation of this baneful water always must be done with *boiling* water. **Always** make yourself immune to these baneful things created with the insertion of the immunity line, given above. Then you can handle them without harming yourself.

## Empowering Beauty
## By the Great and Terrible Name

*(The Palindromic Name is said Three Times)*

Great and Terrible Lord who Disturbeth the Night,
Who Blasts the Sky with Thunder,
Who Unleashes Storms upon the World,
Who Exhales Withering Heat and Chilling Cold,
Breaker of Stones, Who Causes the Waters to Boil,
You Who stirs up the Mighty Deep!

By the Powerful Words I have said here
Let me receive a portion of the Power
That Moves the Sky, Stirs the Depths,
And Drives the blossom to bloom!
Arouse, move, and compel the forces that
Beautify and enliven the eyes, flesh, and limbs
Of men and women, making them irresistible to those
Whom they desire,

*If you are using water:*

Sending them upon this water!
Let this water that seethes with the heat of fire
Receive them and harbor them,
Becoming a water of Beauty.
IO ERBAYT, Let it be so!

*If you are using burning coals:*

Sending them upon these burning coals!
Let these coals that seethe with the heat of fire
Receive them and harbor them,
Becoming a burning field of Beauty.
IO ERBAYT, Let it be so!

*If you are using a container of oil:*

**Sending them upon the oil that is in this (jar)!**
**Let this oil drink them in, receive them**
**And harbor them,**
**Becoming rich and dark with the power of Beauty.**
**IO ERBAYT, Let it be so!**

*If you are enchanting an object:*

**Sending them upon this (cord, talisman, etc)**
**Let this (thing) receive them and harbor them,**
**Becoming a House for the power of Beauty!**
**If a man or woman wears this (or bears it upon their person), let it**
**bless them with its boon!**
**IO ERBAYT, Let it be so!**

✳ ✳ ✳

As always, you must blow three times upon the object or substance of your enchantment after saying the final words. The water in this work, if you are using that vehicle for the enchantment, *should* be boiling or heated. Heating a clay image of a person who wants to become more attractive will work fine, but this working is meant to make waters, oils, or talismans that a person drinks or wears to become more appealing.

## Obtaining Exorcism
## By the Great and Terrible Name

*(The Palindromic Name is said Three Times)*

Great and Terrible Lord who Disturbeth the Night,
Who Blasts the Sky with Thunder,
Who Unleashes Storms upon the World,
Who Exhales Withering Heat and Chilling Cold,
Breaker of Stones, Who Causes the Waters to Boil,
You Who stirs up the Mighty Deep!

By the Powerful Words I have said here
Let me receive a portion of the Power
That Moves the Sky, Stirs the Depths,
And Drives the blossom to bloom!
Arouse, move, and compel the forces that
Cause baneful spirits and demons to lose their power,
Lose their will, scatter,
And flee to lands far away,

*If you are using water:*

Sending them upon this water!
Let this water that seethes with the heat of fire
Receive them and harbor them,
Becoming a water of Exorcism.
IO ERBAYT, Let it be so!

*If you are using burning coals:*

Sending them upon these burning coals!
Let these coals that seethe with the heat of fire
Receive them and harbor them,
Becoming a burning field of Exorcism.
IO ERBAYT, Let it be so!

*If you are using a container of oil:*

**Sending them upon the oil that is in this (jar)!**
**Let this oil drink them in, receive them**
**And harbor them,**
**Becoming rich and dark with the power**
**To exorcise baneful spirits.**
**IO ERBAYT, Let it be so!**

*If you are enchanting an object:*

**Sending them upon this (cord, talisman, etc)**
**Let this (thing) receive them and harbor them,**
**Becoming a House for the power of Exorcism!**
**If a man or woman wears this (or bears it upon their person, or**
**hangs it in their home) let it bless them (or that place and all who**
**live there) with its boon!**
**IO ERBAYT, Let it be so!**

✳ ✳ ✳

As always, you must blow three times upon the object or substance of your enchantment after saying the final words. Wiping the exorcism oil yielded by this work over doors and windows is very powerful; the water can be used to sprinkle the doors, windows, and every room. The coals are meant to heat a clay image of a person inflicted by bad spirits. Water and oil can be applied as usual.

## Final Thoughts on the Great and Terrible Works

It should be clear that, even though these nine workings were given in a format to utilize them via empowerment by the Palindromic form of the Great and Terrible Name, they (or at least workings similar to them) can be done just as well using the other formulas we have discussed. And I *must* again implore you to consider that as an option instead of trying to channel the forces conjured by the Great and Terrible Name. Not every working *requires* or calls for such great power; it can become dangerous or harmful to use such potent things too much. Like the finer tea cups kept on a higher shelf, or the finer china, use the Great and Terrible Name for special occasions.

I did not include a working here that dealt with **Delusion** or **Manipulation**—and yet, the Great and Terrible Name can **certainly** empower such workings. You must create those works yourself, following the examples given here. Delusion or Manipulation is *not* the sort of thing that can be conjured as a Burning Fever or Disease can be. A work of Delusion or Manipulation has to be *spelled out more*; you have to state what kinds of changes you want to force onto other people's minds and souls.

Thus, a Ring empowered to aid in manipulation (to make an example) cannot be simply created to be "A House for Manipulation." That would probably result in a ring that, when worn, attracted manipulative people to you, or made *you* more manipulative than you already might be.

One example of a sort of *Ring of Manipulation* might be empowered like this:

> **...By the Powerful Words I have said here**
> **Let me receive a portion of the Power**
> **That Moves the Sky, Stirs the Depths,**
> **And Drives the blossom to bloom!**
> **Arouse, move, and compel the forces that**
> **Manipulate and bend the minds of men and women,**
> **The powers that deceive with cunning,**
> **Sending them upon this ring.**
> **Let this ring receive them and harbor them,**
> **Becoming a House for the power of Deceit!**
> **If a man or woman wears this ring,**

**Let it render believable any lie they tell**
**To another man or woman.**

This is an example specifically for making a talismanic ring that helps liars to lie better. With a simple application of your devious imagination, literally anything can be worded to endow any object with any sort of manipulative ability; there's more to manipulation than just lies, after all.

Baneful works in the past often included the creation of objects that were enchanted with the power to exert some baleful force on a house and all who lived in it (or upon a specific person who lived there), if they were hidden or secreted in the home somewhere. It's easy to see how simple adjustments to these workings—or the wording of any enchantment, basic or otherwise—can create such objects. The workings of the Witch Bessie Thom provides us with a perfect display of how deadly enchanted oils could be; she reportedly had 'removed' her own husband, and that of her client Elspet Jack. Bessie Thom gave to Elspet a *slaik*—a 'smearing substance' of some kind (likely some kind of oil or unguent) which led to disease and death.

It might be hard for most modern people to grasp this, and we modern folk can certainly be forgiven for this tendency, but not *everything* in life or in Witchcraft has to be madness, deceit, and misery. You may not be the sort of person who could ever engage in such workings, and this is quite fine. Hiding an enchanted object in someone's house doesn't *always* have to be malefic; you might secret a charm you made to exert peace upon the home and all who live there. Whether using the basic enchantment procedures, or the works of the Great and Terrible Name, the sky for what is possible is vast and endless.

A final note of extreme caution: if you ever create a water or oil that is endowed with the awful power of disease, or madness, or anything of the sort—you must treat that substance like it is a fierce and deadly poison, because metaphysically *it truly is*. If you're going to be keeping portions of them for later use, keep them bottled in a safe place and clearly labeled somehow. **Pour out the rest into a hole dug in the earth and then fill in the hole, to disenchant them**, rendering them harmless. If another person chances upon them and gets these substances on their bodies, it can and *will* harm them.

There has been a complete focus on the use of the Great and Terrible Name to create practical results—and this is good and right, as Witchcraft (even of this great strength) should be a useful or practical thing. It is here to *help*, to make changes that need to be made. It is here to help bring justice to the abused, *particularly* to abused women and children, for our society will almost never give them the ordinary justice they deserve.

But if we (carefully) allow ourselves to ponder matters in other realms of consideration, it's obvious that a formula as potent as the Great and Terrible Name formula might easily have the ability to bring about certain personal or subjective-interior transformations. You may say it aloud, and call upon the *Great and Terrible Lord who Disturbeth the Night*, and ask that the powers within Nature itself which *can* alter one's soul or mind in certain ways might come unto you, and change you in those ways.

Here, I refer to asking for interior transformations that make a man or woman's Witchcraft stronger... or which give them the power to more clearly see and comprehend the Unseen world; I mean asking for interior changes that make you more calm, more stable, more patient, braver, stronger, more connected to the Preternatural world, and better able to work your sorceries. In this more subtle realm, your wisdom and imagination is the guide to what might be possible. The Great and Terrible Name—like Nature itself—exists far beyond good and evil. Be cautious with it.

# TRANSVECTION *or* SOUL FLIGHT

The doorway to the world of dreams is the doorway to the World of Spirits. The dreaming space is a dimension of experience and extraordinary encounter that lies at the center of Witchcraft, and it may be thought fitting (or at least expected) that it would be cast aside so thoroughly by ordinary society. There is no possibility of the non-*Witched* truly understanding the *Witched*, and there is no possibility of our society—so dominated by waking logic—comprehending the unawake and surreal language of the dream world. We prefer to ignore dreams or dismiss them, just as we prefer these days to ignore Witchcraft or dismiss it.

The Witched must open the doorway to the world of dreams much wider than ordinary people. The dream is a subtle disclosure of the Unseen World into the waking world; dreams penetrate the waking world like a bizarre rhizome of spectral roots that cannot be seen or measured in any ordinary way.

Dreams are often *traces of vision* that manage to survive the passage between Seen and Unseen, when the rational mind is rendered inert in sleep and no longer able to determine how all experience will be interpreted or governed.

To actualize the full vision of Witching, the adventures and perpetual strange journeys of the *deeper soul*, the Wandering Soul—forever the double to our living selves—must be discovered and witnessed.

The gateway of dreams opens onto *much more* than just personal obsessions, mental ruminations, or unconscious desires being played out in chaotic night-spasms of the brain dulled by sleep. Like a long-shut door opening into a vast underground cavern, the dirt of the surface clinging to the door might be recognizable or familiar, but deeper down another world appears and spreads out infinitely in the dark.

The long and strangely-curved shadows of the Unseen world fall across every dreamscape, no matter how familiar it may be to us. And this is because the more ageless and profound forces of the Unseen World infiltrate and endow reality upon every soul and finally every *body*, no matter how we familiarize those things to ourselves with our stories.

Through dreams, we may find gateways into the Unseen World and into new sorts of freedom that we have yearned for greatly.

Through dreams, we can *fly*; and through flying, we can transition beyond the world of sleeping bodies and enter the world of souls and spirits. Where death will lead one day, dreams might lead every night; what death *will* reveal as a timeless underlying ecology of sentience, only dreams will offer precious glimpses of beforehand.

Through dreams, some might become *Witched*; through dreams, we can chart extraordinary courses for ourselves through this life and into the mind-bending strangeness of the life to come.

The Witch must develop a different relationship to the reality of dreaming than the non-*Witched*. The stronger this new relationship becomes, the stronger the Witch becomes. We will strive with all our souls to develop such a new relationship, whereas the *Witched* men and women who came before us lived and enjoyed deeper and more lucid dreams regularly and organically. Their eyes not cursed by artificial light, they slept differently. Their bodily rhythms tied more intimately to natural cycles of dark and light, of feast and famine, of cold and hot, they slumbered in connection, not in chaos.

Further, the Ancestral worldview was permeated with an ages-old *awe* of the ominous and wondrous power of dreams: a power to bring forth omens, warnings, and even visitations from otherworldly beings or the dead. Lacking that awe, our dreams are walled away behind curtains of banality and dismissal.

The Witched men and women of Early Modern times and before didn't access the Unseen *merely* because they slept in a more organic or healthy manner; that was part of the reason why they were able, but not the whole. Their power to utilize dream as a portal into extraordinary experience was part of their endowment from the Unseen, part of the closeness and familiarity they had gained through spectral intercourse with the Invisible Other. What was sideways and strange to breathing mortals—the strangeness of the visions in the night—was a carpet rolled out for the ghostly feet of the Witched, a bridge as thin as a sword-blade, but eternally binding together the worlds of *Nature* and *Preternature*.

The great reality of the Unseen, with its outer hedges of hypnagogic and hypnopompic trance, its central forest of deep darkness interspersed with clearings of dream-vision and waking dream, it *is* the rhizome that weaves life and into which the dead wander, as readily as the living wander on its perceptual outsides. Dream is an encounter of the permeability of the rhizome as the living are allowed to have; dream is how its own non-linear and timeless nature can be directly encountered or surmised by the breathing. And dream is how the Witched begin to commune with the Great Others, and learn to live and interact as more than just breathing beings with earthly feet.

There is a Word of Power that can transform not only how the Witched man or woman encounters the reality of the dreaming world, but also increase the clarity of their connection to the spectral reality as a whole. Unlike other Words of Power given so far, which allow a man or woman to *assert* themselves metaphysically, this Word is not about assertion as much as *passivity*.

It does not create a Gateway Ring nor a jar of empowering Oyl; it creates not a condition projected outward, but a state of special alertness that can **receive** things of the invisible or deeper world more readily. This Word begins and supports the development of the subtle senses of the Witched man or woman in the face of the Unseen.

That Word of Power is **SAUWENDEI**. It is pronounced *Sow-wen-day*, with the syllable *sow* rhyming with the word *cow*. The emphasis when spoken aloud is placed upon the first syllable of the word.

**SAUWENDEI** is not merely a word of dreams, though it magnifies dream clarity, awareness and memory. It is a word of the *soul*, a word that awakens invisible bridges or connections between the breathing soul of the ordinary world and the wandering soul which perpetually flies and moves throughout the forests and fields of the Unseen world. **SAUWENDEI** transforms men and women as it is used; it deepens perspective in an extraordinary manner.

If any person undertakes to fall into sleep while repeating **SAUWENDEI** to themselves over and over, it shall allow them to maintain a degree of subtle consciousness in sleep, making them more aware of the dreaming world. It will allow them to perceptually move about in that condition

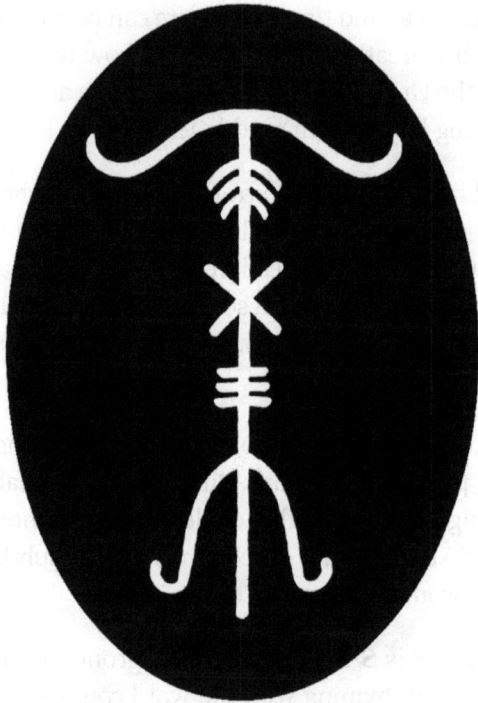

**SAUWENDEI Sigil**

with ease and good fortune, capturing the treasures of that surreal state and transmitting them more readily to the breathing mind of the waking world. It will aid souls in flight, in transition through the Unseen. This same word **SAUWENDEI**, if carved upon a rod of wood in *any* form—*especially* a sigil crafted from it—will greatly strengthen this work.

It will endow the person with increased power to support their subtle and coarse degrees of consciousness in the dreaming world, *if* that rod carved with some form of **SAUWENDEI** should ever lie alongside them when they slumber.

The works of **SAUWENDEI** are to be unlocked and made to live in the following ways.

The basic use of the Word is simplicity itself; when lying down to sleep, make yourself comfortable, and focus upon the sensation of one's entire body lying there, pressed against a mattress or the surface of one's sleep-space, below covers or what have you. Feel the pressure and warmth in different places around the body; focus on nothing but the body. When relaxation sets in, say the word **SAUWENDEI** aloud three times softly, and then begin to slowly but firmly repeat the word **SAUWENDEI** in one's mind, allowing it to obtain a rhythm that is steady and comfortable, drawing out its syllables a bit if one requires. Realize that the rhythmic thinking of this word and the sensation of your body are two aspects of the same thing: this is your being, existing as it does. And your living being is expressing **SAUWENDEI**. This word is part of you.

As the hypnagogic state falls over you, you might notice that the rhythm of your mental recitation of **SAUWENDEI** will change. You might miss thinking it once, or discover that you can't remember when you thought the Word last. This is a sign that hypnagogia is setting in strongly, and the descent into sleep has moved forward significantly. Simply think the word again if this happens, and begin hypnotically repeating it within the interior of your mind. Fall asleep in this manner.

Your dreams may be of a different character that night; more vivid, more strange, easier to remember, or you may encounter characters of an odd type, particularly familiars or persons you know to be dead. You may see those you know and who still live, but they may behave oddly. Over time, falling asleep repeating **SAUWENDEI** will clarify dreams and encounters in the dream state, as well as the power to recall them upon waking. You must go to sleep on as many nights as you can repeating the Word.

The advanced practice of **SAUWENDEI** should commence once you have familiarized yourself with the basic method as given before. To perform the advanced practice, go to sleep doing the basic practice, but set an alarm to arouse you after 4 or 5 hours of sleep. When that alarm wakes you, stand up from your bed and walk about. Move your arms and legs, move as you can to shake off the weight and power of sleep in your limbs, but do not over-exert yourself. Sit, and drink water. Light a candle or a lantern.

Take deep breaths and let wakefulness return to you. Raise your arms above your head and stretch them; rub your hands together to generate warmth between them. Say the word **SAUWENDEI** aloud three times, then say it in your mind at least 18 times while sitting before your candle. Now remain awake in this manner for at least 15 minutes, but not more than 30 minutes; venture away from your sitting area if you like; walk outside, into other rooms of your house, or what have you. Try to avoid artificial light as much as you can, but if you must have it, this will not necessarily thwart the work. Avoid the screens of devices as much as you can. Contemplate the word **SAUWENDEI** and the reality of dreams.

When this short time has passed, return to your bed and get comfortable again. You are to return to sleep, and shall in a short time. Again, as you lie there, focus on feeling the living sensation of your whole body and begin repeating the word **SAUWENDEI** over and over in your mind, steadily, hypnotically.

When hypnagogia finally returns—when you feel the dark descent into sleep and dream truly beginning—cease your interior chanting and imagine a tickling sensation in your chest. Something that was in your chest before, but undetectable because it was not moving, has **made itself known** by moving inside you. It moves up your chest, and up your throat. Tilt your head back and open your mouth and imagine a large white moth coming out of your throat flying out of your mouth.

With your eyes still closed, you can easily "feel" the moth fluttering up above you and into the darkness above your bed. Now, the spaces above and around your bed feel different; they stir with the power of the vanished moth, which is **SAUWENDEI**. Relax as you feel your body **and** the now-empowered wide spaces above your bed and around it. Gently focus on your body and the spaces around you. Start chanting the Word again, slowly and softly inside, and fall asleep this way.

The advanced work of **SAUWENDEI** will likely be a thing you do on special occasions; I strongly urge you to do it at least once a month, if not more if this is possible. The basic practice should be put into place each night, or on most nights. To aid in *both* of these practices, you should undertake to obtain a special talisman which will increase their power tenfold: **you must undertake to create a Riding Pole**.

*** *** ***

The *Riding Pole* is the origin of the famed *Witches' Broom* that is such a fixture in folklore. It is a rod—a staff—of wood that becomes *Witched* itself, through a process you will be taught. To *Witch* this wooden staff is to transform it into a steed of types, a helper upon whom you will ride not only into more dream-clarity, but into lucid dreams and the full experience of soul-flight. Shamanistic practitioners in cultures around the world have utilized special helpers in the form of riding poles since time immemorial to aid in their trance-based journeys out of their own ordinary body-consciousness and into the subtle reaches beyond.

The **soul-flight complex** is a perpetual motif in folklore and myth, and in still-living shamanistic practices today. Its presence deep in the body of folktale and myth is a sign that, certainly owing to ancient cultural experiences and encounters going back uncountable ages, the folk-minds of Europeans throughout Pagan, Medieval, and Early Modern history *expected* (on an instinctive or perhaps unconscious level) to hear tales of certain persons "riding" through the air on pole-like implements, or upon ordinary objects that had, through some enchantment, become "mounts" of some sort for the supernatural feat of flying: agricultural implements, pitchforks, stangs, and even brooms. "Flight" in the received folkloric usage is *always* a circumlocution for the spectral double or the soul of the flying person moving free and apart from the ordinary body. More on this shall be said soon.

## RIDING POLE CREATION: PHASE 1

Obtain a staff of wood, of any type (though Ash should be considered the most potent for this talisman) which is as straight as possible. If it bends or curves a bit, this is fine. It is best to find this staff yourself from walking in a forest. The staff must be as tall as your chin, if you stand up straight and hold it straight against your body. A found staff *cannot* have begun to rot; the wood must be strong and good throughout. If you must cut it from a tree, utilize the same charm used to obtain parts from plants for the creation of the *Green Oyl* (given earlier in this book) to ask the tree for the branch you desire, and pay it with nine drops of your own blood. Then you will have to allow the fresh branch to dry for a few months.

You can leave the bark on the staff, or remove it as you prefer. Remove smaller protrusions from the length of the staff with a cutting implement and smooth them over.

Now you should have what amounts to a sturdy walking-stick; If you crouch to the ground and place it between your legs, and lean back to semi-sit upon it, transferring most of your weight to it, it should support your weight; it should not crack nor strain nor break.

Now you must begin training the Riding Pole to be your companion on journeys. To this end, you must take it on three journeys through the landscapes of our ordinary world. This means you must take it in your hand, and walk away from your home and through a forest, through fields, down roads, through parks, or anywhere of that sort—and then, return to your home carrying it after your outing. It must leave with you, stay with you during your journey, and return with you. If you're a hiker with a place to hike, this is easily accomplished.

If you live in a more urban area, it may seem odd that you should be walking with such a thing, but you'll have to. Hopefully there is a park or something of that nature nearby for you to repair to with your nascent Riding Pole.

If you find that you must put the pole in a vehicle and drive somewhere, that is fine; so long as the pole is in your hand when you leave your door, and in your hand when you return, and as long as you were able to walk around with it wherever you went, all is well.

At least three "ordinary journeys" with the pole have to be taken this way. It must be your companion on these trips. You are teaching it about being your companion, but you are also teaching your own body and soul that when you take this staff in hand, you are *going somewhere.*

At some point during one of these outings, or after the end of the third and/or last one, **use the same charm that was utilized to communicate with the plants in the Green Oyl working** to communicate with the soul of the tree that created your Riding Pole. While sitting with the pole in front of you, say those strange words and then address the soul of the tree that made it. Ask the soul of the tree to bless you with a favor: ask it to be your helper, and if you ever lie down with this staff alongside you and fall into sleep, ask it to help you have dream clarity and lucidity.

Ask it to help you to reach the extraordinary places you wish to go, through the gateway of sleep and dreams. Tell it you have a gift for it, for this favor—then **pour a bowl or a good cup of whiskey** out as that gift, by pouring the whiskey out over the Riding Pole somewhere around the center of the pole.

If you're indoors, have a bowl under the pole to catch the whiskey. The pole will drink in some of the whiskey, but will dry quickly. Doing these three ordinary journeys and making this special offering to the creator of your pole will complete Phase One of *Witching* the pole.

**RIDING POLE CREATION: PHASE 2**

Now you will teach the riding pole to accompany you in the subtle world. Find an outdoors area that you can perform a technique called *The Widdershins Walk* within. This can be a backyard, or a stretch of fields and forest, or a park, so long as it isn't too crowded. It's best if your starting point for the Widdershins Walk is your own front or back door, but if you must go somewhere else to do this, it can still work.

Find a way to either find or create a starting point, which symbolizes your home. Mark it somehow. Turn to the right and walk away from that starting point, and start to gradually walk toward the left, curving your path, as though you are walking on the rim of a huge circle. Stop after a very short while and place or create a marker of some kind. This should be a thing that you can easily visualize—like a big white rock, or a pair of sticks crossed on the ground. Then keep going.

Go a little further, always turning leftward as you go, and make another marker. It has to be different from your first one, but still something easy to visualize and remember. Keep going, and make another marker, and finally one more, before arriving back at your starting point. You have created a large circular (actually more of a rough, semi-circular) pathway marked with four markers, all scattered roughly equidistant about it. The place where the circular pathway ends is where it began: at your starting point.

Remember—this circular path you created is always walked in a counterclockwise direction, which is why you turned *right* to leave your starting point. And it doesn't have to be a perfect circle by any means. In fact, it can meander through stands of trees, go over hills, cross a stream, or do whatever you need it to do, to get back to your starting point. What matters is that you leave by turning right, and come back to the start from the other direction—meaning you had to walk in a big counter-clockwise ambulation. You **don't** have to be able to see all four markers from the starting point.

If you live in a neighborhood that is arranged in blocks, you can walk counterclockwise around the block—literally in a counterclockwise square—to do this, so long as you have some way of creating the four markers you have to make. You might bring chalk with you and make four **different** markings with it, to create your four stations.

The last time I performed this technique, I had a pile of red bricks for my first marker, a large white stone for my second, two sticks in a cross on the ground for my third, and a tripod of wooden branches for my fourth. The path they marked for me began at my back door, moved through a stand of woods, back across a lawn, and then finally back to my door, but not in anything much resembling a circle; it was more of a bent oval.

When you have your course arranged—and remember, your markers have to be very **easy** to look upon and remember, so they must be simple things, and they must all be **different** things—you are ready to begin.

Stand with your Riding Pole at your starting place. Tap your pole on the ground three times and relax. Turn left and walk to your first marker. Stop and deeply gaze upon the marker. Memorize it. Look at every detail. Then, when you're ready, move on your course to the next marker and there, do the same. Move on to each of the markers along the course, stopping to really look at them, engaging them fully with your senses, and memorize how they look and feel. When you get back to your starting point, tap your pole on the ground three times and relax.

Then go inside your home (or return to your home and go inside) and go straight to a bed or couch. Lie down with your Riding Pole alongside you, and close your eyes. Relax and focus on the sensation of your body. After a few minutes—not more than two or three—visualize yourself standing at your starting point, as you just did. Feel and hear yourself tapping your Riding Pole on the ground. Then visualize yourself walking—as you just did—to your first marker.

Bring into your mind's eye as strongly as you can what that marker looked like. Then visualize yourself walking to the second marker, and "see" it, too. Recreate your whole walk in this way—going marker to marker, recalling in your mind what they looked like.

This trick—using the markers—is intended to make your visualized journey very clear and easy, and with practice, it very much does. You don't have to recall *all* the details of your walk; only these four very important details—the markers—is enough to make you feel like you are re-living the walk, making progress from a starting point.

And the memory of these markers should be fresh in your mind, as just a few minutes before, you were physically there with them, gazing upon them.

When your easily envisioned *Widdershins Walk* reaches your starting point again, see yourself standing there, and tapping your Riding Pole on the ground three times. Then visualize yourself going into your home (or returning to your home) and walking rapidly through your home, to where your body is lying, holding the Riding Pole. See yourself from the outside, lying there. See the pole. Then "jump into yourself"—and at this point, open your eyes and get up. The technique is done.

You must do this Widdershins Walk technique *at least* three times with your pole. You don't have to return physically to your walking-course each time before you do it; if you can clearly remember the markers, you can do it anytime you want.

**RIDING POLE CREATION: PHASE 3**

In this phase, you will do the *Widdershins Walk* with your Riding Pole one more time, but something different will happen at the end. Do the visualized walk—lying down, holding your physical Riding Pole as usual—but this time, as you return to your starting point at the end of your visualized walk, something is not the same as when you left. Near to your starting point, **an eight-foot wide hole has appeared in the earth**. It is dark, and clearly very deep—so deep, you can't see the bottom; it vanishes into darkness. You can see roots and things sticking out of the sides of the hole near its top, but under those, the dark earth making the sides of this shaft just gets muddy and smooth.

Stand on the rim of this dark shaft into the earth, and put your Riding Pole between your legs. Now jump forward, so that you fall feet-first into this deep pit. The pit is wide enough that your pole won't be hitting its sides.

The first thing that happens when you jump out is (of course) that you begin falling very quickly. Feel the cavern inside your stomach lurch and tingle as your falling momentum builds suddenly—a sensation that anyone who has been on a roller coaster already knows. Grit your teeth to endure this uncomfortable sensation in your gut, and notice that you have rapidly fallen into darkness. You might have been able to "see" the earthen sides of the tunnel for three seconds before you plunged too deep into the earth to have enough light. You are falling extremely fast, your hands tight around the front of your Riding Pole. And you are falling extremely fast through darkness, air wooshing by your ear, your stomach tingling with the momentum of the fall.

You have to let yourself *feel* these things. It's not the most comfortable feeling, but it forces your body to have a physiological "reality" response that you want. In your visualized fall, you finally close your eyes (it's pitch black anyway), and just focus on the feeling of the rapid fall.

After about 30 seconds of this—and you wondering if you're ever going to find the bottom of this pit; you might wonder if, at any second, you're going to splatter against rocks or an unseen stone floor, or smack into the surface of an ocean that is somewhere in the center of the earth—you realize that you are no longer in a dark pit.

You still can't see, and can only feel that you are moving very fast—but you aren't in a pit. You are in the sky, and still moving "feet first"—you are in the sky laying back, with your pole facing straight up into the sky. Feel yourself leaning forward, "righting" yourself so that your feet now hang towards the ground which is very far below you. The pressure and tingle in your stomach fades as you right yourself, and an exhilarating feeling sets in, instead.

When you open your eyes, you are a great distance above the surface of the earth at night, and flying very quickly in a straight line. Below you are forests that rapidly move under you—even hills and mountains. What you see the most of (because forests and mountains are really just large black sheets or lumps from your perspective) are lights. All over in the dark landscape are the lights of houses, towns, and even cities. They rapidly move under you and away from you.

In the distance, you see super-cluster of lights that can only be a large town; but you're moving very fast, and so it passes under you before you have much time to look at it. The darkness in the distance ahead of you is suddenly illuminated by the moon that came out from behind a cloud—and you can see more of the sky now. A great and vast water is approaching—it looks like the ocean, and you are heading straight towards it.

You must tilt yourself to the left and spin in the air once. It's a feeling that makes your head rush, and your vision blurs, but you right yourself again. Practice doing that a few times, in this visualization. Then, look down and around and notice that the ocean below you is dark and vast, and only clouds on the distant horizon, lit by the moon, can be seen.

Focus on the glowing clouds on the distant horizon and fly towards them. They start to glow even more—like perhaps a sun is coming up behind them. It seems like there might be a huge island or another land ahead in the distance, but as the light gets brighter, you feel quiet inside, and then you open your physical eyes. The technique is done.

You can do this visualized flight three times if you want, but doing it only once completely is enough. If you try and fail to do it, don't worry; just keep on trying until you succeed, because you *will*.

The day after you finished your flight visualization, get a sharp knife, a wood carving tool, or some kind of tool that can carve wood—it doesn't matter what it is—and carve the **SAUWENDEI sigil** into your Riding Pole. You can carve it anywhere you like. It can be as small or large as you like, though the texture and landscape of your Riding Pole itself will show you intuitively how large it should be, and where it should go.

If you peeled the bark off your Riding Pole, you might want to darken the sigil, and this is fair—just carve it first, and then you can use a wood burner to burn its insides, or paint its insides with some dark stain and a very thin brush, or put some other coloring agent inside. You don't have to, of course; it's a matter of aesthetic taste. If you have bark on your Riding Pole, chances are the contrast on your carving will be instant and very nice to see.

When you are done with the sigil completely, prick any finger on your left hand and wipe a small drop of your blood down the central channel of the Sigil. Wipe it up and down, smearing it in there good. It will fade over time, but the essence will go into the wood.

After you have created and blooded the Sigil, your Riding Pole is **complete**. It is now a fully activated and "trained" mount for your subtle body. You should use it when you do the **SAUWENDEI** work as much as possible. If you decide one day to take a nap and want to do the basic **SAUWENDEI** technique, take your Riding Pole into the nap with you.

Take this pole to bed with you on some nights when you do the basic technique. *Especially* try to have it with you any time you do the advanced work. Lay it alongside your body; try if you can to cradle it or touch it, but this is not necessary.

If you like, you can get birch withies and bind them all around one end of your Riding Pole, transforming it into a primitive broom. This is not required; this is as much for aesthetics as it is to honor the spirit of the

Witches of old who, we are told, marked their spectral night-journeys with a broom placed in their beds.

### Analysis and Further Elucidation

**SAUWENDEI** workings are subtle. They might take time to increase in suitable strength for most people, owing to the stressful and disrupted lives most modern people lead. But they should never be abandoned; devotion to these works leads to some of the most important spiritual experiences a person can have in this breathing life.

There is more to these workings than merely following the instructions given in this section. We must train ourselves to understand what sleep and dream really is, or what it *might* be to us if we can change our perspectives slightly. The most powerful support to the **SAUWENDEI** workings is this: **do not be thoughtless about sleep and dream**.

Right now, as you sit wherever you are, look around and deeply take in the room you're in, the vehicle, the park, the outdoors area, wherever you are. *Look* at it. Soak in your surroundings. Realize that all of this is your condition, your state of mind right now, your state of experience. This is real. It's your reality at this moment.

Falling asleep, being asleep, and dreaming—these things are *also* conditions, states of mind, states of experience. They are yours just as much as your many waking moments, and they are just as real. Every opportunity to fall asleep and dream is a **precious chance** to enter into a trance state, an opportunity to have visions or perhaps encounters with extraordinary powers.

Every opportunity to fall asleep and dream is a transition into a trance-condition, into another experience of this world that you can and should want to pay attention to. The tragedy is that so many people sleep like the dead—they arrive at their beds exhausted, stressed, and dazed. They put their heads down and *black out*—enjoying no memory of dreams when they wake, having slept heavily and usually somewhat restlessly.

If they do have dreams, they might be disturbing or so strange that they pay them no heed.

No heed! Heed is indeed the point here—we must avoid falling asleep in utter exhaustion and having no care or concern for *what comes after* falling asleep. Bed should never be that place where we retreat to embrace oblivion for whatever wretched space of hours we'll be able to sleep—and for many, usually not enough hours. Sleep is **not** oblivion; it is a *sacred* thing. It is (or should be) a time of potential visions and understanding, and a time of regeneration and rest. For visions and dreams will not seize upon you all night; your body and soul will cycle through dreamless sleep, too, in which the vitality of your flesh is restored.

Whatever is happening in a person's life to rob sleep of its rightful place of honor and attention, those things should be changed as much as possible. Make time for sleep. Take it seriously. Prioritize it. The *Witched* have little choice in this matter, if they want to strengthen their own power as it should be strengthened.

If you change your ideas about sleep, begin to look upon it with the reverence and excitement it deserves, you will greatly empower the **SAUWENDEI** work.

This work will sometimes result in what people call "Lucid Dreams"—a topic I have written at length about in my work *An Carow Gwyn*. Lucid dreams are a powerful mystery, and have their own very special relationship to Witchcraft, which can never be understated. Lucid dreams are a great blessing when they happen, but, unless you are blessed with the ability to naturally have them often, one must never focus too strongly on them. If you desire them, the best way to get them is through **SAUWENDEI** workings, particularly the advanced work, with a Riding Pole alongside you.

Feel free to bring in other lucid dreaming techniques to support this work, but don't over-do it; you can't crowd your mind and expect to have good results. Those who wish to have more lucid dreams should understand the following things, which will both help them in that goal, but will also help all people engaging in **SAUWENDEI** work to understand some critical points:

Trying to control dreams too much (what people usually mean when they say they want lucid dreams) is a bad orientation, a bad habit. We should **receive** of the Unseen world in dreams more than we assert ourselves. A dream doesn't have to be what is called "lucid" to include elements of journeying about, meeting powerful beings, and yielding many powerful insights and understandings for you. It's often best to let the Unseen World do with us what *it* wills for us in our dreams, than to try to become completely lucid so that we might try and choose our own adventures, as it were.

People who yearn to become lucid often, so they can go off flying or experiencing highly-conscious first-person guided adventures, but who are frustrated in their attempts should realize this: your dreaming soul—your wandering soul—the double of your ordinary self which was in existence before you lived and will be in existence perpetually, is **always flying**. It is always moving, always wandering, always having its own strange and surreal life apart from the ordinary life you know.

Put another way, there is an aspect of your consciousness which you very seldom get to be very aware of, except in dreams, trances, or near-death experiences, which is *always* moving about and adventuring. Change your perspective to embrace this, and realize that your attempt to lie down in your bed and arise lucidly before flying away might be *blocking* you. Instead, realize that what you want is to *become aware of the portion of yourself that is already flying*. This can help many people. In essence, before you've done anything at all, you've already succeeded; what you want to experience is already happening. If you can accept that, it will make your desire more easy to realize in extraordinary experience.

In the meantime, as you go about your daily routines, take time out to look around and recognize that everything around you is just your very real experience right now. When you lie down to sleep, as you become hypnagogic, understand that the weird visions and sounds of hypnagogia are *also* a very real experience, and a precious part of your life, a precious part of your world. Resolve to try to give more gentle attention to them. Don't let your awareness just fall to the wayside when you sleep; try to avoid going to sleep exhausted every night. It is a very bad habit, not good for the body or soul.

It may not often seem possible, owing to the inhuman demands made on so many people these days by our waking world, but insofar as you can, try to arrange a more gentle and aware manner of understanding and approaching the sacred realities of sleep and dream. Every descent into sleep and every dream should be thought of as a possible revelation or sacred vision from the Great Powers. They should all be thought of as potential times of visitation, or empowerment. They should be revered.

Pay special attention to the *Widdershins Walk* technique which was detailed in this section. It has uses beyond just empowering Riding Poles. You can use it as a trance-induction technique to attempt to have visions of the Unseen World itself. To do so, at the point when you are falling in the technique, do not enter a sky; instead enter a great underground cavern lit by a strange glow, where you slow down and land. Then explore.

Aside from dreams and visionary guidance that might come to you unbidden, dream-related workings are the prime ground for incubating *divinatory dreams*. And the Word of Power **SAUWENDEI** makes this very easy to accomplish.

The act of divinatory dream incubation begins in the waking world, when you either put on your Breaching Talisman, or stand in an activated Gateway Ring, or both, and call upon your helpers, familiars, or the Great One who Witched you and *beg for help* in gaining a dream you need. You may ask for help in understanding something that is puzzling you, or for advice to help you in a hard situation you're living through. This begging (and it should be quite sincere) should always be accompanied by offerings, in exchange for the favor of a dream-vision that will reveal what it is you want or need to know. You can ask for a vision of just about anything: a vision of what happened in a place before, or to someone before; a vision of what is happening elsewhere at present; or a vision of what *will be* for a situation that is working its way out at present. You can describe a situation and ask for advice on how to best navigate it, to reach your best possible outcome (or someone else's).

Understand that such dreams are very valuable gifts. After you have asked and given offerings, go to sleep that night doing one of the **SAUWENDEI** works—basic or advanced. And pay close attention, of course, to whatever dreams you get. These kinds of dream-responses, if they come, can have a 48 to 72 hour delay, so if you dream doesn't arrive that night, spend the next two nights watching out for it.

To become more fully aware of the dreaming world is to become more aware of one's own soul, and its strange wanderings and doings. You are succeeding at the most critical work of all if you one day realize that you have as involved and connected a life in *dreams* as you do in the waking human world. If you find yourself looking forward to sleep and dreams, or even dreading what you might see on account of how it has always coincided with waking reality, you are moving into a spiritual condition that history leaves no doubt was occupied by many Witches in Early Modern times, and even long before.

To change one's relationship to dreams—to gain a more entrenched awareness in the subtle world—is to change one's relationship to death, too. Percy Shelley described death in terms of *"Cradles of eternity, where millions lie lulled to their portioned sleep."* Consider how death and sleep overlap. They are not the same, but they are *kin* to one another, as all cosmological states are kin, woven together and co-existent in the rhizome of life or Nature. Life's wearisome changes all lull us to the sleep of death, and death's sleep is a *cradle*, rocking the infant seed of timeless experience, and perhaps even future experiences. But until then, it is a Fatefully-portioned dark trance of profound depth, or poetically, *sleep*.

# THE WITCH FEAST

The notion that Witches travel—often in a spectral form—to extraordinary meetings with other Witches, meetings in which they are greeted by powerful Otherworldly beings and engage in feasting and other kinds of enjoyable activities, is everywhere attested in Early Modern records. An enormous body of folklore, theology, and esoteric theory has sprung up around these accounts, which are universal to every European nation.

These accounts, and the conclusions drawn from them, fall under the broad heading of *Witches' Sabbaths* in most places. The term "Sabbat" is naturally an imported term from the Abrahamic world; it would appear that most Witches did not use the term, or only used it in agreement with their interrogators who applied an understandable cultural label to the accounts they were hearing.

The folklore of The Sabbat may be some of the most recognizable and evocative in the history of Witchcraft, and the largest amount of elite theological interpolations into Witchcraft are found surrounding this topic. The depraved sexual fantasies of religious and social elites enter into the history of Witchcraft at this point; reports of Sabbat meetings often feature lurid descriptions of sexual congress with demons or the Devil himself. To what extent this might reflect what Witches were actually saying—during the times when actual Witches were being interviewed—is questionable. There can be no doubt that Witches engaged with spirit-beings in all manner of ways, but official reports from trials seem to (predictably) come back to sexual behavior on a regular basis, even going so far as to describe (in the interrogation of Isobel Gowdie) the *temperature of the Devil's semen.*

Such confessions and information placed before judges would have been potent condemnations of both Witches and Witchcraft; it furthers the idea that the corruption of the Devil had spread not only to the souls of Witches, but to their bodies as well. The sin of the Witch was not only moral in nature, but biological; their sensual bodies had become containers of tangible otherworldly evil.

It's easy for us to see now that such obsessions on the parts of witch-hunters, along with the learned men who conducted these trials, had more to do with their own twisted psychologies than with the lived realities of their victims. But the dark influence of these pornographic depictions of diabolical 'Sabbats' infiltrated Europe quite extensively and became a fixture of Early Modern Witchlore.

Some contemporary writers on European history and Witchcraft have used this tragic convergence of Christian cultural psychology and Witch-hysteria to claim that Witch Sabbaths and *Witches in general* were never real; that from the start, the idea of "Witches" themselves, or the Witch's congress with demonic beings (sexual or otherwise) was *always* a manufactured delusion or deceit—whether intentionally and maliciously manufactured, or somehow unintentionally arisen through a bewildering combination of many ignorant, paranoid cultural, social, religious, and political circumstances.

These writers point to the fact that reports of the Sabbat are clearly theological in nature—at least insofar as they contain reports of the (theological) Devil and demons, and depictions of intentional blasphemies being committed against Christian holy words, ceremonies, and theological figures. The defilement of Christian burial grounds, the rejection of baptism or all of the Christian sacraments, the "reverse baptism" that washed away the original baptism bestowed upon men and women, pledges to help the Devil to commit harm against innocent persons to stir society into chaos, and finally the fornication with demons: it does indeed sound like all of the worst fears of Early Modern Christians come to life in such an epic and perfect manner that it can *only* be explained by the worst kinds of paranoid delusion.

The truth of the matter lies somewhere **between** paranoid religio-cultural delusion and the ages-old *reality* of men and women encountering Otherworldly beings with whom they forged relationships and pacts, a special encounter and relationship-space that is far older than Christian culture and beyond its moral understanding.

The truth, as I think Emma Wilby has proven beyond a reasonable doubt in her master-work *The Visions of Isobel Gowdie*, is that our official historical records and accounts of Early Modern Witchcraft are (at times) confessions of *real* experiences had by men and women, expressed in the only language they had to express these experiences, and blended in with the interpolations and interpretations of their elite interrogators.

Sometimes the interpolations are more; sometimes they are less. But *all* records are blended things, reflecting how the Early Modern world was itself a blending of folk-culture, folk-animism, elite theology, and often conflicting and even many mutually unintelligible moral and social worldviews spread across the various classes of the time. Society was *not* a singular monolith, but a tangled thicket of stories, moral assumptions, and beliefs vaguely tied together by the prestige positions of the social and theological elites.

The work of trying to unravel what the accused might have said from the manner the elites finally recorded it is a monumental task, requiring a profound understanding of historical psychology and of history itself; for the historical situations surrounding the lives of the ordinary people and their elites represent major influences that condition *why* they may have done what they did or said what they said.

Assuming that the historical men and women who had actual visionary experiences of Otherworldly beings or meetings were driven to confess them, and assuming that certain layers of elite interpolation will have been laid on top of them in the act of recording them, and taking further special note that some—but not all—confessions were coerced by torture, a fair baseline for extracting the essence of the confessions, before they were adulterated with too much elite material, can be established.

*Witched* men and women were real; they were not merely inventions of a Church, nor inventions of paranoid Early Modern societies that were experiencing acute or chronic social strife. Witched men and women were present who experienced (induced or spontaneous) visionary states of meeting with Otherworldly entities. They *utilized* the advantages or insights they gained from these states or these special meetings to engage others in the pursuit of extraordinary goals such as healing, hexing, death transference, or other transformations. This was **real**, and it remains real to this day; this is not a controversial pronouncement of any sort.

The relationships forged between Witches and powerful Otherworldly beings of many sorts clearly exerted a transformative power upon the souls of Witches. Some may have had a pre-existing susceptibility to trance states of visionary encounters beforehand; after being *Witched*, it's fair to imagine that most became more thusly inclined. The idea that certain dream-visions or trance states could feature a journey to a distant metaphysical location where the souls or doubles of other Witches might also gather, or find themselves attracted to, is not terribly far outside of the range of credulity.

Isobel Gowdie provides a powerfully lucid and detailed description of the feasting activities that she and other Witches received at the hands of the Elf King and Queen below the Downie Hills, and she is not the only person whose confessions mention this activity. Agreement in the details of these spectral feasts across many centuries of confessions is easy to find; they almost always include the presence of the bodies—spiritual or tangible—of other Witches, the presence of dead human beings or fairies (which are often the same thing), the presence of other supernatural beings, the presence of "fairy beasts" or animals otherwise, and of course large quantities of food—breads and meats especially, always given in boundless or generous quantities. Dances and sexual encounters are not uncommon in these confessions, but they are not typically the most commonly described forms of activity at these feasts. The confession narratives more commonly center around the sharing of food and co-workings of Witchcraft done by the Witches gathered there, with the direct aid of the powerful Otherworldly beings who are also present.

*Saducismus Triumphatus* presents us with many accounts of Witch-meetings of the "Sabbat" type, often without identifying them as such; they simply emerge organically from the confessions of Witches, such as Alice Duke. In that book we are treated to the following descriptions, all of them centered on food-sharing and co-workings of Witchcraft:

*"(Alice Duke said that) her forehead being first anointed with a Feather dipt in Oyl, she (was) suddenly carried to the place of their meeting. That about five or six Weeks since... she met in (Lie Common) in the night, where were present Anne Bishop, Mary Penny of Wincaunton, Elizabeth Style of Bayford, and a Man in black Clothes with a little Band, whom she supposeth to have been the Devil. At the meeting there was a Picture in Wax* (here is described the baptism of that image and its cursing)... *This done, all sat down, a white Cloth being spread on the ground, and did drink Wine, and eat Cakes and Meat. After all was ended, the Man in black vanished, leaving an ugly smell at parting. The rest were on a sudden conveyed to their homes...."*

Also it is recorded:

*"At another time she was carried to a meeting in the night, to a green place near Marnhull as she was then told, where were present Anne Bishop, Eliz. Style, Mary Penny, and some unknown to her. Then also an Image in Wax was Baptized by the Devil, in the fore-related manner, by the name of Anne or Rachel Hatcher one of Marnhull, as she was then informed. After the Ceremony was ended, they had Wine and Cakes and etc."*

It is perfectly clear that the "sudden carrying" that Alice Duke is reporting here—the sudden manner in which she was transported to the place of this Witch-meeting, was a description of a powerful trance-state caused by the *Green Oyl* that was put on her forehead with a feather. That a feather was used to anoint her is telling; the feather is a symbol of *flight*, of the relationship birds have with the wind that allows them, through the implements of their feathers, to fly. This *Green Oyl* was formulated so as to bring about potent visionary experiences relating to flying. That she and the rest were "suddenly conveyed to their homes" after their meetings were over is further support for the idea that this was a shared visionary state, and that "The Devil"—whoever or whatever he was—was somehow in control of it.

*Saducismus Triumphatus* also contains the following celebrated passage, which has had so much influence on the culture of modern Witchcraft, particularly the modern neopagan *Wiccan* sect that generously claimed such an enormous portion of the reality of historical Witchcraft for itself:

*"She* (Alice Duke) *sayeth that after their meetings, they all make very low obeisance to the Devil, who appears in black Clothes and a little Band. He bids them welcome at their coming, and brings Wine or Beer, Cakes, Meat, or the like. He sits at the higher end, and usually Anne Bishop sits next him. They eat, drink, dance, and have Musick. At their parting they use to say,* **Merry meet merry part***, and that before they are carried to their meetings, their Foreheads are anointed with greenish Oyl that they have from the Spirit which smells raw. They for the most part are carried through the Air. As they pass, they say, Thout, tout a tout, tout, throughout and about. Passing back they say, Rentum Tormentum."*

What begins to emerge from so many of these accounts is the reality that Witch-meetings or Witch-feasts sometimes occurred in a **spectral state**, in a spiritual or dream-visionary condition, and at others times, it's clear that Witches were meeting in the ordinary sense, in waking, sensual in-person meetings. And if you step back from the lunacy of theological interpolation, and its typical fixation on depraved sex-acts, the vision that appears is of Witches meeting the beings who empower them, and **receiving from them nourishment**. There is not just the sharing of food, which is itself an ages-old means of reaffirming community, family, and friendly bonds, but there is also direct instruction or demonstration of Witchcraft, and there is dancing and enjoyment.

Some ancient practices, along with the special experiences of people accused of being Witches in certain regions of Europe, appear to have other dimensions beyond these basic ones. Some scholarship has focused on the folk-cultural and mythological motif of the *War of the Seasons*—the idea that the souls of some men and women are occasionally drawn from their bodies and compelled to participate in an eternal Otherworldly battle or conflict of some sort, a battle between the powers of life and death, or fertility and sterility. These men and women had to participate and help the powers of life to win, else the fertility of crops and other such crucial forces would be hindered or destroyed, and their communities doomed to starvation or disease.

I do not believe that these accounts should be blended in or intermingled with the Folkloric notion of a Witch-Feast or Sabbat. The idea of the eternal struggle of winter and summer, or of the forces of life and death, in which special human beings had to participate clearly extends from a very ancient strata of European culture, and is part of an *agriculture-centered* understanding of the world. To me, this implies that in Neolithic Europe, the first farmers doubtlessly had layers of beliefs and taboos regarding rituals, behaviors, and other activities that were required at certain times each year to assure that the needful powers of life and fertility would be safe or victorious, and that crops would not fail.

That a **shamanistic vocation** could have arisen among those ancient peoples in which certain souls of community members were compelled to join the Hidden Battle of the forces of fertility and sterility is clearly a thing that came to pass. That this deeper spiritual choreography was *still* compelling the souls of certain men and women to participate, even in medieval times or later, has been (I think) satisfyingly proven by scholars like Carlo Ginzburg.

I do *not* believe that the men and women who were entangled in this ancient agricultural spiritual drama should have been considered *Witches*, though they were certainly more than just ordinary men and women. I think the conclusion anyone must arrive at when studying this very interesting phenomenon is that these men and women **never** thought of themselves as Witches until the Church *convinced them* that they were. And it's easy to see why they would be considered Witches; they *flew* in a spectral form not only to battles with otherworldly forces, but to feasts and other such activities that resonate with the reports of Witches in other places.

The idea that some human souls might have to depart from their ordinary communities at times to help win for their people needful outcomes through struggle or negotiation with Otherworldly forces is obviously older than either the Neolithic age or agricultural society. Agriculturalists came to depict this spiritual vocation as a struggle for their crops; it is everywhere likely that the forager and elder hunter-gatherer societies *before* them understood that certain members of society had to enter the Otherworld to ensure that the communities of hunted animals (upon which they all depended) would not only be kept safe, but would be *benevolently inclined* towards the human community, so that hunts could be successful.

This would be the basis for *Fertility Shamanism*, or shamanistic works oriented around maintaining positive relationships with the Life-Giving powers in the Unseen World, the ultimate service of preservation to society. And there's no doubt in my mind that such activities were commonplace across the human world from the dawn of human time. Where this intersects with Witchcraft, however, is clear to see: it intersects only in the minds of much later Christian elites, as a confused mass of spectral experience that their own theological worldviews gave them no means to understand. Thus, it was all mashed together with the already-confused phenomenon of *Witchcraft* with which they struggled so harshly.

The **True Sabbat** is not a spiritual notion of some high or rarified standing; it is not a revelation of some kind of deepest timeless truth; it is not a function of some earlier cultural spiritual psychology concerned with the struggle of Otherworldly forces for the sake of human survival, nor is it tied up with cyclical agricultural rituals. Those things may all individually be real in some manner, but they belong to different realms of experience. The Sabbat or *Witch-Meeting* is an activity of *Witched* souls meeting at times with the powerful beings who endowed them with *Witching*, and strongly re-affirming those bonds or those relationships through shared acts of nourishment or enjoyment. This is the core of the experience.

Those who are *Witched* will probably be drawn into visionary or dream-based experiences in which they (at times) meet with those who empowered them, or with their representatives. Strange acts of nourishment or empowerment will feature in these visions; they may be sexual or intimate in nature, or can take many forms, including the direct transference of power somehow into the body of the Witch, the sharing of food or cups, or instructions in the arts of Witchcraft. Without doing a single thing further, a person who gains Witch Dreams runs a pretty high likelihood of such visionary experiences occurring in an organic and even random-seeming or spontaneous way.

But those who are *Witched* would be wise to take this one step further, and perform special acts, rituals, or workings at special times to either bring such meetings about, or to **symbolically enact** such experiences. Doing so is another manner of "reaching out" to the powers that *Witched* them, demonstrating how much the Witch is thankful, but how much the Witch also desires further and deepening relationship. Deepening relationship means more power; more power to protect oneself and others, or to gain for oneself and others things badly wanted or needed to live well in this world. It also means a stronger soul, and a soul whose destiny will be found with its Masters in the life to come.

On the off chance that Witched souls discover other such souls, and manage to find a common ground upon which to work together at times, the shared experience of the Sabbat or the Witch-Feast can be one of the most potent and enjoyable experiences they can forge together. I shall endeavor now to describe several different forms of Witch Meeting that individuals or groups can conjure, co-create, or engage in, if they are both devoted and diligent.

## The Symbolic Sabbat

The *Symbolic Sabbat* is a potent ritual carried out in the breathing world of our ordinary reality, which allows a *Witched* person (or persons) to enjoy a re-enactment of the *Spectral Sabbat*, or the Sabbat that takes place in a deeper visionary state. What is enacted symbolically here is, if done with seriousness and care, a *potent conjuration* of a very ancient sort; it is a conjuration of the powers that indwell the invisible dimension. It might be thought of as a form of ritual theatre. Done properly, it creates not only more closeness between the person(s) engaging it and their Otherworldly patrons, but it also lays a deeper groundwork for developing more degrees of closeness with the Unseen in the future.

I will first describe the Symbolic Sabbat as a lone person might perform it, because many people reading this work will invariably find themselves doing it alone of human company.

While there are many folklorically powerful "nights" or seasons during which such efforts as the Symbolic Sabbat might be performed, it is the times that stand between the bright half of the year and the darker half that seem to contain the most spiritual strength, the highest degree of liminal strangeness, and which have the most folklore surrounding them. Thus, the beginning of May and the beginning of November are critical times to consider; the times around the Summer solstice and the Winter solstice are likewise periods that exert a great presence in both myth and folklore. *Full moons* create a suitable uncanny presence for the performance of such a rite as this, though it should be noted that a preference for full moons on the parts of secretive groups in the distant past of our world might have had as much to do with how the full moon acts as an ample light source in the forests or wastes at night, as any special metaphysics connected to the moon.

If one is going to engage in Symbolic Sabbats, it's best to do them twice a year. Setting oneself up to perform many more than two runs a risk of becoming bogged down with a difficult "spiritual schedule" that the modern world seldom renders very easy to accomplish. No one *has* to perform Symbolic Sabbats; one may devote oneself to experiencing Spectral Sabbats alone (as can entire covens of Witches) and this will be discussed in the next section. More likely, an individual Witch or a coven

will experience a *mixture* of these two kinds of Sabbats, assuming they choose to work Symbolic ones, of course.

To perform a Symbolic Sabbat, you will need a private outdoors space to work in. They cannot be done indoors. If you do not have such an easily accessible and private outdoors space, or cannot travel to one every now and again, you will have to work with Spectral Sabbats alone—but this is not as grim a Fate as it may seem; the majority of *Witched* souls from the Early Modern era *only* encountered the Sabbat spectrally.

Select a private area in a forest or field to be the place of the Witch Meeting. Around twilight, or at some time in the night, create a Gateway Ring with a larger perimeter. At its center, you'll be building a bonfire, and you must always take care to ensure that the area where you work is safe for fires, or that fires are allowed. Do not worry over the idea of putting a fire at the center of the Ring; when you go to banish it, the fire will be embers.

Inside that ring two features must be raised. The first is a symbol of the Master himself—whether He is understood by you as The Devil in any form, or as the Fairy King, the symbol is the same; it is a wooden pole or staff crowned with a stag's skull or a goat's skull. If you do not have such a skull, then use a forked staff, which will carry the same symbolism. This symbol should stand at least 5 feet in height, but need not be more than 7 feet in height. Erect it in the northern quadrant of the Gateway Ring.

Next, a symbol of the Good Lady of Elfhame must be placed, somewhere to the left or right of the Master's symbol. Her symbol should be a cauldron or a large bowl, placed itself on top of a pedestal made from a tree stump or a few large stones, or hung from a tripod. If this cannot be accomplished, 12 straight branches or sticks (four of them being short, four a little longer, and four even longer than those) can be arranged on the ground so that they create **three concentric diamonds**—which we will call *The Lady's Symbol*—and then a few candles or lanterns need to be placed around that. Then you need to get a plate of cakes or a plate containing a loaf of fresh bread, and put it at the foot of the Master's symbol. A nice goblet or cup of wine needs to be placed near the Queen's symbol. If you can, put a drum somewhere in the circle, or some easily portable musical instrument that you can play—like a flute, or a fiddle, if you have such a talent. This drum or musical instrument isn't necessary, but will add much to the ritual if you can utilize it. Then you can light the bonfire and leave the area.

*The Lady's Symbol*

Walk a distance from that prepared working area. It's even better if you move far enough away to not be able to see it due to landscape features blocking your view of it, but it's fine if it's still in sight. You will of course already be wearing your Breaching Talisman, and you should have your Riding Pole with you. Take out your jar of Green Oyl and dip a feather's quill in it, and anoint your forehead with this, saying **ABANHOU** as usual. Then begin walking with your Riding Pole in hand towards the prepared area with the bonfire you just lit, which should be blazing up in strength at this point.

When you come close to the Bonfire, but still a goodly ways back, put the Riding Pole between your legs and whisper *"Tout, tout-a-tout tout, throughout and about"*, then "ride" your pole towards the boundary of the Gateway Ring. When you reach the boundary, get off the Riding Pole, lay it diagonally across the boundary of the Ring, and *leap across it and over it*, into the Ring. The Riding Pole was not only your mount to fly to the Sabbat, but it was your *bridge* into the Powerful Place where Spirits are met.

Pick up your pole and stand facing the Master's symbol. Place your right hand, fingers spread, against your chest, then thrust that same hand out and towards the Master's symbol, palm facing the symbol. This gesture—

the *gesture of allegiance*—is a symbolic demonstration that your *heart* or *whole entity* is being offered to him, that it *belongs* to him. Then, make the same gesture to the Lady's symbol.

Put your Riding Pole down, walk forward, get on one knee before the Master's symbol, and take a cake or a piece of the bread. Hold it up to the Symbol and say

*"I thank thee, Lord, for this—and I take it into my body, receiving the good that you intend for me."*

Then eat the cake or bread. Go next to the Lady's Symbol, take a knee before it, and take the cup of wine, and say

*"I thank thee, Good Lady, for this—and I take it into my body, receiving the good that you intend for me."*

Drink one or two good sips of it, and then return the cup to where it was.

Now stand and take up the drum or instrument that should be there. Feed the fire if it needs some help. At this point you should pound that drum in any rhythmic fashion you desire, and dance in a counterclockwise circle around the fire. If you can play some other instrument while doing this, that's great. If you don't have a drum or any instrument, and just want to dance and sing, or dance and clap your hands, or dance and make no sound at all, it's fine. This dance is not just symbolic enjoyment or frolicking; it's an offering to the Spirits of the Master and the Good Lady of Elfhame.

As much as it may revolt the aesthetic purists among us, I suppose it is the 21st century now, and so if you have a device that can play music at a satisfying volume (and you can handle this intrusion of techno-modernity into such a ritual as this), such a thing might be used to supply music for your dancing. Otherwise, keep it simple.

Since you will be alone and in a private place, there's no need to be shy about anything. Get worked up; build up a sweat if you can, as this will indicate a lot of bodily energy increased and given away. If such physical motion is not on the table for you, sitting and playing an instrument, or beating a drum for a good long while, will be well. If you wish to have a mask in the Gateway Ring for you to put on while you drum or play an instrument or just dance, feel free to include it; assuming a masked visage while in the Witch Meeting Place is a symbolic way of *shape-shifting*, which adds much to the experience (particularly when more than one person is sharing this experience with you.)

After your dancing and performances are done, and any works of Witchery that you might want to do in this Witch-Meeting Ring, you should depart.

Take your riding pole and lay it again diagonally across the boundary of the Gateway Ring, and leap across it and over it, landing outside of the Ring. Pick up the pole, put it between your legs and whisper *"Rentum Tormentum"* and then ride away. When you're a reasonable distance away, take it from between your legs and just walk with it normally, *back to where you started* in the first place. When you reach there, the Symbolic Sabbat ritual is completed.

Wait for a while then return to the area where the Sabbat took place; the fire should have died down, and you can finish extinguishing it, or rake its embers aside to beat the ground seven times to banish the Ring. Pour out the rest of the wine on the ground, and leave the rest of the bread there. Then collect your things (and make sure the fire is completely out) and depart.


**The Symbolic Sabbat with Multiple Persons**

If you are fortunate to have other *Witched* persons with whom you can perform Symbolic Sabbats, a lot of things can change with this ritual, and a lot more things become possible. If you only have two people, then the Symbolic Sabbat is performed just as written above, only you'll have a partner who does all of the actions mentioned: saluting the symbols, kneeling to take the cakes and wine, and then dancing or playing instruments with you, and so forth. You'll both ride to and away from the Gateway Ring in the same manner, entering it and leaving it in the same manner.

But if you have three or more people—a *Coven* in fact—the ritual can increase along new and more powerful lines. If you have three people, one of you can be chosen to assume the Role of the Master or the Lady of Elfhame. That person, who will be in a certain costume, will be in the

Gateway Ring to greet the others who come "flying" to it. If you have four or more people, two can be chosen to assume the roles of the Devil or Master or Fairy King, and the Lady of Elfhame.

Before I continue on to this, something must be stated which each person (or group of persons) reading this will have to work out for themselves. The Symbolic Sabbat ritual you just read, written for a lone operant, included symbols for the Master and the Lady of Elfhame. This should be considered a standard sort of ritual outlay, but it's not the only possible one. If a small group of Witches are all empowered by the Devil or the Master, they may choose to meet *only him* in Symbolic Sabbats. This means that only his symbol will be in the Gateway Ring, and the cakes or bread and wine will *both* be taken from him. Just so, if *every* member of the group received their Witch Dreams from the Lady of Elfhame, *She* may be the only entity they choose to meet in the Ring. Only her symbol will be there, and the cakes and wine will be taken from her. And of course, even if every member of the group was Witched by one Patron, the symbol of the other can still be included in the ritual, just as it was written. It's up to the members of the working group.

All of this holds true if you have a human member of the group who will assume the role of the Devil/Master or the Lady of Elfhame. If a group chooses, they don't have to meet *both* characters. But one thing *does* remain true, always: if some members of the group have received their Witch Dreams from the Master Spirit, and some have received their Dreams from the Lady of Elfhame, **both have to be met** when that group conducts a Symbolic Sabbat. It would be insulting to do otherwise.

A further "aesthetic twist" occurs if some members of the group received their Dreams from the Devil or Master classically considered, but some from the *Fairy King*. This becomes a matter of what kind of metaphysical agreement they can reach regarding how they understand the relationship between the figures of the Folkloric Devil and the Fairy King. If they can agree that these figures are the same spirit, but called by different aesthetic names, then all is well. If not, it may be that the *Fairy Witches* need to operate on their own and only with others who have sought and received their empowerments from the Fairy King or Queen.

I will give notes now for how a Symbolic Sabbat might be conducted with multiple people, assuming that one person is going to be assuming the role of the Master Spirit, and one woman will be assuming the role of the Lady of Elfhame, and two or more others will be flying to them to perform the ritual. If your group only has three people in it, meaning that only one human will be greeting the others, **or** if your group will only be meeting with a human representative of **one** of these great powers for whatever reason, it will be easy to surmise how you have to re-write this ritual to perform it.

The human dressed as the Master Spirit should be in black or dark robes or clothing, and be wearing a full-face covering mask of a goat or a stag, or an abstract mask of some sort of a horned or antlered beast. A human representing the Lady of Elfhame should be in a long white gown or robe of some sort, and her face should be made pale with some kind of makeup or paint. If she does not have long hair, a long-haired wig (usually black or golden) should be used.

The two humans representing the Great Powers are the ones who will create the Gateway Ring, and light its central fire. Symbols for the Master or Lady of Elfhame *don't* have to be made if humans are portraying them. They will make certain that the cakes or bread and wine, are present and safe. Any other things needed for the night's activities will have to be there as well. They should go out some time before to prepare this space, and the others who will be journeying to them should have a pre-determined time at which they will approach the area, so the representatives of the Master and the Lady of Elfhame should be sure to leave early enough to do all that they need to do.

After they have made the Gateway Ring, before the others arrive, the man and woman playing the roles of these powerful entities should make invocations asking the Underworldly King and his Queen to bless the space, and hear and see all that will happen there, giving their blessings to all who attend. Then they should await the coming of the others.

When the others all approach and arrive in the Ring, the representative of the Master and the representative of the Lady of Elfhame should be standing in the north of the circle, watching the arrivals. After all of the arrivals are in the Ring, they will all make the gesture of allegiance to the representatives. When the representatives see someone (or the whole group) make that gesture, offering their hearts and entities to them, they respond by holding out their left hands with their palms and fingers open towards the celebrants, showing that they are **receiving what was just offered to them**.

After the gestures are made and received, the man representing the Devil or Master steps forward and says

**"We greet you, our chosen, and bid you happy welcome to this good place of meeting. We have given you our dreams, and we protect those who dream our dreams."**

He then takes a plate of the bread or cakes and offers them to the celebrants, saying:

**"Take, eat, receive the good that we intend for you."**

The celebrants each take a cake or a piece of bread, saying *"I thank you, my Lord, for this"*, and then eat it. Then the representative of the Lady steps forward and offers a cup of wine, saying:

**"Take, drink, receive the good that we intend for you."**

Everyone takes a sip, saying *"I thank you, Good Lady, for this"* when they receive the cup and before they drink. If the cup runs low, the Lady re-fills it so that it can continue to be passed about.

When the cup is done being passed and taken away, the Lady says:

**"The Good Powers have blessed you. They will walk alongside you unseen. Now make music; dance. Let your hearts be free of anything that burdens them."**

The gathering should now begin their drumming and dancing, or any instrument playing. The Lady always watches; if the space or location renders it possible, she should have a "throne" or chair/seat of some sort to sit on as she watches the proceedings. The Devil or Master Spirit may join in dancing or instrument playing, or watch as he desires.

After the merry-making is over, co-workings of witchcraft that need to be done can be performed together. When the gathering prepares to leave, the Devil or Master of Spirits says to them:

"Merry we greeted you, Merry we part now. Merry we will meet again."

And then the Sabbat-goers leave as described before. The two representatives who stay behind should close the Ring, and each have some of the bread and wine left over. They should be joined by the others to clean up and move away anything that needs to be taken away.

It is **critical** that the representatives of the Master Spirit and Lady of Elfhame *never* remove their costumes or "break character" while the Ring is in place. They must *never* be treated as their human selves by the others who arrive to participate in this. Any requests they make of Witches in the Ring should be honored as though one of the Great Powers themselves actually asked—though the representatives should never talk too much, preferring instead to behave quietly and mysteriously in most cases.

### The Spectral Sabbat

There are three methods or "routes" towards having the experience of the Spectral Sabbat. The first is the **Hypnagogic Technique**, a simple technique in which a fairly detailed Hypnagogic journey is taken on a special night, with the hope that, after sleep arrives, one's dreams will be blessed with further chapters of experience.

The second method is the **Free Dream Technique**, in which a sequence of nights is put aside in which one does the advanced **SAUWENDEI** work on *each* night, with their Riding Pole in bed alongside them, hoping to obtain a *Sabbatic Dream*. The third method is the **Shimmering Technique**, in which a lucid dream is sought, and in that lucid dream, the Witch literally flies on their Riding Pole in an attempt to find a Sabbat meeting-ground, and join it. This final method is by far the most advanced, and may take some time to master, assuming it ever can be.

### *The Hypnagogic Technique*

To perform this technique, one needs a fully created Riding Pole. Before going to bed, you should anoint your head with Green Oyl, using a feather to do so, and of course saying **ABANHOU**. You should also be wearing your Breaching Talisman—but that should go without saying at this point.

Lie down with the Riding Pole alongside you. You will *not* be doing a **SAUWENDEI** working this night; this is a pure hypnagogic experience, so make sure you go to bed with a store of extra energy of alertness, because the hypnagogic visualization takes some time and you don't want to fall asleep in the middle of it.

Relax and focus on the sensation of your body, lying there. As relaxation deepens, you will begin to sense the signs of hypnagogia beginning. The first moment you sense them, begin the following visualization:

*It is a damp, dark night. The stars are burning very bright in the black sky, and the ink-dark shapes of trees can be seen in every direction. You are walking down a well-worn gravel road away from some rustic country houses, leaving a small village behind which is sleeping in the night. Your Riding Pole is in your hand as you head away from the houses and towards the wider shadowy forest ahead.*

*The pathway crosses a field, an abandoned field once used for farming, and there, in the open you stop and look to the sky. Here is where you will do the spell of flying to reach the Sabbat; here you are sure no one will see the sorcery that the Devil made.*

*You put your Riding Pole down and take a small jar of Green Oyl out of a pouch you have, dip a feather into it and anoint your forehead with it. Then you replace the lid on the jar and put it back in the pouch, tossing the feather away. You pick up your Riding Pole and take a deep breath.*

*A strong wind begins to stir deeper in the forest on the far side of this field. An owl suddenly hoots a cadence of its dark calls aloud. You begin to feel light headed. You put the Riding Pole between your legs and whisper the words* **Tout, tout-a-tout tout, throughout and about.**

*There is a suddenly lurching feeling in your chest and stomach and back, and you are lifted off the ground with great force, and you accelerate directly upward into the sky. You squeeze your hands around your riding pole tight and clench your jaw. Suddenly, like a stone hurled from a catapult, you are launched towards the dark horizon north of you. You begin flying very quickly in a straight line high above the dark forest below.*

*The wind blasting against your face is ice cold and exhilarating. Oddly, cold seems warm somehow. Below you more and more of the dark landscape passes; you see isolated lights from farms, and an occasional fire in a forest clearing. The land below you begins to glint with moon and star-light, as it becomes boggier, and full of lakes and ponds and marsh.*

*After a while, the land becomes water completely—a vast dark water that you realize is a river, a terrible river of immense proportions that separates the human world from the Netherworld beyond.*

*You begin to look side to side in the dark air, hoping for one of the Pale Ones to come and help you, for you know that you can't make it across this river—even flying, as you are—without their help. Sure enough, you see the ghostly form of one a Pale One coming towards you. She is wispy, as though her body is made of fog or mist, and her face is indistinct. She flies like a wraith through the air, attracted by your Spell of Flight.*

*She flies up behind you, and you suddenly feel a boost in your speed. You begin to fly forward so fast that your vision blurs, making you squint closed your eyes. Then she releases you, and your speed returns to normal. Below you, there is no more water; she has carried you over the Dark River that separates the living from the dead.*

*There is a new dark land below you instead, which seems to glow with a dark green, even though there is little light. Far ahead, you see a light on the horizon. A tiny light, a beacon, is visible, and you focus on it and turn the staff of your Riding Pole to fly directly towards it.*

*Soon, the little beacon light comes into view for what it is: a massive fire blazing atop a huge mountain. This is no ordinary fire and no ordinary mountain; the fire is many times larger than any human-created blaze could be, and the mountain has a very truncated, flat top—the surface of this "flat top" mountain is so large it has clusters of dark woods in places on top of it.*

*As you begin to fly over the mountain, and directly over the fire, you look down from your great height and see three rings of dark human figures dancing around the massive fire. The ring of human bodies closest to the fire is turning counterclockwise; the next ring out (the middle ring) of humans is dancing clockwise, and the outer ring—which must have hundreds of people in it owing to its great size—is turning counterclockwise.*

*But then you see that there are other fires, much smaller than this mighty central fire that has three concentric circles of humans dancing around it. Stretching away from the central fire are nine other fires, very tiny compared to the central colossus of flame. Three of them stretch away from the central fire in a line to what you surmise is the north; three run away from it in a line towards what must be the southwest, and three stretch away from it towards what must be the southeast.*

*And around each of those nine smaller fires are big, dark crowds of human bodies or shapes. The top of this mountain—the Field of the Sabbat—is clustered with thousands of reveling bodies, which you take note of as you pass over it. You aim your Riding Pole downward towards a dark stand of trees near one of the outside smaller fires, and land softly.*

*You lean your Riding Pole up against the tree, and with excitement in your heart, head towards the dark crowd of laughing and chattering beings who are gathered around the small fire nearest the wood you landed in. You can now hear the music of drums, pipes, flutes, fiddles and harps coming from all directions—and all of the tunes are enchanting.*

*The people in the joyful crowd that you enter are mostly humans, but some are clearly not human; they have horns bursting from their foreheads, some of them, and eyes that glimmer a luminous green or sometimes blue. Some are elves—pale-faced and cold or dark-eyed, but still most of them are grinning and dancing or drinking from horns and tall stoneware cups.*

*As you're moving through the crowd, a dark-haired woman suddenly blocks your path and hands you a cup carved with snakes all around its rim. "Drink", she says, "And be one with the Great Powers." She smiles and walks back into the crowd. You drink what she handed you in one long draft. It has a sweet, honey-like taste, and you immediately feel warm all over. Everything seems brighter and you feel a peace inside you.*

*You walk forward, smiling, past another fire and its reveling crowd, and another, and find yourself outside of the "outer ring" of dancers who are making circuits around the towering inferno of flame that is at the center of the Field of the Sabbat. Their bodies—some of them naked—are dancing and rushing from left to right, from your perspective. They are dancing to a deep, droning drum and weird pipe music that seems to come from the great central fire that the entranced people here seem to be worshipping.*

*You push your way through their ring, and find yourself facing another ring of dancing bodies, these going from right to left, the opposite of the outside ring of dancers. You push through them as well, and find yourself facing a final ring of dancers, whose bodies move from left to right. All is bright here, because you are close to the center fire now. You push through the final ring and find yourself facing the towering blaze around which these three rings of dancers are turning.*

*You've never seen a fire so huge, and oddly, it does not radiate the killing heat you'd imagine it would. It towers gold, orange, white, and blazing bright at least 60 feet above you. Then you see a wonder: from the heart of the fire, a ten-foot tall figure steps. The giant is female, and has smooth, deep brown skin, slender long legs that end in pointed hooves, and majestic crescent-curving cow horns spreading from her head. She has long black hair spilling almost all the way to her knees. She is naked, and has dark eyes that still shine somehow.*

*You hear hundreds of voices shout out behind you in unison: **KEUEMORI! (kyoo-ay-mar-ee) QUEEN OF THE GOOD EARTH!** The giantess begins to prance around the immense blazing fire, so you lose sight of her as she passes behind it. The shouts and cheers of the dancers grow louder.*

*Then, from the heart of the massive blaze, another wonder emerges: A massive muscular white stag, easily seven feet tall with wide, spreading antlers, comes striding out. It paws the earth with its massive hooves and begins prancing around the fire, too. The screams of the people all around become wild, and you see the giant pair racing around the fire together. You hold your hands out to them as they pass and think "Take me with you to your feasting table, for I belong to your hidden company..."*

And you fall asleep like this, watching this scene of the giant ones racing about the fire.

This involved visualization may seem hard to sustain or remember, but I assure you it is not. Read this multiple times and the details will sink into you, and become easy to recall. Let your imagination fill in any other details you want as you move through this visualization in your deepening hypnagogic state. Remember—you cannot fall asleep until you reach the end.

The hope here is that through this hypnagogic visual invocation, your dreams will be of a *Sabbatic* character later that night. If they are not, feel free to repeat this for the next one or two nights, then stop. Simply doing this visualization aligns your inner soul to the current of the *Witching* powers, so it is useful all by itself. Also, if you wish to alter the visualization to be more in line with a different aesthetic sense—if you'd prefer to see different beings emerging from the Great Fire—feel free to alter it. You may wish instead to behold the great black *Sabbatic Goat*, or something of that nature. Whatever inspires you most should be visualized.

### The Free Dreaming Technique and the Shimmering

These two techniques overlap greatly, because they begin in precisely the same manner: you go to your bed on the propitious chosen nights, and you perform the advanced **SAUWENDEI** work. You do it fully: Riding Pole laying at your side in bed, your breaching talisman on, and you wake 4-5 hours after going into your first sleep, and after the brief interruption, you go to a second sleep. If you are Free Dreaming, you are simply watching for dreams of a special (or *Sabbatic*) character as it was defined here: visions of your helpers, familiars, empowerers, or even dream-visions of other potent beings (such as the dead) or any *other-than-human* or strange beings interacting with you.

In Free Dreaming, your special dreams can arrive at any point during your first or second sleep periods. It is also possible that you may arise in a lucid dream, and if this happens, you would apply the advice about to be given when we discuss *Shimmering* or lucid dreams specifically.

Understand that you don't have to utilize this technique (or any other) only on one specific night.

If you will be Free Dreaming for a potential Sabbatic Dream around the beginning of May, around the time of Walpurgis Night or May Day, there's no reason not to extend your Free Dreaming attempts to the few nights before *and* after May 1st.

As with all dreams of this nature, the very *best* ones will likely come on their own, seemingly spontaneously arisen, surprising you with dream visions featuring extraordinary encounters.

Before you attempt to do either a Free Dreaming night, or a Shimmering night, it is enormously helpful—and I might even say necessary—to spend a few precious moments or minutes communicating to the Unseen Powers your wishes and desires to become aware of the sort of dream-vision-experience you are seeking. This might be thought of as a *Sabbat Prayer* of types, a moment of communion in which you make your goals and desires clear, in hopes that you might increase the chances of obtaining your oneiric goal.

On any night that you will be doing a Free Dreaming technique, or attempting to arise in a full state of lucidity (what we refer to as *Shimmering*), I would suggest sitting up in bed (or standing next to it) before you lie down, wearing your Breaching Talisman, anointing with *Green Oyl* via a feather, and saying something like this aloud:

**"I go to this sleep in the Devil's Name**, (or name of your chief Patron, i.e. *the Fairy King's Name* or *in Antiochia's Name*, etc.) **not to wake till the Good Powers please again. Let the eyes of my soul open wide and behold the strange glories of the Unseen. Let a vision of meeting with *Them* who help and protect me come unto me in the dark places. Let me behold them face-to-face. Powers Unseen, be merciful to me. Be kind to me."**

Anything like this will do. Short, deep, and sincere is the key. If you are doing the Free Dreaming technique, you simply go to sleep in your first and second sleep periods, cultivating openness to your dreams. The Word of Power **SAUWENDEI**—which you should be using regularly anyway, will have helped to develop this capacity in you.

If you will be working to arise in full lucidity/Shimmering on a particular night, again, you perform the advanced **SAUWENDEI** work, and in your second sleep period, you will expect to become lucid. You may use other lucid-dreaming techniques to support this work, but again make certain that they don't overwhelm your mind with complications. If you succeed, you will either find yourself standing or lying in the room that you fell asleep in, or in another landscape.

Your Riding Pole should always be with you. If you arise in lucidity in your own bedroom, it's lying right on your bed. If you appear in another landscape, it should still be with you or nearby, as it is talismanically bound to you. Take it and go to a place where the sky is visible. Put it between your legs and fly away. Such is the nature of lucid dream states that you might be able to levitate or fly through walls or any other obstructions, if you will it so.

When you are aloft (however you get there) in the sky or any other wide-open space, you will have to find your way to the Sabbat-stead or the place of meeting. With good fortune, the Deeper Powers will have provided you with an easy way to get there; there may be guides, or signs you should follow. If not, you will have to call out—aloud—for help in getting there, for guidance. There will almost always be a response. You might also try spinning around very fast, so that the lucid dreamscape blurs, while holding the desire in your mind to be transported to the Sabbat. When you stop spinning, you may find yourself in strange—but deeply desired—company.

Do not take it as some great sign of failure or "breached contract" if your attempts to obtain the vision of the Sabbat here and there fail. There is no spiritual schedule, after all, that the Unseen Powers are working on. When you need to see the vision of the Sabbat, you *will*.

At very unexpected times, you may find yourself in the grip of strange dreams of meeting, even lucid ones, whether or not you prepared for them, expected them, or wanted them. Cultivate a sense of trust in the Unseen in this regard.

Over time all of the practices of Witchcraft will begin to change and transform your dreaming life. This is one of the main ways we know that success in Witchery is coming about or working out in the deeper levels. No one has dramatic visions of Otherworldly helpers all the time. If they did happen frequently, they would lose their power to enthrall us, enchant us, and move our souls into better and deeper states of connection.

## Feeding the Familiars

When a person obtains Witch Dreams and enters into a relationship with a Patron power in the Unseen, deep transformations will occur, no matter how obvious or subtle the transformations may be to the ordinary senses of the *Witched* man or woman. Over time, the changes that have taken root in their souls *will* become more obvious, assuming that some of them didn't begin that way.

There is no way that a book can discuss or encapsulate *all* of the possible changes that might come with being *Witched*. There is truly no way to satisfyingly talk about the endless varieties of relationships that might form between human beings and spirit-beings who will act as empowerers or Familiars. When we discuss the reality of the Sabbat, we are discussing the reality of nourishment—of meeting with one's helpers, Masters, or empowerers, and receiving of them the gift of nourishment, or vitality, or knowledge, or power in some other form. But the Witched man or woman might have a duty to act as a *nourisher* or a giver to their Familiars, too. This may not be the case for all, or then again it *may* be, but the forms of nourishment or power taken from the Witch by their helping spirits may be of a sort that lies outside of the Witch's ordinary perception, such that the Witch doesn't feel like they do anything out of the ordinary for their familiar or familiars.

In *Saducismus Triumphatus*, we are told that Alice Duke "fed her familiar" in the most common manner recorded in Early Modern literature: by allowing the spirit to **suckle directly from her body**. It is written:

*"Besides the plain agreement betwixt the Witnesses, and the Witches own Confession, it may be worth the taking notice here how well her confession of having her Familiar suck her in the shape of a Cat, agrees with Eliz. Style's Confession, that she had seen Alice Dukes Familiar suck her in that shape."*

And:

*"She confesseth that her Familiar doth commonly suck her right Breast about seven at night, in the shape of a little Cat of a dunnish colour, which is as smooth as a Want, and when she is suck't, she is in a kind of a trance."*

It is important to note that Alice Duke's report of being in a *trance* when she engages her familiar to feed it is a critical clue as to what is occurring here, metaphysically. The familiar is a spirit. The visions of the spirit assuming a feline shape and sucking from her right breast to gain nourishment—a direct donation of life force from Duke's body—are happening while she is within an altered state of consciousness.

Not *all* familiars will want to take life-force directly from the bodies of Witches that they aid or empower. And yet, the familiar's presence implies that it does gain benefit, co-created with its human partner, of some sort. When you obtain your Witch Dreams, you may learn who your familiars are to be, and what they may want from you. You *will* have to comply on some level with their requests for payment for their services.

And yet, these "payments" need not be so linear and finite as allowing them to latch on to your own body or soul and take a share of your vitality at times. These offerings given to the familiars can assume countless forms, and that's assuming that they take some form that is within your understanding *or* power to give consciously.

I know for a fact that entering into the sorts of pacts and covenants that you enter into when you obtain Witch Dreams means that your *wandering soul* enters into a new sort of society in the Unseen World. Whether or not your breathing soul and mind realizes it, your deeper soul enters into a new condition of activity at times, in which it may be interacted with, moved about, or even sent on errands for the Great One or Great Ones who empowered it with the power of Witching. It is in these strange night-journeys, or other conditions, that your soul may be used to bring about ends that the *Others* desire—and in those conditions, your soul may be paying familiars their due in ways that the ordinary mind can't comprehend.

If there was *ever* a sort of reality to the Christian hysteria about men and women "selling their souls", it comes back to just this: the soul cannot be "sold" or traded because it is not an object or some bag of goods. It is a *fundamental aspect* of the relational system of life itself. But it **can** enter into new or more extraordinary relationships, and find itself tasked with new responsibilities, a new society, and a new destiny through those things.

If, in the process by which you come to obtain familiars—usually dream meetings with them—you do not also receive instructions about how these familiars wish to be "fed" or repaid by you for their services, understand that they probably *are* getting fed by you or repaid by you somehow, just on another level. If they ask you for something during the formation time in your relationship with them, don't *ever* fail or cease to give it to them, else you may lose the benefits that they bring to you. Also, it is a **very good idea** to assume that your familiars will want offerings from you from time to time. So don't hesitate to go out and make offerings to them on a semi-regular or regular basis. This can *only* increase your connection to them, and by that, your own power.

To sum up—*nourishment* is a critical exchange of power; it binds together Witches with their own Patrons and their familiars. You will receive it in various forms after you are Witched; you *may* be instructed or come to knowledge regarding how you are meant to give it; and if you do not, you can assume that you are *still giving it* in an unknown or preternatural way, and you should *also* choose to make offerings to your Familiars on a regular or semi-regular basis just to be sure.

The best offerings for familiars, aside from nine drops of your own blood (or more) put onto nicely peeled and smoothed twigs of wood, will be strong liquors, eggs, whole cream, aromatic pipe tobacco, wine, whole butter, or meats. You should already be able to figure out how to give these things to Familiars; you can use a Gateway Ring to call upon them—describing them just as you saw them in dream-visions if you don't have names for them revealed to you—and putting these offerings in bowls or on plates or directly on the ground, telling them the vitality in these things is your gift to them, that your relationship with them will be strong and good.

If you don't use a Ring, just wearing your Breaching Talisman and going off to a private spot outdoors will do fine; leave their offerings in small circles of stones or twigs you make to surround the gifts.

# THE DARK GLASS: SCRYING

The complex act of *scrying* into a dark glass mirror, or through the dark and still surface of a vessel filled with water, or by one's gaze fixed steadily into the polished surface of a *shewstone*, is an advanced act of divinatory art. And while the art of scrying through the particular methods mentioned above usually falls more within the purview of historical practitioners of *magic* or divination-specific *seership* than it does the repertoire of Witches, Witchcraft in the past certainly evinced a relationship (across all cultures) with the art of scrying and provoking divinatory visions or awareness through many methods.

*Saducismus Triumphatus* does mention a man—described as a magician or a local mage of some sort—who was able to show another man a vision of his wife (though she was many miles away) in a shewstone or a dark mirror of some sort. Glanvill goes on to defame these arts, reporting his belief that *Witches*, or any others who claim to have revelations or visions through these devices, are being fooled by demons who can (of course) easily deceive the senses of human beings.

The act of scrying in a dark glass mirror-surface, or on the surface of water held in a dark vessel in a dark room, or even into a polished globe of a substance like obsidian must surely concern us here, and must attract our attention most powerfully, because the act of scrying itself has many deep and powerful overlaps with the reality of **dreams** and **dream-visions**. To the extent that dreams and dream-visions are central to the mysterious heart of Witchcraft, the capacity for visionary scrying of the sort we are about to explore is a natural and useful outgrowth of the *Witched* soul's evolving ability to perceive the world of dreams with more clarity, along with the Unseen world as a whole. *Witched* souls who increase their visionary capacity, whether through the works detailed in this book or otherwise, will usually develop an aptitude for scrying in some form or fashion, often without realizing that they have.

We shall begin with a discussion of scrying in the service of pure divination: that is, divination for the purpose of discovering things that are hidden, for discovering the truths about layered situations which are concealed from ordinary understanding or knowledge, discovering the best or wisest courses of action to take through uncertain situations for yourself or for others, and even discovering the *shape of things to come*.

**HESTUVIKET Sigil**

Then we shall transition to an even more radically advanced form of divination, covered in our next and final chapter, which involves spirit contact and communion.

There is a Word of Power that will enable and empower a Witched man or woman to perform potent acts of scrying, so long as these acts are assayed under the specific circumstances described herein. The Word of Power itself does not simply empower devices of scrying; it also does something mysterious to the deep mind and deeper soul of the Witch, allowing the trans-rational contents of the soul to spill forth into visionary revelation through the *mediation* of a scrying device.

That Word of Power is **HESTUVIKET**. It is pronounced as such: *Hess-too-vee-ket*. When spoken aloud in ordinary circumstances, the emphasis falls upon the syllable *vee*; it is spoken *Hess-too-VEE-ket*. When chanted or intoned for use in scrying, that emphasis can be kept, or all syllables can be given equal emphasis, in the act of drawing the word out in a droning chant, if one chooses.

If ever a Witched man or woman should say the word **HESTUVIKET** aloud thirteen times before a mirror or a dark surface—which is to say a dark or black glass surface, or the surface of a quantity of water poured into a dark bowl, cauldron, or container otherwise, or a dark polished stone, and **so long as** that device of scrying is inside of a darkened room lit only by one candle or lamp, or outside under a night sky (still only lit by a single candle or lamp), and **so long as** that device of scrying is placed somehow into a triangle (the triangle can be drawn around it with chalk or charcoal, or created around it with wood, stones, or flour), the mirror or the dark surface will become endowed with the power to mediate the powerful event of visionary scrying.

**Once the Word of Power has been said thirteen times**, the Witch must explain aloud before the scrying device what the subject or topic is that they are presently seekingguidance or divinatory revelation about. Then they must gaze into the darkness of the scrying device's surface at length. This activity will win for the Witch *visions of truthful and accurate guidance, or divinatory revelation*. This powerful act has important dimensions that must be carefully elucidated for success to be assured.

## Analysis and Further Elucidation

Dark surface scrying causes a trance state to set in very quickly. Those new to the practice—even with the support of the powerful word **HESTUVIKET**—may find that it takes in the range of 10 to 15 minutes for the first signs of trance to show themselves. The amount of time required for the trance to manifest *rapidly decreases* if you utilize the Word and attempt this practice on a regular basis.

You must be outside under a night-sky with a single candle or lantern, or in a darkened room—which means that if you work during the day while in a room, nearly all daylight *must* be blotted out from the room, and you will still have the one candle or lantern in the room. This single light source must be placed away from your scrying device—even as far off as the corner of the room if you need—such that it does not directly reflect in the device, or make your surroundings so bright that they reflect in it.

Also, the device must be at some kind of angle which will prevent your dimly-illuminated face from reflecting in the device. If you are using a round *shewstone*, this can seem challenging, but if the light-source is behind you or off to an angle behind you, the *shewstone* will be plenty dark enough for scrying.

You will know when you have the proper light situation, because the dark surface of your scrying device will be very easy to make out, even with the extremely dim lighting, and it might even seem to take on a strange subtle luminosity. But it will also be the deepest black you can imagine—inky black, much more dark than the rest of the environment.

You will have to put the device in a triangle of some sort, as described; I use three straight, sanded-down branches to make my triangle. It is almost required that you be seated when doing this; you should be comfortably seated and able to gaze into the inky blackness of the device.

When you gaze into the deep darkness of the scrying device, imagine that you are looking into a window of some sort, and look *through* the darkness. Look deep within the blackness—this extremely dark space might be conceived of in the imagination as a tiny chasm, abyss, or black hole that passes through the earth and enters directly into the Underworld or the Unseen World.

When you begin you should be wearing your Breaching Talisman and you should announce aloud *"I do this work in the Devil's name"*—or in the name of your Patron or your Empowerer. This is a practice that should have set into your sorcerous routine from the time you gained your Witch Dreams. It *always* helps a work, and in some cases, it might be thought *necessary* to declare that you are working in the Name of the Patron with whom you have pact and covenant. After all, when you sent your request for a pact down into the Underworld through the burying ritual, you asked them to give you the power to *do Witchcraft in their Name.* Try hard not to skip this declaration before any working.

After your declaration, you should relax and then intone the word **HESTUVIKET** thirteen times strongly and clearly in front of the device, leaning to be a bit closer to it, if you must. Some find it difficult to keep track of how many times they've said a word, when they are required to say it so many times. The solution to this is very simple; Put your fists out or in your lap and each time you say the Word, extend one finger out. This will easily keep track of ten of the recitations. Once you've said it ten times, you know you only have three to go.

After satisfying the requirement to say the Word of Power thirteen times, you must speak aloud to the device a brief couple of statements explaining the situation that you wish to gain divinatory revelations or guidance about. You can draw it out, if the situation is complex, but try to make it clear exactly what kind of revelation or guidance you are seeking. Avoid questions seeking a "yes or no" answer; you are looking for visions of what will be, or what was, or what is, or visionary guidance for how you or another should proceed through a difficult situation. Consider this carefully.

Then you simply look into the center of the dark field of your scrying device, and gaze. Look *through* the darkness, as though you are trying to see something deep inside it—but don't strain your eyes in doing this. Focus there in the blackness and do not look away.

It is completely normal for your eyes to wander a bit, focusing in different spots on their own, and things of that nature. Just don't stop looking deep into the darkness. A few minutes of this focus on the deep darkness will begin to cause a trance state to emerge inside you—and you will almost never realize that the state has begun, or that you are tumbling into it faster than you consciously realize. This act of darkness gazing *itself* provokes a trance state.

What actually occurs when you successfully scry is this: you are entering into a **hypnagogic visionary state**, with your eyes wide open. It's the same kind of hypnagogic state that you encounter as you are beginning to fall asleep on any ordinary night, but the special conditions surrounding scrying force this hypnagogic state to occur differently. The dark surface of the scrying device acts as a mediation-space, in which the many hypnagogic visions projected by your mind and soul can seemingly appear *outside of yourself*.

The Word of Power **HESTUVIKET** impacts your mind and soul, forcing the hypnagogic images that appear to be **relevant** to the divinatory request that you made. In short, it blocks many of the somewhat random-seeming images that tumble wildly through the hypnagogic mind ordinarily, and forces more specific or relevant images to emerge and show themselves to your awareness.

As your scrying begins, you may quickly notice "tingling lights" in the darkness of your device, little sparkles or white tracer-like lights. You may see what resemble clusters of little sparks, or pin-points of light. Soon, you may see what look like ghostly, white blur-shapes, which move around the device, vanish into it, re-appear, and look like strange white blobs or jellyfish, even.

Any of these phenomenon can form themselves into shapes—whether geometric shapes, or the clear outlines or ghostly forms of ordinary objects, or animals. They can form into faces, of strangers or of people you know. If you begin to see this, understand that your scrying is beginning to reveal information, albeit at an abstract early stage. It is no less important for this, so take careful note of the things you see, even at this phase.

What will eventually happen is something I call the **Overflow**: the blackness in your device, the zone of dazzling or deep darkness, will seem to overflow out of your device and fill the space around you, making you lose visionary perception of the device, the table you are sitting out, the triangle around the device, and so forth. Then, the wide black field that filled your vision might recede, allowing you to see your device again. Then, it may repeat, overflowing again. This is a very good sign that you have entered into the early middle of trance state, and that it is getting stronger.

At this point you will begin seeing things in your field of vision—whether they appear in the space of the device, in the "overflowing darkness" that takes you at times, or even *inside your own mind*. There is a curious effect that happens in this dark moment, in which it's no longer clear if you're seeing things in your head or in your device. It doesn't matter *where* you are seeing them; what matters is that you *are* seeing them.

Finally, when you reach the apex of your trance, you *may* discover that you begin to experience the phenomenon I call **Deep Blinking**. Without knowing how it happened, you may discover that your eyes have slid closed and you don't remember anything from the last few moments or seconds. You will open your eyes and tilt your head up, for your head will likely have leaned forward somewhat (again, often without you realizing it) and you'll become suddenly a bit more aware.

When this first happens, you may discover that you feel heavy or tired. You may wonder if you're too tired to scry. You are doing fine—you had a *deep blink*, which is part of this *Awake Hypnagogia* that you are experiencing. And while the deep blinks can seem frustrating at first, they are actually a good sign. Because almost without fail, the moment you return to awareness from a deep blink, if you turn your gaze back into your scrying glass you *will* see something very clearly. Sometimes, the only visions I get are visions I spy in the glass *after I've deep blinked*, and generally, the visions gained at moments like that are the most crucial or informative to my divination.

But deep blinking—and this whole process of scrying in this quiet, dark, relaxed space—can make you feel like you're tired, or sinking like lead into the earth. It's not always a comfortable or pleasant feeling, but unless you actually *were* tired before you began, this is the **false tiredness** of the trance. Allow yourself to accept it and continue. Otherwise, *never* scry while tired; you will fall asleep. If your eyes begin "jerking" in your eye sockets, this is another good sign that your trance is working.

If you are scrying using a dark bowl filled nearly to the top with water, you ordinarily can't see the water if you have arranged the lighting and the room just right. But when you are in your deep scrying trance, another thing that might occur is a vision of the water suddenly seeming very *clear*. It suddenly appears that you can somehow tell that there's water, or "see" the shape of the water in the bowl as though the bowl's sides were transparent, and the water seems *vivid* in some manner—and you can see something inside of it. That *something* down in the water is a vision for you.

There is one more phenomenon that can occur when your trance has progressed to its apex or beyond: spirits and other non-ordinarily-physical things can appear in the room with you. They will seem to be as physically present as your scrying device or anything else in the room that you can glimpse in the dim light. This can be extremely disconcerting the first times it happens, but you must stabilize your mind in the face of both the possibility and the occurrence.

I was scrying in a bowl of water in a darkened room once, when I was suddenly shocked by a large spider that came walking by, onto one of the pieces of wood that made the triangle around my bowl. I recoiled in shock and surprise, and even in the dim light I could clearly see the spider's eight legs, the glistening from the distant candle on its shiny black body, and see the way it scurried and scuttled as spiders do. It ran and burrowed under one of the pieces of wood that made up my triangle's sides.

I put the candle near that spot—without taking my eyes off the spot—and lifted up the wood, but the spider was not there. I felt all around my bowl, thinking it had gotten on the bowl, but it wasn't there. I lifted the bowl up and looked at it. There's no way the spider could have scurried off without me seeing it. It was not a physical spider, and yet, it was *real*. In my trance, I had seen it.

But this trance state is quite special—you can be deeply entranced and deeply hypnagogic *without realizing that you are*. It is a form of the *waking dream*, but it is not as advanced as a dream—it is closer to *waking hypnagogia*, and so I have called it thus. Your mind will be able to project tangible-seeming things into the room with you, which will appear to your senses to be as real as anything else. And further, spirits of many sorts will be able to manifest themselves to you and your awareness with maximum ease. This is a topic we will discuss at length in the next chapter.

You should cease scrying after you've obtained anywhere from two to four or five visionary revelations. Once you have seen a sequence of images numbering thus, get up and take a break, or stop scrying for a while. Write down the things you saw, in sequence, and see if you can surmise a message from them. Study the symbolism if you want or if you can, but beware—modern lists of symbols and their meanings are almost always terrible. It's better to let your intuition tell you what a symbol or a visionary article you saw might mean, if you can't obtain a trusted source for the obscure language of symbols.

It should be mentioned that when you Deep Blink, you might have miniature visions or fast, surreal dream-like experiences in your mind. Pay attention to those. Much information can suddenly surge into your consciousness and body through these *micro-hypnagogias*.

If you keep your scrying device in a box, try to paint, burn, carve, or otherwise somehow decorate the box with the **HESTUVIKET** sigil. If you keep a cloth over your device, see if you can embroider or paint that sigil onto the cloth. It adds to the power of this process and to the power of the device when scrying.


## The Dark Vision, Dreams, and the Dead

There is a powerful overlap between the act of scrying and the reality of dreaming. The range of consciousness or the trance-condition in which scrying occurs overlaps in some quite mysterious way with both hypnagogia and dreams.

Thus, if you have developed your dream clarity and insight with the regular practice of **SAUWENDEI**, you will have developed your power to scry, too. Just so, if you practice scrying a good bit, and develop your power to be aware in the strange, dark states that it required, you will increase your power to be more aware of dreams. There is a synergistic effect here, binding these things together. And that means that scrying is a pathway to the most sublime attainment of all, just as gaining more awareness in dreams is; both scrying and the **SAUEWENDEI** work increase what I call *The Dark Vision*.

"The Dark Vision" is just a poetic reference to being able to extend awareness into more subtle spaces or situations than ordinary eyes or non-Witched people can see. It refers to **extraordinary sight**, the kind of sight that unveils the presence of spirits, and allows one to begin feeling that they have altered their very entity, their own soul, in some profound or more ineffable sort of way.

And that's what this all comes back to: the alteration of the Soul, from a thing of lower power, awareness, and insight, into a living convergence of much *deeper* power, awareness, and insight. Meaningful dreams will occur to you more often. You will remember your dreams more. Lucid dreams will occur seemingly unbidden. At some point, even dreams of *foresight* may occur, and while those occur at times even to non-Witched people, the way the *Witched* soul encounters them and receives them is of a different character, from a different origin.

The walls between the worlds seen and unseen will seem thinner for a Witch who has developed The Dark Vision. It's subtle; it's hard to rationally explain. They will feel different within themselves, and the world around them will feel different, too. Things may seem *darker* and *slower* on some very slight or subtle level, and deeper connections between things may become more apparent.

Earlier in this book, I mentioned the relationship between sleep and death. I quoted Percy Shelley's beautiful line about the dead of this world being in "cradles of eternity, lulled to their portioned sleep." I also said that **to change one's relationship to dreams was to change one's relationship to death**. I must expand a bit more on this, for it is a critical point glimmering within the heart of all of the metaphysics of Witchcraft.

Developing The Dark Vision means that you have altered your relationship to sleep and dream. Whether through mastery of scrying, or the powerful **SAUWENDEI** work (or hopefully both), your mind and soul becomes used to being active and conscious in special ways when all is dark, when the breath-soul is paralyzed or gone, and when a deeper world or reality is emerging for you.

This very attainment—being in possession of a mind and soul which is used to operating in such conditions—means that death will lose some of its power to "lull you" into the deepest states of death-sleep, when it finally occurs. Death's poetic sleep is (as stated before) a profound sort of trance all its own, but the minds of ordinary people are often totally unaware of what's happening to them while they are slumbering in it.

When death's equivalent of dreams finally does dawn for those souls, they may or may not comprehend them, or recognize them, or realize what is happening. This is not true for the *Witched* Soul that has become practiced in the darkness and in the dream. The Witch, in death, has a special grasp of subtle conscious states that can allow them to somehow **maintain their awareness-continuity and activity** in certain mysterious ways that do not apply to most of the dead of this world. While all lie "asleep" in dreamless sleep of death, the Witch may be lucid. While all face death's visions, often without comprehending them, the Witch may recognize them.

This is an inescapable benefit, or at least a highly likely transformation, that will unfold within all whose path through the Witching Way includes the regular use of the **SAUWENDEI** work, or regular scrying, or visionary state attainments of any sort. Even some non-witches who practice various esoteric strains of meditation or lucid-dream development can forge a soul within themselves that will encounter death in a different, perhaps more aware shape.

Throughout Early Modern history (and even long before it) folklore and beliefs across Europe and much of the rest of the world included an idea that Witches needed to be *killed* in special ways, and have their bodies *disposed* of in particular ways, to stop them from returning from the grave to wreak havoc on a community, or to prevent them from continuing on after their deaths as a dangerous and vengeful spirit..

Obviously, the executed Witch would never be placed in a churchyard or any 'holy' ground, where the community of the Christian faithful all lay in wait for the Last Day; the Witch, like the suicide or the unrepentant sinner, was excluded from burial in such a place.

The Witch, like others of the *cursed dead*, would be buried instead at a crossroads, or some lonely and unmarked plot of ground elsewhere. But unlike the others, the Witch's remains needed *special* attention: in some places they had to be buried face-down, if they were buried at all; often their bodies had to be burned. If buried whole, they might have their heads removed; they may have a spike or stake driven through their hearts or chests to "fix" them into the earth. When the remains of the Witch were burned, other charms might have to be brought to bear: a *basket of live cats* might be burned over the witch.

Why all this fear? Whence comes the ages-old belief that Witches might still be dangerous even after death *and* burning or dismemberment?

The answer has already been given. Witches didn't *live* like others; they didn't belong to *quite* the same society as others (they treated with the forbidden society of spirits while alive); and they didn't *die* like others. In death, the Witch might *still* be awake and aware. They might still be capable of doing their Witchcraft, even from beyond the grave. As a dark and wrathful spirit, the Witch would be more terrifying, further beyond the ordinary reach of humankind's understanding or justice, and flush with a spirit's supernatural abilities and powers of perception.

*The Dark Vision* is **more** than just expanded awareness into the subtle world of spirits or dreams; after it becomes strong enough, it becomes a kind of partial immortality or a preternatural resistance to death itself.

We mustn't deceive ourselves; death is hardly the kind of cosmological power that can be resisted in some *absolute* kind of way. But below the ancient legacy of Witchcraft there lies a hint, a rumor, a *reality* that a man or woman, if they are cunning or devious enough or empowered enough by their helpers, their Patrons, and their special deeds, *need not die* in the traditional sense of the word, or in the ordinary way.

The burial of Icelandic and Norwegian practitioners of *Stave Magic* with their books and implements of magical art is good evidence that at least *someone* in their societies believed they'd need those things, as their magical work continued in their post-mortem condition. The burial of magical wands, staffs, and bags of sorcerous implements alongside dead *Volvas* or Shamans from much earlier times suggests the same belief.

It's an ages-old belief that those who get proficient in the Strange Arts will somehow alter their destiny beyond the grave into a destiny distinctive from that of others. When the *Strange Arts* finally became the truly *Despised Arts*, that ancient idea carried with it a deep spiritual menace and threat for the frightened people of Christian Europe, at an often unconscious or atavistic level.

Image detail from *De lamiis et pythonicis mulieribus*, 1489

# THE DARK GLASS: SPIRIT AUDIENCE

Now we shall proceed from the act of scrying for the purposes of divination to the act of scrying as a vehicle for communication with spirits, or *spirit-audience*, and even the legendary feat of **necromancy**, or the conjuring of the dead that they might be consulted and experienced across the dark wall separating life from death, in the ordinary meaning of those words.

These kinds of operations are more advanced than the divinatory scrying we discussed in the previous chapter, but many of the principles remain the same, particularly with regard to what you will physically and mentally experience when you sit before your scrying device in a sufficiently dark space. These are certainly the most advanced operations detailed in this book, and only suited for those who have gained the Witch Dreams and good empowerment from the Unseen world.

Earlier in this work, I mentioned the realities of **psychism** and **mediumship**—the fact that psychics and mediums *do* exist in our world. While there is no metaphysical direct connection between the actual phenomena of psychism, mediumship, and Witchcraft in the historical sense, any man or woman who can reliably manifest psychism or have mediumistic visions of the dead or spirits is clearly in possession of a capacity of mind or soul that is not common. What that capacity might be, or guesses as to its origins or what it might *mean* in some cosmological sense, is far beyond the scope of this work. I can say that those with psychic potential who become *Witched* will have great advantages with it comes to scrying, just as those with mediumistic potential will have advantages when it comes to scrying in an effort to perceive and communicate with spirits or the dead very directly.

Psychics and mediums of any strength or development don't have any need to become *Witched* to have these kinds of visions or experiences. If all they wish to do is speak to the dead, or to ghosts or other spirits, or practice developing clairvoyant abilities or suchlike, their natural inborn capacities should be enough. No need to pact away their souls for such things! Of course, entering into pact and becoming *Witched* could lead to a dramatic increase in such odd abilities, so I guess some modern psychics or mediums might find this prospect tempting in a way that the psychics or mediums of our past seldom would have. Most people with psychic or mediumistic abilities in the past would have looked upon Witch-pacts and Witchcraft with the same cultural or metaphysical dread as anyone else.

'The Dark Vision' developed by men and women who become *Witched* is not psychism, but it can resemble it in many ways. It might be considered a form of **sorcerously-provoked psychism**, a kind of special development of awareness that is ultimately caused by spirit-helpers, familiars, and deeper forces in the Unseen with whom the Witch creates and maintains potent connections. This has led, in the past, to a certain kind of confusion between the Witch and the people who *naturally expressed* different degrees of extraordinary mental or spiritual sensitivity. It has also led the people naturally expressing those odd ranges of mental or spiritual sensitivity to come under suspicion of evil society, or to end their days swinging from a rope in very rare and tragic circumstances.

Witchcraft begins in visionary states and special dreams imparted by spirits, and it unfolds steadily from that point. It is *certain* that nearly all Witches will go on to encounter and communicate with spirits, often including the spirits of formerly living humans. Here, the special occult awareness developing in the Witch starts to overlap with the special awareness of the medium—but again, they are *not* the same thing.

The *Witched* soul is **endowed** by powerful spirits with whatever it needs to receive visions from the Unseen world in a conscious manner; the medium is **born** with some metaphysical capacity that renders similar feats possible. Whatever mysterious thing makes this possible in the Witch may not be the same mysterious thing that makes this possible in the medium. The nature of their visionary experiences can be radically different. The *context* is certainly very different.

Since psychics and mediums in the past could find themselves mistrusted or even shunned by communities, it makes sense to imagine them being prone to seeking Witchcraft in the sense of seeking allegiance with the *Shunned Powers*, or even (more commonly) falling into a simulacrum of Witchcraft—of being considered Witches by people who didn't know any better. But it's just as likely that Witches in the past sought *them* out, wanting to see them *Witched* or allied otherwise due to their natural psychism or mediumistic abilities, which any Witch would know can be quite advantageous to gaining extraordinary insight or power.

One way or the other, in regard to the arts of scrying, and particularly feats of scrying for the purposes of direct communication with spirits or with the dead, psychics and mediums who manage to gain *Witching* will have enormous advantages. But all who become *Witched* will have access to this spectral window into the Unseen.

* * *

Using Witchcraft for gaining Spirit Audience—whether with spirits in the ordinary sense of the word, or with the wandering souls of formerly living men, women, children, or beasts—can be accomplished in many ways. Here, we will focus on a method utilizing scrying devices, the very **same** devices mentioned in the previous chapter. But this operation is aided by and made much more powerful through the use of a Word of Power.

Unlike the other four Words of Power this book has detailed, this one will take some extra explaining, and will require certain extra efforts on the parts of those who use it. It helps to render incredible things possible; it unseals very rare and powerful spaces of mind and soul.

The Word of Power that renders Spirit Audience through scrying possible is **ABARITUM**. It is pronounced *ah-bah-REE-toom*, with the emphasis, when ordinarily spoken, being placed on the "ree" as indicated. When used in acts of scrying it can be spoken forcefully in just that way, or the emphasis can be spread out equally to all syllables, for the purposes of chanting if a person prefers.

If ever a Witched man or woman should say the Word **ABARITUM** aloud thirteen times before a dark glass scrying mirror, before a shewstone, or before a dark bowl or container filled with water, while in a darkened room lit only by a single candle or lamp, or outside below the night sky (again lit only by a single candle or lamp), **and** if that device of scrying is surrounded by a triangle created from earth, or drawn around the device directly onto the earth, **and** if the device and this triangle has a bowl of water to its left, and a piece of quartz crystal to its right, the person who said the word thirteen times will be granted the attention of

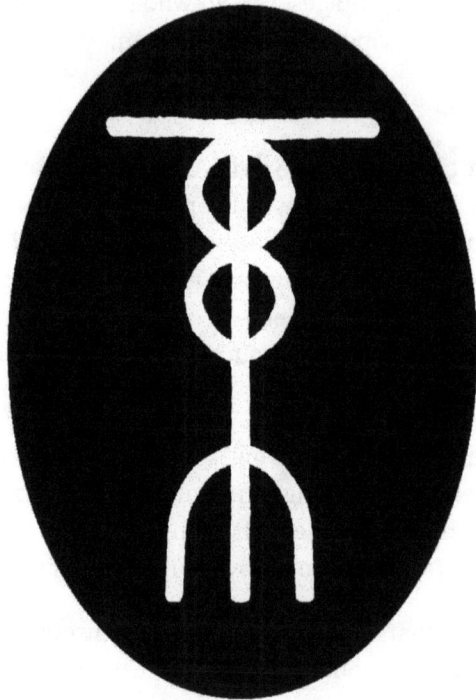

**ABARITUM Sigil**

a spirit or spirits, and granted visions of that spirit or spirits, *if* they call their name or names three times aloud after saying the Word thirteen times.

This is the basic form of the operation, but there is much more to be understood through a detailed analysis, which we will proceed to now.

## Analysis and Further Elucidation

Before giving specific instructions that will lead to ritual clarity, it would be prudent to mention now that Witches who will be focusing much effort on the art of scrying—of any sort—should create their own scrying mirrors. Scrying is a powerful thing to do, with regards to developing The Dark Vision. It aids in dream clarity development just as much as dream clarity development aids in scrying. It is a never-ending source of insight and wonder, though it can be a strain on the ordinary human social mind if it is done at a bad rhythm or with too much obsession.

Making one's own scrying mirrors is very simple, and creates a device that is connected to you at a deeper level. Obtain flat, round, and clear pieces of glass with ground or polished edges—and they are easily available in many places. Glass that is eight inches in diameter is an excellent and manageable size; I don't suggest making a scrying mirror larger than twelve inches in diameter, though a twelve inch mirror is quite workable as well. Of course oval or square glass can be used, but round is best.

Obtain the glass, and cover one side of it completely with three or four coats of flat black paint. Spray paint makes this task very easy. Once the paint dries, you have a dark glass scrying mirror. If you will make two—one specifically for divinatory scrying, and one for spirit-audience scrying, you can paint the **HESTUVIKET** and **ABARITUM** sigils onto the backs of the respective mirrors, with white or red paint. This will make the mirrors more powerful. Keep your mirror or mirrors safely in a box or wrapped in a cloth that is used only for them—and as before, if you can embroider the proper sigil onto the cloth, do it.

There is naturally nothing at all wrong with using or preferring to use a *shewstone*, which is a polished black round globe of obsidian or rock crystal; just so, there's nothing wrong with scrying in a dark surface of water that has been poured into a dark bowl or cauldron. Some of my most powerful feats of scrying were done in a bowl of water. But the glass to make scrying mirrors is very easy to obtain and inexpensive, and so is black paint. And few things are as satisfying as the wide and perfect ebony black surface of a well-appointed *shewglass* or scrying mirror coming to life with visions and revelations from the Unseen.

As we proceed into these scrying instructions, I wish to mention the importance of what I lightly call "The Trinity of Preparation"—the three things you can do, and *should* do if you can, before every working of Witchcraft.

The Trinity of Preparation isn't just about gaining Spirit Audience through the act of scrying. There's no working of Witchcraft so small or minor that it shouldn't follow the Trinity I'm about to mention. If at all possible, before you do any sort of Working, **put on your Breaching Talisman** and keep it on throughout the working; **declare that you are doing this work in the Devil's name** (or the name/title of your Patron-empowerer as you know it), and **anoint your forehead with *Green Oyl*,** saying the Word of Power **ABANHOU** as you do. Remember, anointing with the Green Oyl makes your body and soul stronger in many metaphysical ways, and endows not only a form of occult *protection*, but makes spirits better-inclined towards you. It helps in every way in any kind of working.

The only time you use a feather to anoint your head with *Green Oyl* is when you are about to ride your Riding Pole to a Symbolic Sabbat, or when you are attempting to gain the dreams  that will allow you to experience a Spectral Sabbat. *Any* other time, you use your finger to anoint your forehead with the Oyl, or to anoint other people or objects with it.

This is the Trinity of Preparation; there's never a time you should fail to do it, insofar as you are able. This goes for *every* work mentioned, described, or suggested in the Workings section of this book.

✳ ✳ ✳

When you are preparing to utilize the Word **ABARITUM** to create an audience with a spirit or spirits, the area of your working has to be set up a certain way. Your device of scrying, if it will be on a table, a floor, or a place such as this indoors, has to be surrounded by a **triangle of earth**. This is very easy to accomplish. Take three straight sticks, poles, rods, or even very straight branches, and make a triangle with them (ideally with sides that are as equal as possible) wherever you will be working. Then take a jar of earth and gently pour the earth along the inside edges of this triangle of wood. Then remove the three pieces of wood, and what will be left behind is a beautiful triangle of earth. The size of your scrying device will determine how long these three guide-sticks will have to be, and thus how large the resulting triangle will be.

To the left of that triangle put a bowl of water; to the right of it put a piece of quartz crystal. The crystal here represents a *fire*—a petrified flame. But this kind of crystal has, since the Neolithic era of Old Europe, been connected to graves, the places of the dead, and communication or transition between Seen and Unseen; it brings a certain influence to this work that makes it easier for spirits to assert themselves visually and in other ways.

If you are working outdoors under a night sky, you can just get a sharp stick or blade and draw a triangle in the earth around your scrying device, assuming it's sitting on the earth. If you have a table outside, or a large stump or something, you'll have to make the triangle of earth as described above.

Once you have done this, you're ready to light the single candle that will illuminate this working, and position as described in the last chapter, such that its light does not directly strike the surface of your device, and so forth. Make yourself ready (do the *Trinity of Preparation*) and then relax and begin.


### Conjuring Named Spirits:

Say the word **ABARITUM** 13 times directly into the dark surface of your scrying device. Then, say the name of the spirit that you'll be calling up **three times** into the dark surface. *Then* say something like this:

**"Come forth and grant me thy audience. Treat with me, Good Spirit; appear to me, who wishes only good on you and your kind."**

Then begin your scrying session. Know that the Word of Power **ABARITUM** assures that the spirit you call will **not** be harmed or hindered in their conjuring by its power. The spirit, not being harmed by the power of the word, will give you its attentions and appear to you without rancor, malice, or spite.

The spirit will not harm the person who has spoke aloud the word **ABARITUM** thirteen times, nor will they harm anyone that person loves. Nor shall they harm anyone else who is present, if those persons wear around their necks a cord knotted with nine knots. The spirit so conjured will be inclined to communicate with *and* help the person who has said the Word thirteen times, or to offer that person truthful guidance on any subject. So feel free to speak aloud to a spirit who has manifested, and prepare for any responses they make to you to come in the form of more images appearing in your scrying device or vision; actual sounds you hear outside of yourself or inside your own mind; or—sometimes—in *dreams* that you may have if you sleep soon after your scrying session is over.

This spirit audience **ends** when the person who said the word thirteen times speaks aloud the word **ASHOONA**, pronounced *uh-SHOO-nuh*). The spirit will then depart without rancor or malice. This word *must* be said at the end of each scrying session of this type.

After the word **ASHOONA** is said, the person who said the Word **ABARITUM** thirteen times **must pay** the spirit who gave the word **ABARITUM** to the world. From the time the word **ASHOONA** is said aloud, that person has exactly **one hour** to give an offering of **nineteen drops of fresh shed blood**. If that person fails to give this offering within the allotted hour, this Word of Power will *never* work for that person again.

To give the offering, all one needs is a smoothed-off twig or stick, and a lancet or needle. Prick a finger, and squeeze out 19 drops of blood, one at a time, putting them along the length of the stick. It doesn't usually take that many pricks from the needle or lancet to get out 19 drops. When they are on the stick or wood, place it right next to the triangle of earth and say:

**"This is given to the Powerful One who Imparted the Word."**

This **has** to be said—that sentence exactly. Again, if the person who said the word **ABARITUM** thirteen times fails to do this within one hour of saying **ASHOONA**, the word will never work for them again. So make the offering as soon as you finish.

The Wise and Powerful spirit who gave me the word **ABARITUM** would not give it unless I agreed to this condition. It was willing to impart this word only on the weight of knowing that it would be receiving offerings of fresh, vitality-filled blood from many people around the world who would engage in these workings empowered by **ABARITUM**.

Somehow, in some way that I do not understand, the spirit who imparted it to me *also* plays a role in making it have the effectiveness it has, so this spirit can eliminate that effectiveness for certain people, too, or refuse to help if it chooses. The recitation of the word thirteen times by someone wearing a Breaching Talisman (or being in a Gateway Ring, or what have you) *clearly* attracts the attention of this spirit. The spirit is **not** dangerous, and it is providing an invaluable service for which it deserves a rich reward. This spirit is, in a sense, a kind of mercenary scrying familiar for anyone who uses the Word. And though I have no way of knowing this, *Abaritum* might even be the spirit's name.

If for some reason the scrying session empowered by **ABARITUM** fails, or does not work at all, the person who said **ABARITUM** thirteen times does *not* have to pay the nineteen blood-drop toll. But one had better be certain that the failing came from the "other side", and not some human foible or ordinary world stress or nonsense. It's probably wiser and better to just pay the toll each time the word is used, to assure that you'll be able to use it again in the future.

What I have just described are the basic dimensions of scrying via **ABARITUM**, and particularly if you are trying to conjure a spirit whose name you know. If you have both the spirit's name, and a sigil for the spirit, your task becomes easier or more powerful; have a copy of the spirit's sigil somewhere near your scrying device, usually to the right of it, or you might place your scrying device on top of a small round or square parchment bearing the sigil.

Earlier in this book, I gave the names and sigils of eleven real and powerful spirits—the **Seven Fairy Sisters** and the **Four Serving Men**

**of Oberion**. If you managed to get dreams of them asking in the method I suggested, you can then attempt to use this working to conjure them and treat with them for various purposes. But they are addressed in special ways; at the point in this working when you call the name of one of the Seven Fairy Sisters three times, you then say:

**"You Good Lady who serves the Queen of the Little People Below, Mighty Tytam, in the name of your Queen, grant me an audience with thee. Come and treat with me, who desires the good pleasure of your company."**

These things have to be said—Tytam's name (or some form of the Fairy Queen/Good Lady of Elfhame's name) has to be said, and the Sister has to be asked to come *In the Name of Her Queen*. You can be more elaborate in this request if you like, so long as those things are said.

If you say the name of one of the Four Serving Men three times, you should then say:

**"You strong and noble counselor to the great King Oberion, come forth in His Name and grant to me an audience. Come and treat with me, who wishes only good on you and your kind."**

In this case, you *must* use the name **Oberion**. It doesn't matter what you personally call the Fairy King, or the Devil, or whatever power you conceptualize as being the ruler of the fair and dark dimension below. In this particular invocation of these spirits, Oberion has to be mentioned.

### Conjuring Spirits When Names are not Known:

If you do not have or know the name of a spirit or a group of spirits, so long as you can with **precision** describe the dwellings or expressions of that spirit or spirits, you can conjure them with this methodology. You do not have to make this precise description three times; you only have to say it once. Thus, if you wish to conjure the spirit of an oak tree that you visited earlier that day, and placed your hand upon, then that's all you have to say. And so, you'd say:

**"Come, spirit of the great oak tree that I visited earlier today, and placed my hand upon. Come forth and grant to me an audience.**

**Treat with me, Good Spirit. Appear to me, who wishes only good on you and your kind."**

The same is true for any spirit or group of spirits whose dwellings or expressions you can precisely describe, such as "Spirit of the deer I saw in the woods today", or "Spirits of the woodland grove I walked through today" or "Spirits of the pond I placed my hands in today."

If you are present at the location where spirits indwell, it's even easier. You'd say "Come, spirits of the pond before me..." or "Come, spirit of this mighty tree before me..." or what have you. If you can describe a place a spirit dwells, that will do; "Come, spirit of the ancient tree that sits atop the hill behind this house..."

### Conjuring the Wandering Souls of the Dead:

Here we reach the acts of Necromancy via scrying. You can attempt to conjure the *known dead*, the dead whose names you know, or the *unknown dead*—but to conjure the unknown dead, you must be in possession of some piece or part of their earthly bodily remains, or in possession of some object they owned in their breathing life, and better it be if the object was something they likely cherished.

If you know the dead man, woman, or child's name, you have all you need—though it would be much more powerful to address them along with the name of the woman that made their breathing life possible. Thus, if you were attempting to conjure the spirit of John Amos, and you happen to know that his biological mother's name was Anne Smith, you would conjure him like this, after saying **ABARITUM** thirteen times, of course:

**"John Amos, who was once given a breathing life by Anne Smith; John Amos, who was once given a breathing life by Anne Smith; John Amos, who was once given a breathing life by Anne Smith; come, honored guest, from the place of the dead. Come forth and grant me an audience; come and treat with me in the name of the King of Spirits and his Queen."**

Notice that "John Amos, who was once given a breathing life by Anne Smith" was said three times. The known dead are *always* called three times. If you do not know the name of the woman that granted them the breathing life that they once had, you can try to conjure them simply by their names, but again, three times.

Sometimes, when names are too general—both for the named dead and their biological mothers—you may have to increase the power of the call by adding elements to your working space that leave no doubts as to who you are calling. Having a picture of the named dead alongside your scrying device is the best way to accomplish this; having a piece of their mortal remains inside the triangle of earth is also powerful—perhaps the most powerful thing you can do. In lieu of a piece of their bodily remains, a personal possession of theirs placed inside the triangle of earth will be mightily powerful.

You can change the wording of your call such that the call can **only be to them**—by saying something like **"John Amos, who perished in the town of Franklin on the first of June in the year 1967..."** This is often a good tactic when other ways of being very specific are not forthcoming.

When it comes to the unknown dead, you must have a piece of their earthly remains, or some object that they owned and hopefully cherished. That piece of their remains or that object has to be placed inside the earth triangle, and you have to say three times:

**"Come, honored guest, from the place of the dead."**

Then say, once:

**"Come forth and grant me an audience; come and treat with me in the name of the King of Spirits and his Queen."**

This will attract the wandering soul of the man, woman, or child (or even a beast, if it is part of a non-human creature's earthly remains) who once lived in connection to that portion of earthly remains, or who once owned that object.

Please note the phrase **"Come, honored guest, from the place of the dead"** *must* be used, as a condition for **ABARITUM** workings to conjure the dead.

Some have wondered what would happen if a person tried to conjure the wandering soul of a dead person who was no longer in the "place of the dead." It is believed by many that while some of the dead may indeed *sleep* in the strange dream or trance of death for what we would call ages upon ages, others of the dead may pursue different destines. What if some of the dead are no longer in that condition, but moved on to others? What if they have obtained breath souls and live again, but as different people now, or even non-human creatures?

The answers here are very simple. If a dead person is somehow beyond the reach of necromancy, then they simply won't show up to your attempt to conjure them. If they have undergone some transformation in the Unseen that has led them to a powerful range of new experiences or embodiment in some other condition of existence, it is possible that their spirits or wandering souls in those conditions can still be called to your necromantic working. And if they have obtained a new breath soul and now live again as a breathing human being or some other creature in our ordinary world, then your necromantic work will *still* potentially conjure their wandering soul/separable soul to presence.

A living person or being somewhere else on earth—who themselves may never consciously become aware of this—will have their separable soul drawn to your working. When they appear, they may not be who or what you expect. And from their side, the most that might occur is an experience of some strange dreams (or nightmares) of odd people calling them and then trying to talk to them, or dreams of dark rooms with weird people in them.

✶ ✶ ✶

These are the methods of using **ABARITUM**. When you actually begin scrying after making these calls according to their various particularities, the scrying experience is very much the same as described in the previous chapter—though when the desired results begin to emerge, you will see that they can be quite distinctive.

During my first uses of the word **ABARITUM**, I conjured **the spirits of the forest that lies just outside of the walls of this house**—the very same spirits who I reported befriending and seeing in dreams

217

in an earlier chapter. I will never forget the experiences I had with them through this method of spirit-contact; I will share them on the off chance that others may have similar experiences, and will appreciate the information.

When I conjured them via **ABARITUM** into my scrying device—which was then a bowl of water—I felt that the scrying session began as a normal divinatory session would, but when I reached the point where I began to notice the darkness **overflow** effect (described in the previous chapter), the overflowing darkness did not behave as it normally did. The darkness surged out of my scrying device, but didn't just blot out my whole sight; it seemed to "snake" around like a living column of dark smoke, and dance around under my face. I thought this was strange, and perhaps even a touch distracting, but I kept my firm-yet-gentle focus on the darkness of the device and kept scrying.

Fifteen or so minutes in, that "snaking darkness" from the overflow had performed many fine stunts, but I was still trying to focus on the larger experience of scrying—and I was beginning to see many of the expected pin-points of light and strange clusters of sparkles in the darkness. Then I noticed something I had never seen before—some of the clusters of pin-points of light, and some of the clouds in the darkness of my scrying device were not white light as they usually are; one particular group of clouds or cluster of lights had turned a rich brown-orange color, which was very surprisingly vibrant.

I noticed this oddity with pleasure, because I had never seen *color* before in my scrying sessions, at this stage. And it was a very stand-out cloud of sparkling brown/orange. And then it moved upwards, and from the perceptual "top" of it, a *face*, a non-human face of such intense beauty and detail, unfolded before my sight. Soon, others did too.

I was shocked and of course thrilled with deep pleasure that this working was *working* so well. But you have to take care in situations like this —getting too emotionally stirred up can sometimes break the subtle fabric of your trance. Still, by the time this session was over, my eyes watered with emotion, and my lips were curving in a very excited smile. This is only a small part of the tremendous joy that *Witching* can sometimes contain.

## Conjuring Familiars

Though I have endeavored to keep a light touch on the topic of Familiars, choosing instead to allow each man or woman's dream-experiences of them govern how they understand the identity and roles of familiars in their own lives, there are some who will not gain detailed dreams of familiars up-front at the time of their Witch Dreams. Even the following dreams that come, usually soon after the initial Witch Dream, might not feature strong revelations or appearances of Familiars.

As I said before, you *asked* for Familiars in your pact, and so if you gained Witch Dreams, you *received* Familiars. If you have not seen them or come to know them very directly, they have likely been spectrally aiding you all this time, sight largely unseen. They are also likely collecting a toll or tithe of some sort from you, or reaping some benefit from you, which is outside of your awareness.

Speaking from my own dream-visions, Familiars did come and I was aware of who and even what they were. And I do maintain my own kinds of offerings to them. But this won't be the case for everyone, and indeed, so long as your Witchcraft is progressing or working nicely, it's not a very big deal.

And yet, I am aware that some people will crave to know Familiars granted to them on a deeper level, and so I will mention certain ways one can gain insight into such a thing, if the insight is taking its time coming the more natural way, in dreams and visions.

The best method for gaining visits from Familiars bound to you is not using this scrying method to gain a Spirit Audience with them. It's actually in incubating dream-meeting with them—a process I described in the chapter on Transvection. Perform, as described there, acts of *divinatory dream incubation*, all aimed at getting your Familiars to appear to you. That will usually do the trick nicely. I would only try to conjure a Familiar or Familiars into a Spirit Audience after trying without satisfying success quite a few times at getting a dream.

Since you won't know the names of these Familiars, you will treat them as spirits whose names are not known. So, you will have to describe them with precision:

**"Come, you spirit or you spirits who were made Familiar to me by the power of the Witch Dreams I gained."**

That's about as specific as you can be, as in all of human history, only you have had dreams in precisely that shape. Please fight the urge to be too obsessed over this matter; it can drive people a little over the edge.

### A Final Word: Broken Pacts and the Sale of Souls

If you ever fail to give to your Otherworldly Patron what you **promised** you would give when you made your pact, you are in critical danger of losing your ability to perform Witching feats. In most cases, the broken pact will simply fall by the wayside, and whatever *Witching* was imparted to your soul will unravel and be withdrawn. If your relationship with the Patron and the familiars that came to you was developed over many years, and your own Witched soul gained much strength over that time, you *may* be able to apologize and make twice the offering to repair the situation—but if you make that mistake again, I don't imagine it will matter how great things were before; I fear the *Witching* will flee you.

Humans have a tendency to be sentimental about these things, particularly regarding relationships that have gotten close and deep, but I don't believe that the Unseen World of other-than-human powers is as sentimental as we are. In the Deeper World, there is a sense of power and debt, of exchange and reciprocity that is developed beyond what humans ordinarily realize or can imagine. And the powerful beings there don't operate within our mental and socially-conditioned boundaries of propriety or morality, either. This is not to say they are all the spirit equivalent of sociopaths, nor unfair, nor uncaring; this situation isn't a simple "either/or" dichotomy. It's just that things in the Deep are very strange, alien in ways to most people, and beyond our power to predict easily according to a simple set of rules.

Thus, if you are preparing to give a yearly or bi-yearly offering that you promised to give in your pact, and suddenly you get into a car accident and end up in the hospital for weeks (quite unable to give your promised offering), you may be thoroughly out of luck. And there is no more comfort I can offer; it seems unfair, but life isn't always fair. We can *hope* that the Great Powers will keep your human hide safe *especially* around the times you're about to make a great offering, because they *will* want your offering—but Fate is inexorable and strange. Dark things can happen to anyone, even Witches of great power. My best advice is to never break your promises to *Them* in the Unseen, and try to be careful out there.

Some people, imagining themselves quite clever, feel *safe* thinking that they can intentionally break their pacts and "escape" from the *Witched* life at any time. After a few years of living the hell-raising and exciting life of a Witch, some imagine that they'll just toss their pacts, get right with Jesus, and try to get into heaven or something of that nature.

Sadly for them, it might not be quite that simple. If your pact has been maintained for quite a long while and your soul *Witched* and transformed greatly over time, just breaking a pact might not save you from anything. Some relationships, when formed and pursued for a long time, have a way of impacting us profoundly. They can change us *so much* that we cannot return—in any meaningful way—to who or what we were before.

Thus, if a Witch man or woman has lived a goodly while in the dark grace of their Masters or Patrons, and the company of the Unseen, and their souls have developed The Dark Vision, and they have been altered into a *Witched* shape that anyone would struggle to explain, the loss of their pact will **not** alter the destiny that has been set into motion by all of these powerful changes and transformations. Even if they lose all or some of their power for Witching, the soul-level transformations are **not reversible** in their lifetime, or perhaps not in *many* lifetimes, if such a thing is possible.

This means that their original promise of allegiance *in this life and in the life to come* is still very much in force, even without the pact still being present. As confident as I am that a truly *Witched* soul, so deeply transformed by the regular company of spirits, will never fall into the rancid fear and weakness that would lead a person to seek shelter in the comforting lies of the human social world and its transparently manufactured religions, I must still admit that our world *does* produce some real messes of human beings, and one never can tell just how deep fear might bite.

This brings us to the deep cultural dread that our Western Christian society still maintains around the idea of "selling one's soul" to the Devil. This old folkloric saw, which is so deeply tied into the folklore and myth of Witchcraft, acts as both an **empowering dread** in our culture, filling the "pact with the devil" with its own great excitement and numina, as well as a form of **hindering dread**, when it leads weaker people to *fail* in the face of what they promised the Unseen World, or make attempts to evade their commitments made to the *Others*.

At this fairly nice point in my life, the idea that anyone could be terrified of the reality of making "deals" with powerful spirits (or even pledging soul-allegiance to them) is hard to imagine. As I said in an earlier chapter, souls cannot be "sold"; they are not sacks of potatoes or nice pieces of jewelry. They are not objects of trade or barter. They are powerful metaphysical constituents of this living cosmos, timeless in some ways, and as natural to the universe as stars, rivers, rain, or meadows full of flowers.

All we can do is enter our souls into relationships with different powers, and then undergo the transformations that these relationships will bring. And those strange transformations will of course impact our destinies—but this potent arrangement that the Witch brings about, while it *is* different in its context and tangible expressions, is not so metaphysically different from what **everyone is doing** when they create any kind of relationship at all in their breathing human lives.

The Witch enters into relationships with extraordinary persons and powers, or spirits in what we call the **Unseen World**; these relationships alter the destiny of the Witch. They transform what is going to come after, both in the breathing life of the Witch and after their breathing comes to an end. The Witch is *bound* to this extraordinary community of beings that they pledged themselves to. And this extraordinary company will influence their future, even beyond the grave.

But the ordinary person enters into relationships with only ordinary other persons or beings, all in what we'll call the **World that is Seen**. These relationships alter the destiny of the ordinary person; they transform how the person's life goes, and they influence what will come *after*. The ordinary person is *bound* to this ordinary community of beings that they pledge themselves to every day of their lives, and this ordinary company will influence their future—yes—even beyond the grave.

The Witch's *unimaginable* destiny will be found with the spirits that were familiar to them, and with the Fairy King or Queen, in that time-bending and mind-bending space of existence we call *Elfhame*; or perhaps with the Devil himself in his own grim and dark caverns, or in his aerial army of flying spirits. The Witch *made* these connections, and the timeless, eldritch realities within and behind these connections will shape them always.

The ordinary person's quite *imaginable* destiny will be found with the souls of the human beings who influenced them so much in breathing life; their bosses, co-workers, the politicians and billionaires that they foolishly worshiped and helped to wreck the human world, their spouses, their children, you name it—*these* are the beings that ordinary people *sell their souls* to, who they become bound to, and who shape their destinies. These are the people that accompany them to the grave, into the earth, the common tomb of all human beings, and these are the people they share the dark dreams and slumber of death with.

So *everyone* is giving their soul to someone or something; it's not just Witches. Witches just have enough cunning to give their soul-relationships to powerful entities that can make their breathing lives into occasions of more strange joy, more extraordinary capability, and more power. And by power, I mean *actual power*—the power of spirit-aided feats and rare insights that might even build a bridge over the dark river of death.

This is not to say that Witches have dumped all human relations, or that human relationships of a deep variety won't influence or shape the destiny of the Witch. Of course they will; Witches are still humans and the shaping of our destinies is a very complicated matter, forever mysterious. Destiny is *always* a child of a million parents.

This is a call to examine what relationships are strongest in our lives, what ideologies obsess us the most, and what connections and donations of power or precious vitality those things lead us to make. In this, we will see the hand of Fate writing away in the book of life and death.

Some wonder if the "Other Side" can break pacts: can The Devil decide that he's done with the pact and relationship he made with a Witch? Can the Queen of Elfhame—or any Patron who granted Witch Dreams—ever withdraw their favors and empowerments, cause a man or a woman's familiars to flee from them or abandon them, and then fade as an influence from someone's life, as though they never were?

While the abstract answer to such questions will always be "*Yes, technically*", the *actual* answer is no, this will almost never happen. The Great Powers do **not** break pacts or agreements. When they invest the power that comes with *Witch Dreams* into you, you become (in a way) an extension of their presence, an ally to them which helps them somehow fulfill their unimaginable goals or their deeper cosmological roles in this world or other places. Joining the company of the *Witched* is both a thing of integrity and part of a much larger natural chain of relationships and power-transactions that has its own fitness, its own timeless integrity. The Ancient Powers do not flippantly toss agreements or relationships of this nature; too much power is invested in these things, too many ageless connections and older agreements that we can't fathom.

People may take it quite hard if an act of Witchcraft they performed failed for some reason, or if several acts do, and begin to wonder if their Patron has failed them or abandoned them. They do **not** fail or abandon anyone. They and your familiars *might* be unable to overcome the dark chain of Fateful forces surrounding a situation by Witchcraft; **no** entity and no Witch is all-powerful and some situations are Fatefully tangled up in very dense ways. But Patrons and familiars are always going to aid you in doing all you can in any situation—and they may have other ways of wiping away any tears you shed as well.

**Witch Riding to the Sabbat** from *Hexen Meysterey*, 1545

# APPENDIX

## Unawake and Unsleeping: Hypnagogic Prayer and Invocation in Witchcraft

\* \* \*

### Pre-Modern Witchcraft and the World of Sleep and Dreams

The most profound difference between modern witchcraft and the witchcraft of Early Modern Europe lies in the primary experiential stage that the witchcraft itself is encountered upon. For people practicing most of the forms of modern witchcraft, the primary encounter with "The Craft" lies within **ceremony and ritual**; "magical tools" with elemental associations are utilized within circles drawn and 'quarters' called, either indoors or out—and this is because most modern witchcraft is a recent descendant of European ceremonial magic, albeit a simplified form of ceremonial magic blended with heady doses of spiritualism, Neopagan Goddess worship or the worship of other divine figures from pre-Christian times, and a vaguely Eastern-flavored brew of "all is consciousness/energy" mentalism-monism and ideas of spiritual development through karma.

But the people living before the Industrial Revolution (and some living for a good while into it) who were mediators of the complex cultural phenomenon of historical witchcraft primarily encountered the agencies and powers that stood behind witchcraft in **sleep**, in **vision**, and **dreams**. This difference, and the many reasons why it is critically important, can never really be emphasized enough.

For many modern witches, regular Otherworldly contact and congress is sought or initiated "from their own side"—through their own visualizations of divine or otherworldly beings, wed to exercises of *will* and speech through invocations. The mainstream path to modern witchcraft itself is largely inaugurated through personal interest, the seeking of books, teachers, or working groups, and an eventual arrival at some form of initiation. One might even initiate oneself, declaring their belonging to modern Witchdom (again in a ritual or ceremonial context), and proceeding along from that point in a free-form, self-guided manner.

There can be no doubt that pre-modern practitioners of the countless forms of Early Modern Witchcraft also utilized invocations in the attempt to gain the attentions of familiars and helping spirits, or even other spirits perceived to be more powerful. The critical difference again brings us back to the world of sleep, dreams, and the visions that may occur within these compartments of experience: Pre-modern Witches often encountered the spiritual forces that endowed them with their future power in dreams or visionary states that came unbidden, unsought, or which arose during times of great peril or trauma.

Their *ongoing experience* of spirits or otherworldly beings likewise continued through special forms of dreaming and trances found in or between the various stages of sleep. Some of these dreams or visionary states could have been intentionally provoked through certain techniques or the use of certain substances; others may have been just as spontaneous or unchosen as their initial "witch dreams" were.

Pre-modern Witchcraft's relationship to the reality of dreams, alongside the visionary conditions provoked by hypnagogic paralysis and lucid dreams, is finally emerging into the mainstream of scholarship, and it's about time. Emma Wilby's groundbreaking work *The Visions of Isobel Gowdie* offers a thorough analysis of the reality of *Dream Cults*, alongside very thoughtful arguments and pieces of evidence that the origin of many of the accounts given by witches of spectral travel to Sabbats and meetings with spirits (including the spirits of deceased humans) originated in their own dreams.

Edward Bever's seminal work *The Realities of Witchcraft and Popular Magic in Early Modern Europe* is likewise an encyclopedic walk through the consistentlyemerging solid connection between accounts of Witchcraft and witch-experience and the shadowy-but-universal reality of sleep and dreams which we still have little understanding of in the year 2020.

Beyond these two sources mentioned, I have amassed a small library of writings on the connection between Early Modern Witchcraft and the phenomenon of sleep and dreams. My own personal practice of sorcery or witchcraft, and those of my closest allies, has come for years to focus upon the strange world of dreams and the occult techniques and pathways to unsealing its hidden potentials. We figured out long ago the critical distinction between the "two stages" of witchcraft-experience that I gave above.

In my recent work *An Carow Gwyn*, I give a very detailed discussion on using dream-states for fundamental acts of sorcery and spirit-contact. My essay here intends to ultimately detail a potent (and very accessible) practical technique that strange-souled people (or people of any interior proclivity who engage in some interanimistic lifeway of friendship with spirits) can use to increase Otherworldly connection, contact, and sensitivity.

Let me clear up some very important points, here at the beginning. The idea that Pre-Modern Witches or the widespread (and many-shaped) phenomenon of Witchcraft could have been *primarily* focused around dream-states, trance states, or extraordinary states of mind and soul that came about through sleep and dreams, is not the same as saying "witchcraft was all just a bunch of people dreaming stuff up."

As I hope I will show (and as only extraordinary experiences can truly teach), dreams are **not** merely meaningless mind-noises that echo through a person's head in the night. I have done a thorough analysis in multiple writings of my own of the association of dreams and the world of dreams with what Anthropologists call the *separable soul* or the "Free Soul"—the aspect of the human psyche and body complex that can activate and move through various relational conditions during sleep, during traumatic moments, or even near-death moments.

My extensive personal practice has revealed and manifested consistent experiences that can most *simply* be explained through reference to this model or this anthropology, experiences whose features line up with the reports of informants from primal cultures around the world, and with what can be surmised from Early Modern European and Early American folklore regarding the apparent presence or activity of the Free Soul. The idea that one of our souls activates and has encounters in dreams, and that dreams (and states related to sleep and dream) can be **portals to extraordinary encounters** with spirits or Otherworldly beings is easily one of the most universal and ancient beliefs known to humankind, and this is because it is backed by hundreds of thousands of years of direct experience across all cultures.

In dreams, and particularly the special dreams whose nature or character stand out or apart from ordinary dreams, we are face-to-face with an ancient phenomenological encounter that has served as the trans-cultural origin of organic human spirituality since the dawn of our human time. Sorcery, or Witchcraft (which in its pre-Modern forms originally referred to special abilities or insights gained by men or women who made extraordinary relationships with spirits or other-than-human powers) has **spirit contact** at the heart of its entire central endeavor.

And dreams can be a powerful and accessible method of spirit contact—of creating and maintaining relationships with spirits. In full truth, dreams *always were so*; in the accounts of every primal people contacted in the last handful of centuries, Anthropologists have consistently found their understanding of dreams to be intrinsically tied to their understandings of spirits and human contact with spirits.

Of course, creating and maintaining relationships with spirits isn't something that only "witched" people did in ages before now. In the Pagan past, the cults of local spirits, the cults of Ancestors, and the cults of many other entities of that sort required communities of humans to create and maintain relationships with them—relationships that were demonstrated and maintained through certain customs and practices. The *presence* of these relationships had many different degrees of impact upon the ordinary and extraordinary mind-states of all the members of those communities. It formed a silent, wordless interanimistic background which made their belonging to a place or to their own communities a powerful and even sacred matter.

Spirit-contact is **not** just for witches or sorcerers; it is for all humans who hearken to the critical importance of interanimistic relationship with the powers of places in the modern day, and the importance of reverencing the great Indwelling powers of the majestic landscapes, skyscapes, waterways, and the *Netherworldly* landscapes that we all *dree our weird* upon: the places to which we belong, and within which we unravel and wear out our human Fates in life and death.

The perspective I always approach these matters from is simple: the witches of the Early Modern period (and doubtless the witches from every culture who existed in the centuries before them) sometimes experienced extraordinary dreams (or through dreams, extraordinary conditions of mind) that were **points of contact** between them and other-than-human tutelary entities that they had relationships of power-exchange or information-exchange with.

They sometimes incubated or induced these dreams or states; sometimes they came unbidden. Their *initial* encounters with the spirit-world through these dreams or states were often enough not provoked by any ordinary means, though some might have sought out power through sorcery or witchery, and been taught by others how to incubate dreams of an initiatory character.

I take the position that all dreams have the potential to be of an extraordinary type, and anyone who can dream can potentially incubate or provoke dreams that become points of contact between the human world and another world entirely: the extra-sensory world or continuum indwelled by what we can call "spirits". This continuum of reality is part of our life-world. It is not wholly separate from anything; it is an **integral** part of the world of our ordinary sensory experience.

The spirits who dwell in this range of extraordinary encounter may seem "supernatural", but they are every bit as natural (in a broader sense) as the other living beings we encounter in our ordinary daily lives. Their motivations and ways of interacting with the relational world that we all inhabit are unique to them, but spirits are not all the same; they have an infinite range of motivations and different powers of communication and interaction. The same could be said of the human and animal persons that wander through the more familiar world of our ordinary senses.

**From Fantastic Flights to Fantastic Delusions**

The idea that the reports of Early Modern witches—who claimed that they "flew forth" in the night and interacted with spirits (recall the oft-repeated report of "flying to the Sabbat")—might have been based on things they experienced in dream-states is not a new idea. While it seems that witches, or those accused of witchcraft, were often enough literally believed by some local authorities when they said they "flew through the night" or traveled to far-away lands to join in demonic revels, throughout the 16th, 17th, and 18th centuries the notion that witches were *dreaming their experiences* was suggested more and more frequently, and gradually became the chief official explanation for the phenomenon.

And it's not hard to see why cultural authorities would finally conclude that witch-flights and other spectral encounters were occurring in the dreams of these men and women. In 1663, in the small town of Wildbad, Germany, an eight-year old boy named Hanss Ferner was arrested for witchcraft. Hanss confessed that he had flown to a place of music, dancing, and feasting where the Devil met him, and that he had given the Devil his allegiance. Hanss described the Devil as a black-skinned man with horns, and further reported that his own mother and grandmother (and lots of other people) were present at these celebrations.

Hanss' Devil was apparently quite amiable; he carried Hanss on his shoulders and gave him large quantities of bread and meat—a feasting menu that Isobel Gowdie likewise reported when she was in the halls of the Elf Queen and King. Hanss called the Devil his "father", and was in turn called "son" by the same.

This was of course enough to get anyone arrested in those days, and depending on where you were, could lead to being executed. Hanss was arrested and placed into a cell, but he swore that he was still traveling at night to the place where the Devil and other witches were—so the local authorities had Hanss watched in shifts, all around the clock. Hanss was watched while he slept, and his observers took notes of the struggles and sounds he made in his sleep. He woke after being watched all night, and reported his nocturnal journeys, the same as always.

The people watching Hanss sleep through the night *knew* he hadn't left his cell. And the case of Hanss Ferner is certainly not the only case in which the authorities realized that witches—or people accused of witchcraft—were reporting physically being somewhere else when everyone knew (for certain) that they were not. This did lead, quite early on, to a lot of theological and legal debating and cultural soul-searching.

If these witches were not *actually* flying off to meet the Devil, or the Queen of the Fairies, or the dead, what was happening? Different explanations arose; in some places (and particularly early on) it was believed that the Devil or other spiritual agencies (none of them seen as "good" by

Christian cultural authorities) were taking the *souls* of witches from their bodies for their nocturnal excursions. This explanation maintained the gravity of the crime of witchcraft, and still allowed for people to be executed at times for making such reports. Others suggested that witches were being given "hellish dreams" or visions by demonic forces, which could still be seen as dangerous or criminal enough.

Other explanations ranged, as you'd expect, from delusions to outright insanity. Over time, European authorities (starting on the Continent, and gradually moving outward) began to dismiss "spectral evidence" gained from confessions that were believed to be drawn from dream-experiences. In some places, such confessions were no longer believed or entered in as evidence of witchcraft or demonic doings. They became a matter of "deluded women" who "believed they flew at night with Diana or Holda", or "madmen who say they dream of the Devil and flying through the air in their sleep."

Ironically, it was these same skeptical authorities that not only (eventually) brought an end to many of the trials and executions of witches, but who laid the foundations for another kind of skepticism prominent today: **the idea that psychic, visionary, or mystical phenomenon is all "in the heads" of people claiming to have such things**. By being "merely" a product of the minds of men and women, the reality of these matters was condemned to insignificance or meaninglessness, at least with regards to community affairs, to legal issues, and other interpersonal dimensions of social life. It was shunted off to a place where it was no longer felt to be a danger or a threat, nor indeed to have any power at all.

It was no longer seen as possible that a man or woman could actually harm another person, merely because they dreamed that they had shot them with a magical arrow, or killed them in a dream-visionary state. It was no longer seen as credible that a person was actually in league with the Devil merely because they dreamed they had met the Devil.

We have all inherited this same skeptical worldview today, though we've gone even further than the Early Modern skeptics; in the halls of our own sciences and academic institutions, we've also banished devils, demons, ghosts, fairies, and witches altogether. Most Early Modern skeptics still believed in different aspects of the basic Christian theological worldview; they still believed in God, and that the Devil or demons were probably real. They simply doubted that peasant men or women from rural backwater villages could actually be meeting such beings in their dreams, or conducting direct pacts or working relationships with them. The modern world has dismissed even The Devil himself, replacing him with brain chemistry, schizophrenia, repressed urges and drives, and fear of the darkness in ourselves and in our culture.

The Devil, for us, is now relegated to the status of "psychological archetype"; he is a function of psychology, an image of the "shadow", the embodiment of our condescendingly-labeled "animal nature", the bearer of our violent proclivities, of our addictions, of our greed, or perhaps just a remnant of Early Modern superstition. In my mind, this is a dismal end for The Devil. It's the end you'd expect for the transparently culturally-manufactured **Theological Devil**, for he was always a needful product of the over-rational Christian conquest of the worlds seen and unseen.

But the **Folkloric Devil**– the Devil or Master-spirit who emerges as a very fluid mask for earlier spirits and powerful entities venerated or known in pre-Christian cultures—he was tossed out with the bathwater, too. And since it was He who witches and sorcerers from so many times and places were often enough *actually* encountering, and since His existence is not a matter of institutionalized religious manufacture but an organic product of countless millennia of visionary experience, you can be sure that *He's* still around. I know from my own personal experience that He is.

Some wonder if this entity—or the wide range of entities attached to him—can play any kind of positive, needful, or practical role in the interior or relational lives of modern people. This is a question that only modern people could ever ask, and it shows the extent of their disconnection from the earlier world of spiritual-ecological relationship. The question is *never* whether or not spirits can serve our collective human ends, or nurture our fragile modern human psychology in some "positive" way. If spirits exist—and they *do* exist—then they have a share of this world, and are kin (on some level) to all the other beings who come from this world.

We organically owe them recognition, a degree of general respect, and we're very unwise to ignore them, or seek to domesticate them or "use" them just to further our human agendas. If they are there, then we must relate as well as we can with them. In exchange, some *may* help humans to learn more about what it means to belong to our world, or more about the Unseen reaches of our world. They may endow some humans with healing or harming powers, or special insights.

Spirits can do this; they are capable of interpsychic communication, and most are very aware of hidden dimensions and realities of this cosmos that even the most brilliant human minds cannot comprehend. And many can use our dream-states as experience-regions through which they can reach out to us and communicate with our souls via asserting various influences upon the shapes of our dreams.

This reality of spirit-relating is as old as mankind. And I think that should provoke a bit of "Sympathy for the (Folkloric) Devil", and all that he represents. If we wish to use him as some kind of icon (never forgetting that He is also a Person, and the spirits clustered in his entourage and relational systems are also Persons), he is *best* understood as an icon of our shamanistic past, an icon of a time when humans, their dreams, and the spirits that fill our world existed in a cycle of conscious co-creation, co-singing, co-experiencing, and co-operating for various personal or collective ends, on both sides of the Hedge.

**Towards the Death of Dreams**

Our modern cultural "intellectual elites" (our academics and scientists) dismissing the Devil, right along with God, angels, demons, fairies, and spirits as a whole, did not empty out a world that was subsequently found to be lucid and explicable to them. They have not come near to understanding the reality of human consciousness, nor its many mysteries. Their (predictable) attempts at creating reductionist, materialistic models to explain the existence of consciousness have yielded nothing but unsubstantiated claims; some have given up and actually taken to insisting that *consciousness isn't real at all.*

My purpose here isn't to cast more (well deserved) scorn upon the laughable lostness and blindness that characterizes the mainstream of our modern intellectual stalwarts. They *still* manage to manufacture enough miraculous technologies which our populations greedily snatch up, more conveniences and technical addictions which, though they yield a negative and non-sustainable impact upon our world, still keep everyone shrugging and agreeing that the scientists must be doing *something* right, and that their mechanistic explanations for everything must be *somehow* correct, even if scientists can't quite explain all the details. The covert logic, I believe, is "if they can make rockets and smart phones, they *must* be onto something." The other logic appears to be "well, they've invented more life-saving and convenience-granting stuff than anyone else in any age of the world, so... we're with them."

And besides, certain cultural dogmas are programmed into everyone from kindergarten, and rejecting them too publicly might get you socially executed: scientists have the hallowed **scientific method** which is the key and gateway to anything that is *really* real– and if there's something it hasn't explained yet, it *will*. You just have to be patient. There's *peer review*, the ultimate act of learned collective discernment, to keep us safe—to make sure we always have the *best possible* truth about anything... or at least the truth that will declared acceptable to express trust in for the time being.

The modern religion of Scientism is quite a show, and while it's busy putting on performances and throwing techno-bread to the insatiable crowds, it's also intrinsically tied up with our legacy of Western rationalism, colonialism, and fatal near-sightedness to the greater, deeper needs of our intricate living environment. In this sense, Scientism and our chief intellectual institutions of academia and science today are products (ultimately) of Christianity. What we call *secularism* is likewise a product of Christianity, and *secular humanism* a continuation of the myopic anthropocentrism of the same.

Despite what the modern myths that have been created say, there was no heroic, dogged team of brave skeptics and scientists who were just "ahead of their times", and who challenged Christian superstitions and finally managed to banish the Devil and his imps and demons from our cultural psychological stadium. Some abstract class of "scientists" or "rationalists" didn't evict God and the Devil from the Western world; *Christian culture itself* lost its overall deeper belief in them and let them fall by the wayside. Collapsing social orders and extreme social revisions, alongside endless religio-political social strife and enormous economic transformations in Early Modern times lie at the heart of why the Devil lost his place in the details of life.

This Christian culture didn't spend its first 15 centuries cultivating a deep understanding of pre-Christian spiritual beliefs or worldviews; it didn't have an anthropology of the soul that was in any way adequate to the task of describing the richness and depth of human dreams, trances, and interior-type experiences. If anything, Christian traditions and cultures from their foundation have been profoundly distrustful of their own 'mystics' and visionaries.

When God and the Devil were kicked to the margins, the over-simplified Christian notion of the soul was too, and any possibility of comprehending the true depths and nuances of dreams went with it. The soul or *psyche* became nothing but the mind, and later that mind was itself viewed— as it is now—as a mere epiphenomenon of the brain, electrical and accidental synaptic noise, or accidental self-awareness arising from meaningless and random combinations of chemicals.

And so we sit here, now, with dismissive guesses about the role and meaning of dreams in our embodied existence. We fruitlessly seek to understand them by primarily observing the brain's chemical and electrical behaviors in sleep, not heedful that dreams (like any other phenomenon of experience) are *co-created by much more* than a single organ in one part of the body.

Before I can set to the task of giving some instructions on how to use certain states of sleep and dream for extraordinary purposes (including a specific technique that I have utilized, whose efficacy is well-verified) we will have to briefly analyze some aspects of how sleeping and dreaming seem to regularly manifest within our human experience. I will do the unthinkable and draw upon not only anthropology and experiential-metaphysical angles on sleep and dream, but also share some observations into the biology of the same—biological observations won for us by scientists who are making a brave (but I fear futile) effort to win their own kind of answer to these mysteries.

In the interests of clarity, I will say it simply: I do *not* believe that dreams are meaningless. I do not believe they are simple rehearsals of worries from our wakeful hours, nor random emergences of anxieties, desires, or cultural materials that we have ruminated often upon. I do not believe that dreams are mere evolutionary junk side-effects that came along with developing a big brain, and the supposed power of special creativity or imagination that comes with such a brain.

And I do not believe that dreams happen "merely in the head" or in the brain. When you wake up from a dream, and tell others a story of it (after reconstructing the memory of the dream filtered through your own rational, breathing mind) you are *not* sharing a dream; you are sharing an *account* of a dream that you experienced, which is itself an event that **took place within this world**.

That your body and your organs were part of the system that aided a dream-event to arise within the world is without a doubt, but they are a small compartment within the multi-compartmented system that makes dreams possible. What we experience when we dream is a thing—or a complex of things—that *must* necessarily arise from many other conditions and factors, some of them existing (perceptibly) within the organs of your sensual embodiment, and many of them extending quite a bit beyond the ordinary boundaries of your body. We ordinarily interpret dreams as entirely subjectively-generated phenomenon, and yet they arise at the behest and under the influence of many intersubjective forces. Meetings with spirits within dreams would indicate that some aspect of dreams is transpersonal, or that more than a few aspects of dreams may be.

**Dreams are relational, systemic experiences that deeply involve the body and one of our souls**. They rely on many factors, but chiefly the existence of the separable soul/free soul and its relationship to the very seat of our conscious awareness, alongside its inherence in a surreal world that is ordinarily invisible to us. As countless primal voices have made clear, what happens to the free soul always impacts the body, for the body is a sensual expression of the free soul. Sleep and dreams (as they relate to the free soul) *can* and *do* have measurable and fairly consistent biological impacts on the body. And yet, dreams themselves are too complicated to discern the full reality of their nature simply by observing the body. More scope is needed.

**The Four Stages of Sleep**

When we lie down to sleep, it doesn't take long for us to enter into the first stage of sleep, which is the **hypnagogic** state. This state is characterized by the sensation of relaxing and "drifting off", or drifting "deeper down"—of the many sensations of falling asleep. Depending on how tired a person is, they may pass through the hypnagogic state very rapidly. But most of the time, people have a short while of drifting, of experiencing chains of free-association thinking, which can include thoughts about the day just ended, or anxieties or expectations for challenges that will await the next day.

Eventually, this free-association type thinking begins to give way to images—one may begin to "see" images from the day just finished, or any of a vast range of random images that can surface during this time. In this state, a person has fallen into what amounts to a very real and potent trance; it is a liminal state, a transitional state in which one is neither awake, nor asleep—**unawake and unsleeping**. If one were to enter the hypnagogic state with any measure of mental energy, one might use this state for some very profound works of spirit-contact, which is what this essay is ultimately about, at the practical level: **hypnagogic prayer and invocation**. This we shall discuss soon.

If one has a measure of mental energy—if one is not "dog-tired"—the hypnagogic state is often characterized by visualizations and interior visions of many different varieties. Artistic inspiration can be sought— and is often reportedly found—by artists in this state. Associations can sometimes spontaneously emerge between different topics and subjects that create surprising links and suggest solutions to difficult problems. Time appears accelerated in the hypnagogic state; auditory and visual hallucinations can occur.

The name "Hypnagogic" means "Initiator into Sleep" or "Sleep initiator"— and in simple terms, this condition acts in the way a human initiator might act when leading a candidate for initiation into a chamber of the mysteries. The hypnagogic state is a border-place, "neither here nor there", in which the subtle influences of the Unseen world can impress themselves on the not-yet-fully-faded conscious mind. And the conscious mind at this stage is "dulled" a bit, put partly out of commission or relaxed, such that it becomes surprisingly receptive to things it never would have been open to before.

Every "schema" of something so organically intrinsic to our entities (like sleep) always has an overlap with a larger cosmology. Sleep and dream have often been compared to the rhythms of life and death, and for good reasons. The Hypnagogic state is a parallel to the transition-state between being alive and being dead, which all must experience one day. In that state, we are not yet fully dead, but no longer able to return to the fully integrated, ordinarily operating condition of life.

In this state (not surprisingly) dying people report visionary encounters, report seeing spirits or deceased persons, or report coming to terms with life and death as a whole, as though they were in a place of profound realizations. I poetically refer to the hypnagogic state as **Twilight Sleep.**

When the descent of the hypnagogic state is over, we enter into **nREM** sleep, or as I poetically call it, **Deep Shadow**. nREM sleep is the most ancient form of sleep, and is known to occur in reptiles, birds, and mammals. When we are in the nREM state, we have no conscious awareness of it. This is the great "dark void" that we spend most of our sleep in, but it has a very critical role in our health. When we enter the Deep Shadow, our bodies begin to undergo the needed biological regenerations that we require to live.

The brain's activity changes dramatically in nREM sleep, and mentation is either absent, or reduced to a very simple, primal level—and is often repetitive. Bever notes that in this state, "the body replenishes and restores itself in a variety of ways, repairing damage, growing new tissues, and resupplying itself with chemicals depleted during wakefulness. The limbic system is active, but forebrain activity is low." Some dreams *can* rarely occur during nREM sleep, but "it is usually brief, closely connected to waking concerns, and **verbal and conceptual rather than visual and emotional.**"

nREM sleep is as critical to maintaining our lives and health as getting adequate food and hydration. This "plunge into the darkness", in which we become "void of self", is a needed regeneratory experience, which creates a profound parallel with the process of dying. When a dying person finally passes the threshold of death, the release and permanent loss of the breath soul leads to a loss of consciousness. Something about the dreaded "darkness" of losing the breathing self, and the fear we have of eternal loss of consciousness, hides a reality that is tied to regeneration.

I am reminded here of a story I once read, in which a dying elderly grandfather was spending time with his young grandson. The grandfather knew he would likely die that very night, but his grandson, bouncing around with the fresh and abundant energy of extreme youth, was unaware of this. When bedtime came, the grandson didn't want to go to bed, but his grandfather helped to tuck him in. The grandson complained about having to go to sleep, and the grandfather gently told him **"You need your sleep, and I need mine."**

This is a very profound story, obviously, for in the fewest possible words it captures an organic reality of how necessary the "deep shadow" is— both for people sleeping, and for those who have passed beyond the boundaries of the breathing, waking world. What regenerates us in a nightly small death rehearsal may point to a deeper cosmological reality that waits to regenerate us beyond the larger death. Both require a surrender of conscious, ordinary aspects of experience.

At various points during nREM sleep, birds and mammals enter into a stage of sleep called **REM** sleep, or *Rapid Eye Movement* sleep. It is during one of these REM sleep sessions that most of our dreams occur. REM is a very strange state, for brain activity during REM changes drastically from the near non-register of nREM, into a condition that is very similar to being awake.

The breath soul that ordinarily vitalizes and controls the body in times of being awake has become paralyzed by the time a person falls into nREM sleep, and so during REM, the portions of the brain that control motor activity are (normally) shut off. If they were not, people would physically act out their dreams. Bever mentions that cats whose brains lack the mechanism of "shut off" paralysis get up during REM sleep, and stalk, capture, and devour invisible prey.

REM sleep is the central mystery of most sleep and dream studies. Studies show that theta waves are very active in REM—the waves most active when critical matters of survival are being focused upon in a creature. Dreams that arise during REM sleep are often of a visual and emotional nature—and very often far beyond rational rules and expectations. Bever reports that in REM sleep, "higher executive systems which normally imbue human thought with logical coherence and propositional structure, and constrain perceptual possibilities on the basis of established knowledge of the world are switched off. Production of aminergic neurotransmitters, which play a role in maintaining focused attention, stops, while large amounts of cholinergic neurotransmitters, which promote diffuse associations, are produced."

Further, Bever points out that the right cerebral hemisphere becomes more active than the left, putting the part of our brain responsible for sequential-temporal processing at detriment. He says "the limbic system and associated areas that play a central role in emotion, memory, and visual and auditory associations are more active than during waking... and finally, mentation during REM takes the form of complex, episodic, vivid, emotionally charged multisensory experiences, in other words, what we think of as dreams."

Bever concludes, in line with the research he utilized in his own work, that REM sleep serves a critical function in human health and in the human ability to relate to our human and other-than-human world: the brain might be integrating into itself things that it needs to learn, or "coding in" new things that have been learned during the day—things necessary to survival and thriving. In this way, REM sleep may be when the brain trains itself, creating new neural architecture to embody new knowledges and interaction-strategies. People who have recently studied or set about trying to learn complex bodies of knowledge will have longer and more intense REM sleep at night.

Those who cannot, for some reason, enter REM sleep in a normal, healthy way (or who get deprived of it) are apparently not as able to learn complex material, and they "recall material of personal and emotional importance more poorly, show greater emotional brittleness, and exhibit a "rebound effect" of increased REM sleep when allowed to sleep uninterrupted." It's worth noting—and telling—that younger creatures remain in REM sleep for longer periods of time, and more frequently than adult creatures.

Human infants, likewise, have been shown to REM often, and display a wide range of emotions and facial expressions that they clearly demonstrate in REM, long before they socially demonstrate them with other humans. Dreams shape us, and help to make us who we are. We learn and change through them.

I call REM sleep by the poetic name **Visionfast**- the time of vision-strength, when the free soul, itself connected to the emotional and surreal, non-linear depths of our deeper entities, becomes active. The rational and measuring breath-soul is entirely out of commission during most REM sleep, leaving only the free soul's strange perceptions and adventures in a timeless or time-meaningless condition. But visions—whether they are communications from spirits or simple reconnections to the Unseen—are *always* about learning and further development of connection or insight on some level.

Visionfast corresponds cosmologically to the stage after death in which the free soul, no longer bound to the breath and body it once sensually manifested, becomes aware again of the deeper world and relational system that is its origin and home.

In *An Carow Gwyn*, I discuss the "two sleeps" method of obtaining lucid dreams—which is to say of obtaining the experience of regaining a degree of conscious awareness and seeming control when you are in the condition of Visionfast. To become lucid in a dream is to have a small portion of the breath soul awaken and permeate the experience, allowing for more consciously-directed activities and efforts, while you are submerged perceptually in the surreal world of dreams and visions.

How such a thing is possible should be quite clear at this point; after completing a cycle of sleep, and waking up well-regenerated, returning to sleep allows a person to carry a significant portion of energy into the sleep state. This excess energy of the body corresponds to a kind of excess energy of awareness and attention—and when the Visionfast/ REM state begins, and the brain's activity corresponds closely to being awake, that excess energy can birth a wakeful or lucid overlay on the experience.

It is in this state of lucidity that I believe "out of body" projection and travel ("Shimmering") can perhaps be launched or created—a thing I discuss in *An Carow Gwyn*. Some very fortunate people have (for whatever reason) a simple trait or proclivity towards provoking lucid dreams frequently, with or without any special efforts.

The final state of sleep—the **Hypnopompic** state (which I call the **Rising Light** state)—represents our transition out of sleep and back to the waking world. Like the hypnagogic state or the Twilight Sleep, the time of the Rising Light is a very liminal time. It is another liminal-transitional stage, and like those sinking in the hypnagogic descent, a person in the hypnopompic state can see and hear visual and auditory hallucinations, can see jumbled images or hear strange sounds, and gradually becomes aware of lying in bed, and of being awake again. Hypnopompic means "sleep guide"—though it is a guide that takes one away from sleep and towards waking.

Awakening means re-integrating with the ordinary world of sensual encounter and experience. It is a re-assertion of the breath soul's control over the body, and a resuming of the brain's ordinary daily functioning. During the times of hypnagogic descent *and* hypnopompic ascent, a very special thing can occur—the phenomenon of **sleep paralysis**. This condition (often thought to be very painful or frightening) occurs when a person discovers that they have mentally awoken, but their bodies are still paralyzed in sleep.

They may believe they are awake—and may feel in every way fully awake, but in reality they are still in a form of sleep, and in what I would call a powerful trance. Some people attempt to understand (and treat) sleep paralysis as a medical condition, but I think this fails to capture the entire portrait of the experience. I am one of the people who is prone to sleep paralysis, and though I did "suffer" from it initially, as a young adult, I rapidly learned to utilize it as a means of gaining out of body experiences.

The folklore connected to sleep paralysis is very telling and interesting. I wrote a treatment on it in *An Carow Gwyn*, and even gave a technique for consciously provoking a state of sleep paralysis, with the intention of using it as a "launching point" for lucid dreaming and out-of-body travel. Julian Goodare and Margaret Dudley wrote a superb essay entitled *Outside In or Inside Out: Sleep Paralysis and Scottish Witchcraft*, which gives the best treatment I've ever seen of the historical connections between the sleep paralysis experience, accusations of witchcraft, and reports of supernatural encounters.

Those "trapped" in sleep paralysis often report feeling a malevolent or treatening presence in the room with them, an evil or dangerous being approaching their bed or standing over it, who sometimes exerts a painful pressure on their chest. The extreme fear that people feel in this state can be an overwhelmingly negative experience, but in reality, the "sleep paralysis demon" or the "old hag" who was thought to attack those in their beds is a hallucination born from what is called *threat hypervigilance*, a state in which your emergency-wracked midbrain interprets any sound in your room at all as a potential threat, or simply imagines a threat, in an attempt to panic itself into waking up.

The painful pressure in the chest—thought in ancient times to be a sign that a spirit was stealing vitality from a person—is in reality born from the fact that in sleep our breathing slows down, and the (uncomfortable) pressure on the chest is natural; we are just ordinarily asleep before it appears, so we never feel it.

I certainly believe—from personal experience—that episodes of sleep paralysis can be times in which spirits can be encountered. Not all experiences of "the old hag" can be explained merely by negative reactions to the biological stresses of sleep paralysis. It can simply be hard to discern the presence of actual spirit-beings from the emotional extremes of fear and anxiety that occur at such times, and regularly generate a sense of a (threatening) presence near to the sleeper.

Eventually, awakening means re-integration with the breathing world. Re-integration, in the wider cosmological sense, refers to the wandering soul or free soul finding a new home, a new condition of stable interaction in line with the fateful powers influencing it or compelling it.

This may be conceived of as a wandering soul coming to rest with its kin in a subtle condition beyond this world, or deep within the metaphysical depths of the world; it can refer to the free soul arising as a spirit-being of some sort after its post-death transition and metamorphosis; it can mean the wandering soul has re-expressed itself sensually in a more tangible form, or even refer to the idea of "rebirth" into another human shape, or into an animal shape, or the many other possibilities that lie beyond our range of easy knowing.

## Prayer and Invocation in the Soul's Twilight

Utilizing the Hypnagogic State—the *Twilight Sleep* that we pass through every time we lie down to sleep—for sorcerous and otherworldly contact/communication purposes is very powerful, and very easy. One needs no special tools, no special preparations, no special anything at all except a mind and body that's ready to go to sleep. The only thing you need beyond *that* is a small or a somewhat significant amount of energy; this technique cannot be used if you are feeling extremely tired or worn-out.

When I say "a small or somewhat significant amount of energy", I mean the kind of energy you have when you go to bed when you know it's time to sleep, or when you feel the need to turn in, but before you're completely exhausted. Those who make it exhausted to their beds every night will have to leverage whatever changes they can make to their daily activity cycles, to allow themselves to reach bed with something other than a dead soul and the desire to drop down and pass out.

You will need one very important *intangible* thing to accomplish this work. You will need an **image**: an image of the Otherworldly being or beings you are attempting to make contact with and communicate with. Whether or not this technique could be used on a being who is breathing and living in this world is a conversation for a future essay; for now I can say that it *is* likely possible to contact the free soul of a human or animal with this technique, but at present, our discussion must be about Otherworldly entities.

The image you will need can be found in several ways. But **it must be gained or found**- it cannot be simply made up. The ideal image is one you will have gained through a visionary experience or a dream in which you are *very* certain you met an Otherworldly being. How that being (or beings) looked in your dream or vision is the image you will have to utilize in this technique.

Images can also be found in traditional sources—normally folkloric, historical, or mythical sources—that describe the appearances of

Otherworldly beings. Earlier in this essay, I talked about Hanss Ferner and gave his account of how the Devil appeared to him. From his description, you could build an image to use if you were going to use this technique to attempt to reach out to the Folkloric Devil. But the same is true for any of the countless descriptions we have in history and folk-accounts from people who met Fayerie-entities, the Queen of the Fairies, and so forth.

As a sorcerous practitioner, I have obtained over the years more than a few Familiar Spirits that I met and created relationships and agreements with in visionary states. I keep their images in my mind, of course—how they revealed themselves to me—for use in techniques like this. But not everyone is a sorcerous practitioner, and those who are not still have enormous resources to draw from to reach out to spirits, through the accounts of their appearance in folklore. Those who practice the Ancient Fayerie Faith (to make an example) have an enormous gift in the form of *The Romance of Thomas Rhymer*– a lengthy and deeply descriptive romance that I give (and analyze thoroughly) in *An Carow Gwyn*.

In that romance, the appearance of the Fayerie Queen herself is described in exhaustive detail. That *image* of her can be used by a member of the Fayerie Faith, in conjunction with this technique, to reach out and potentially establish deep contact with her, and the spirits close to her.

I will give the step-by-step instructions for the **Hypnagogic Prayer** technique now, and follow the instructions with a detailed analysis—and a checklist of ways you will know that you have succeeded at using this technique.

✱ ✱ ✱

### THE METHOD OF HYPNAGOGIC PRAYER

1. Lie down comfortably, close your eyes, and focus for about a minute on the sensation of your body, lying in bed.

2. Relax for another minute or so, but have a caution—depending on your level of energy, only two or three minutes in a comfortable position in bed can cause a rapid descent into the hypnagogic state. You *want* to begin descending into the hypnagogic experience-level, but you have to be very aware that you're doing it. You must be mindful of what's

happening to your mind and body. Most people don't pay attention at this time, when lying in bed, and so they slip into the hypnagogic condition unawares, pass through it relatively quickly, and then fall into the unconsciousness of deep shadow.

3. When you can tell that you're relaxed and feeling slightly "sinky", you will have to use your powers of visualization. This technique makes use of intentional visualization or envisioning. You must visualize yourself taking a journey to **reach a dwelling-place, where you will meet the entity or entities** you are intending to reach out to. It's best if you're walking on this journey, and best if their dwelling-place is in some wilderness area. You can "see" whatever you require, but these are the basics.

Let yourself experience the sensations of walking, as you move along whatever trail, road, or through whatever landscape you need. It's best to visualize this happening at night, because the darkness means you have less details to worry about visualizing in the landscape around you. At some point—**and don't let the visualized journey be too long, else you may fall asleep**– you will see yourself reaching the house, cottage, cave, castle, riverbank, forest (or whatever) where the being or beings you're seeking out dwell.

4. If you must knock or do something to gain entry to a building, do it; the door will be opened for you, or someone will come and let you in, or you will be called in or invited in somehow. If there's just a cave or something, go in. The entity or entities you are trying to reach will **be there**, looking just as your image of them depicts. Begin a conversation with them—but this is a special conversation.

This conversation is like a strange (and I think fun) game. When you speak—whether you are speaking a greeting, or responding to things said to you—you must *always* **greet or respond exactly as you would "in real life"**, if you found yourself in the physical presence of this being or these beings. There is no room here for anything else—treat this visualized conversation/interaction as though it were **100%, absolutely intersubjectively real**.

You are visualizing this conversation, and that means **You will decide** what the being or beings you are meeting will say to you, when their time comes to speak or respond to you. You must judge—based on all that you know about the folkloric, mythic, or legendary character of this being or beings—what they would **most likely say**, at any given time. And then you have them say those things to you.

At the beginning, it's easy; you will make some kind of greeting, and their return greetings are easy enough to imagine. But as the conversation continues and develops, then perhaps you must be careful. They will, at some point, inquire about why you traveled to see them, and you must answer very honestly regarding what your true goal for the visit is. You probably will (at some point) ask them questions or seek help regarding some topic or issue. How they respond again is something **you'll decide**—but right about this point, you should notice some odd things beginning to happen.

The time you took to visualize your journey to the dwelling, and the time you've spent having the conversation that you're creating with this envisioned being, was time you were sinking in hypnagogic transition. More time may have passed than you realized, when you busied yourself with a focus on the visualizations. By the time the conversation is happening, you may feel like you're slipping into an actual dream of this conversation. Things may be easier to visualize than you expected, or things may become vivid.

But more than that, you may find that you no longer have to decide very much what your conversation partners are saying in response to you—you may find that, without much effort on your part, **they make responses that you didn't consciously plan to give them, using words and phrases that you didn't spend much time planning to put in their mouths, if you planned it at all.**

This is a good sign—a sign that you are in a potent trance state. I think of it as a cognitive form of "automatic writing"—call it "automatic thinking" if you like; you begin by creatively conducting a conversation for two or more parties (yourself and your Other or Others) but then, as your hypnagogic state deepens, the conversation begins to take on a life of its own. You might find that "They" say things to you that suddenly make you remember things you haven't thought of in a long time; that's a good sign. You may make connections you hadn't made before.

If your conversation partner or partners direct you to do something, or ask you to accomplish a task, do it. They can even ask you to leave the meeting place and come back after performing an action elsewhere, or retrieving something. That is all fine and well—it doesn't have to happen, but it might.

5. By this point, you will probably be very near to falling asleep. You will want to continue conversing with the one or the ones you came to visit, and **let yourself fall asleep from within that conversation, or from within the experience wherever you happen to be**. You won't remember the last thing you said to them, or that they said to you; you will simply black out, fall into deep shadow, and be within your nREM sleep state. And with that, the technique is finished.

∗ ∗ ∗

It might seem like a bit of an anti-climax to just black out in the middle of a conversation with an envisioned being or beings, but there are special reasons why this is important. First, let me say the most critical thing I can at this point: when you creatively visualize a conversation between yourself and some powerful Otherworldly being or beings, you must remember **You are creating it**. You are not, within the boundaries of your hypnagogic state, *actually* speaking to them in this exchange. And yet, you must speak *as though you are*, and allow them to respond in as realistic a way as you can creatively imagine.

Because the whole visualized interaction **is itself a prayer**. It is itself an **invocation**– by being in the powerful trance-state of hypnagogia, and creating this visualization while using a real image of real beings that you either gained or found, **you are sending out a signal of types to them**– seeking their attention, and demonstrating what kinds of things you're wanting to ask them. In the liminal state of Twilight Sleep, your whole visualization is a beacon to them, containing your desires and needs.

Now, whether or not they receive it or respond to it, is up to them. Their response can come in two different forms, at two different times:

1. They can infiltrate your hypnagogic state itself, usually near to the end, and cause the visualized conversation you're having to take surprising,

unexpected turns. If you find this happening, or find yourself "seeing" or "hearing" things you didn't expect to see or hear in your visualization, particularly meaningful things to your present concerns, goals, or problems, this may have happened.

2. They may appear in your dreams later—in your first or second REM state of Visionfast—and speak directly to you, or simply shape those dreams to show you things you need to see, to answer the concerns or desires you brought to them in your visualization.

One or both of these things may happen, or neither may happen. You never can tell until you try it. This hypnagogic prayer technique *is* a form of dream incubation; it has the potential to incubate potent dreams of communication, communion, contact, or messages from the beings you visualized in your Twilight Sleep.

When you fall asleep in the middle of your visualized conversation, if you *had* gained the attentions or influences of the entity or entities you were seeking, then don't worry at all about it; your free soul will *continue having* the interaction you were just visualizing with them. Your breath soul has simply finally lost consciousness, but your dreaming soul is just fine. What your dreaming soul might be learning in communion with them will be outside of your conscious awareness temporarily, but you might see hints or direct visions of it in later dreams. The goal to "make contact" and commune is all that matters—alongside the hope of receiving insights and dream-visions.

If for any reason you find yourself failing as you try to do this visualization-sequence, beginning with your walk to the meeting-place, it is a sign that you don't have the mental alertness or energy needed for the technique. There's nothing wrong with starting over if you find that you've lost the visualization, but if you find that you have to start over multiple times and can't make it far, stop trying. You don't have enough energy. You may have gone to bed more tired than you realized. Try again another night.

∗ ∗ ∗

I have a few tips for making this whole process much easier, beyond what I've already given. The last time I performed this technique (and you can do it as often as you want, though understand that "doing it simply to do it" isn't likely to yield much in the way of results) I visualized a journey to a cottage in the forest. It was snowy, and it was nighttime.

As much as you can, have your visualized journey happening in a seasonal setting that **matches the one around you in the real world**, at the time you do it. If it's a snowy winter where you are, let your journey happen through a snowy winter night. Also, let small details aid you. I know what my snow boots feel like when I have them on. And I know what they sound like when they crunch through slushy or stiff snow. I was able to "feel" and hear that in my visualization, which made it seem very real to me.

When I arrived at the cottage, a dead woman opened the door to let me in; she was a servant or attendant to the One I was there to meet. There was a fire in the hearth, and I could see that orange glow through the windows as I approached to knock on the door. The moment she let me in, the feeling of the warm inside, versus the cold on my face outside, was very pleasurable and noticeable. If you've ever passed from a chill cold outdoors into a warm house, you know this feeling. When I felt that, it made the whole environment of the cottage interior seem very real, like a real space of interaction.

Bring in little elements like this—sensations that are easy to "visualize feeling." They add a reality element that is very conducive to the experience. Remember that trying to over-visualize details is not good; you are already "on a clock", as it were—no one's hypnagogic state lasts for very long. Taxing your mind which is already on a 'down slope' with too much visualization can ruin this technique. When I stood in the cottage I traveled to, it was lit only by firelight in a hearth, and candlelight. That means it was largely shadowy—and that means less details to visualize, both in the environment, and in the beings you're talking to, whose images you place within the setting.

∗ ∗ ∗

This technique of Hypnagogic Prayer has many layers of use. One of the primary effects of using it on a regular basis will stem from how it orients your soul towards Otherworldly beings, and to subtle contact with them. This makes "waking world" intuitions and feelings of connection stronger, over time. This is important not only for the sorcerously active people of our world, but for anyone who maintains relationships with spirits in the modern day.

We may desire friendship, empowerment, or relationships from spirits or beings we gain or find images of; this technique can unlock the potential of that. We may need guidance or help from spirits that we have long-standing relationships with, and who we have encountered in previous visionary states and conditions; this can help to facilitate that. Seeking dreams and visions of guidance is as old as humankind; this technique is another manifestation of that seeking.

## A Final Word: Hanss The Devil's Son

Earlier in this essay I gave the story of Hanss Ferner, the eight-year old boy who claimed to have met the Devil and pledged his allegiance to him back in 1663. Hanss reported, in the course of his various confessions, that the "Black Man"—the Devil—had been appearing to him for some time before he (Hanss) gave him his allegiance. He had apparently been pestering Hanss somewhat, appearing to him at different times and scaring him.

Hanss didn't turn himself in after he made his deal with the Devil; his case is unique. Hanss was *in custody* when he claimed to have traveled to the demonic feasting place, and made that offer of himself to the Black and Horned Man. Not only was he in custody, but he was being observed around the clock.

For the people (then and now) who take the story of Hanss and use it as a way of dismissing the claims of witches (for many people today *still* insist on dismissing dreams as potential vehicles of power and relationship), a strange detail emerges from the story of Hanss Ferner. While he was being observed in his sleep, he was seen to struggle and call out early in the night, and then later in the night. Upon awakening one morning, he reported (with fear) that he had pledged himself to the Devil—and that a celebration had been thrown in honor of his pledge.

After feasting with the Devil, the Devil flew Hanss back "home"—but before Hanss parted company with him, he expressed to the Devil that he was afraid he'd never be able to go to heaven now. The Devil became quite angry and stabbed Hanss in the foot. He awoke crying and in pain.

The Barber-Surgeon of the town, along with the town scribe and two other men examined Hanss and found that he had a cut on his foot, in the same place that he said the Devil had stabbed him. No explanation is given in the records for how Hanss could have gotten the cut, and the men who did the examination had no answer.

For those worrying about Hanss, his family was investigated, but no one was arrested or charged with anything. The local magistrates and judge were not willing to believe Hanss on the basis of his reported experiences, as they had obviously happened in dreams. I suppose they just ignored the mysterious foot injury, and really, it's hard to blame them.

Hanss was found to be a "very bad boy", a troubled boy, an immoral boy, and his family system (upon investigation) was found to be broken and troubled. He was sentenced to be beaten, to "impress upon him the wicked depravity of magic", to be "scolded for his slanders", and to have the town preacher visit him regularly to "lead him in earnest prayer."

And with that, Hanss Ferner leaves the pages of history.

# WORKS CONSULTED

**The Book of Oberon: A Sourcebook of Elizabethan Magic,** by Daniel Harms, James R. Clark, and Joseph H. Peterson. ISBN 978-0-7387-4334-9

**Cunning Folk and Familiar Spirits: Shamanistic Visionary Traditions in Early Modern British Witchcraft and Magic**, by Emma Wilby. ISBN 978-1-84519-079-8

**Fairies, Demons, and Nature Spirits: Small Gods at the Margins of Christendom**, edited by Michael Ostling. ISBN 978-1-137-58519-6

**Magic, Witchcraft, and Ghosts in the Greek and Roman Worlds**, by Daniel Ogden. ISBN 978-0-19-538520-5

**The Realities of Witchcraft and Popular Magic in Early Modern Europe**, by Edward Bever. ISBN 978-1-349-54664-0

**Saducismus Triumphatus: Or, Full And Plain Evidence Concerning Witches And Apparitions, In Two Parts**, by Joseph Glanvill, Henry More, and Anthony Horneck. First published in 1681.

**Scottish Fairy Belief**, by Lizanne Henderson and Edward J. Cowan. ISBN 1-86232-190-6

**Scottish Witches and Witch-Hunters**, edited by Julian Goodare. ISBN 978-1-137-35593-5

**The Visions of Isobel Gowdie: Magic, Witchcraft, and Dark Shamanism in Seventeenth Century Scotland**, by Emma Wilby. ISBN 978-1-84519-180-1

**Witchcraft and Belief in Early Modern Scotland**, edited by Julian Goodare, Lauren Martin, and Joyce Miller. ISBN 978-0-230-50788-3

## About the Author

Robin Artisson has been writing books on the topic of Witchcraft and related occult topics for a goodly while. He is one of the co-founders of *Covenant DeSavyok*, a society of peers created in 2015 to preserve, practice, and develop sorcerous arts according to pre-modern and Early Modern historical understandings. He and his family live in Maine.